500 THINGS TO DO

with Your CHILDREN *Before* THEY GROW UP

Linda Williams Aber and Corey McKenzie Aber

WEST
SIDE
PUBLISHING

Linda Williams Aber
As the mother of two sons, Corey and Kip, and the author of more than 150 books for children, Linda Williams Aber has devoted her life to inspiring children to be curious, adventurous, confident, and secure in the knowledge that each and every one of them is special and loved. One of those children is all grown up now and is the coauthor of this book.

Corey McKenzie Aber
Corey McKenzie Aber is a graduate of Brown University and a fifth-generation writer. In addition to working on a novel relating to art and architecture, he is the coauthor of *Scooby Doo and the Skeleton Key.* Most importantly, he and his wife Katie just had their first child, a little girl named Audrey, who helped inspire this book.

Factual Verification: Marci McGrath and Chris Smith

Cover Images: Getty Images; Shutterstock

West Side Publishing is a division of Publications International, Ltd.

Louis Weber, CEO
Publications International, Ltd.
7373 North Cicero Avenue
Lincolnwood, Illinois 60712

ISBN-13: 978-1-60553-481-7
ISBN-10: 1-60553-481-1

Manufactured in U.S.A.

8 7 6 5 4 3 2 1

Contents

Don't Waste a Single Second!

"Enjoy every minute of it, they grow up so fast!" How many times has someone said that to you? The fact is, they're right. And though we wouldn't want our children to stay in diapers all their lives, we might certainly have moments where we wish we could slow them down so we can really enjoy every minute of their childhoods.

We may all know 500 things we *have* to do with our children before they grow up—feed them, bathe them, clothe them—but there's more to parenting than these daily necessities. We all want to create warm childhood memories, to foster our children's sense of wonder, to explore and discover the world with them and experience interesting, awe-inspiring, fun and funny places, events, and moments. There's nothing quite like experiencing something old and familiar through your child's fresh, new eyes. The first time your child rides a roller coaster or visits the zoo or sees the ocean, it's almost like it's your first time, too. That's where this book comes in. With 500 ideas for things to do together, you'll be making treasured memories and building relationships that become the foundation for happy and healthy children and a stable family.

Some of the ideas you'll find here are as simple as catching lightning bugs in a jar, teaching your child how to set a table, and having a picnic indoors on a rainy day. Others may take you to foreign countries, to wondrous sights in your own country, or to attractions in your own town that you hadn't noticed before. You'll find guidelines for building confidence, making friends, ending arguments peacefully, behaving properly in social situations, and being a good steward of our planet. We've covered the practical and the not-so practical. Things like playing in the mud or playing with your food may not seem important to you in the grand scheme of things, but we bet you'll get more out of such activities than you'd expect. Remember: Each and every thing you do with your children is a brick in the building they'll become. What those bricks are made of is your choice; this book gives you solid materials with which to work.

Alongside each activity, you'll find a ballot box where you can keep track of the activities you and your child have shared. Take pride in your accomplishments as you check off item after item. Think of all the wonderful memories you are creating!

As a parent, you are a mentor, a friend, a confidant—the one who is always there to love, guide, and care. You'll share thousands of experiences with your children in your lifetime, but these 500 have been hand-picked as things you should make a point of doing before they're all grown up. Spend the time while there *is* time, because they really do grow up so fast. The last thing you want is to find yourself wishing you'd taken the time to do more, to go more places, to have more experiences. Many of the activites in this book are free—or cost very little. So what are you waiting for? Why not get started right now?

▲ ▲ ▲ ▲ ▲

"This time, like all times, is a very good one, if we but know what to do with it."

—Ralph Waldo Emerson

▼ ▼ ▼ ▼ ▼

❑ 1. Visit the Ocean

The ocean has a mysterious draw that has nothing to do with the tides. The sand, the sea breeze, the rhythm of the waves—what's not to love? The ocean covers approximately 71 percent of the earth's surface and is home to a vast and varied ecosystem, making it a great place to learn about all kinds of plants and animals. Children will take great delight in watching pelicans nosedive for fish and seeing sandpipers skitter along at the edge of the tide. They'll also have a blast playing tag in the waves along the shore and splashing in the salty water.

There's plenty to do on land, too. Wander the beach collecting seashells—the homes of some of the ocean's creatures—or just relax on the sand and watch the waves rolling in and out. Build elaborate sand castles, and let your children bury you in the sand. You'll be creating memories that will last a lifetime.

▲ ▲ ▲ ▲ ▲

"Just as the wave cannot exist for itself, but is ever a part of the heaving surface of the ocean, so must I never live my life for itself, but always in the experience which is going on around me."
—Albert Schweitzer

▼ ▼ ▼ ▼ ▼

❑ 2. Experience the Big Time at the Big Top

Let's face it: Life with kids can be a bit of a circus at times. And the kids probably feel the same way about life with Mom and Dad! Sometimes everyone needs a time-out, and what better place to take it than under the big top? The magic of the circus is that it has something for everyone—young and old, boy and girl. Acrobats, clowns, and trained animals will keep the whole family on the edge of their

What's almost as much fun as a trip to the circus? A trip to a circus museum! Believe it or not, the circus is celebrated at many museums across the United States. Here are some that we found:

- Barnum Museum, Bridgeport, Connecticut
- International Circus Hall of Fame, Peru, Indiana
- Circus World Museum, Baraboo, Wisconsin
- International Clown Hall of Fame, Milwaukee, Wisconsin
- The John and Mable Ringling Museum of Art, Sarasota, Florida

seats. Whether the circus that comes to your town is one ring, two, or three, the ringmaster sets the tone for excitement, glamour, laughter, and a couple of hours of nonstop entertainment. Ringling Bros. and Barnum & Bailey Circus, Cirque du Soleil, Big Apple Circus, Cole Brothers Circus of the Stars, and many, many others set up their tents and fill up stadiums all over the world. Chances are good there's a circus performing near you right now!

❑ 3. Sail Off into the Wild Blue Yonder

Have you ever wondered what it would be like to float on air? A trip in a hot-air balloon will give you a chance to find out! You'll ride underneath the balloon in the gondola, or wicker basket, with a pilot who controls the craft by manipulating the temperature inside the balloon.

Believe it or not, the first hot-air balloons were used as military signals in China as long ago as the third century A.D. But the first crewed flight, which took place in France in a balloon built by the Montgolfier brothers, didn't happen until 1783. Balloons have come a long way since then and are now shaped like almost anything, including bees, turtles, or even some favorite cartoon characters.

You can find hot-air balloon operators in your local phone book or by visiting a local ballooning festival or air show. Be sure to allow at least three to four hours for the adventure, and don't forget to bring a camera—you don't get to see sights like this every day.

❏ 4. Celebrate Summer with a Fun Festival

The sun is shining, the air is fresh, and summer festivals are popping up in a neighborhood near you. You'll find jazz festivals, renaissance festivals, and film festivals as well as festivals celebrating art, religious holidays, agriculture, different nationalities, a variety of historical events, and just about anything else you can imagine. These events offer an opportunity to sample other cultures as well as exposure to creative ideas, music, crowds of revelers, and new foods. Watch the newspapers for announcements of festivals in your area and then make a family outing of it. Wear good walking shoes, the right clothes for the weather, and bring a good supply of water. Part of the fun of a festival is sampling the foods, but you can still soak up the atmosphere while choosing a picnic spot and eating lunch brought from home.

Plan ahead for the souvenir temptations that might spoil the day if you haven't set your ground rules before leaving home. Perhaps you'll give each child a specified amount to spend and let him or her decide how to spend it best.

❏ 5. Bake Cookies Together

The kitchen is the heart of any home. Because it's a center of activity and family meal making, it's often the place where laughter is the loudest and memorable moments are shared. Baking cookies together is a shared learning experience with a sweet reward. Let your children help with all the steps, from mixing the dough to rolling it in sugar to shaping the dough into round balls. Whether you prepare these treats for holidays, rainy days, or any day, make an extra batch for a neighbor, and teach your children a fun and tasty lesson in spreading good cheer!

YOU WILL NEED:
- 1 box lemon cake mix
- 2 cups Cool Whip
- 1 egg
- Large mixing bowl
- Measuring cup
- Wooden spoon
- $1/2$ cup powdered sugar
- 2 cookie sheets
- Oven mitts
- Metal spatula
- Cooling rack or plate

1. Preheat the oven to 350 degrees.

2. Mix cake mix, Cool Whip, and egg together by hand in the mixing bowl.

3. Spoon-drop mix into the powdered sugar and roll into balls.

4. Place balls 1 inch apart on cookie sheet.

5. Bake for 10 to 12 minutes.

6. Remove cookies to cooling rack or plate.

7. Eat and enjoy!

❑ 6. Create Stepping Stones

Making your garden more personal is a family affair when you and your kids add homemade stepping stones. Handprints, footprints, finger-paint designs, or dog's paw prints add a personal touch to this garden art that you'll appreciate for years to come.

Where to start? Well, you could purchase a stepping-stone kit at a craft store, but that can become pricey if you want to make more than one. The alternative is to buy your own supplies, all readily available at craft stores.

YOU WILL NEED:
Newspaper or plastic sheeting
Goggles
Rubber gloves
Stepping-stone concrete
Mold
Old screen or hardware cloth
Old spoon
Decorations

1. Protect your work surface with newspaper or plastic sheeting. Protect yourself with goggles, rubber gloves, and old clothes. Set your mold on your work surface. If you are using a special stepping-stone mold, follow the enclosed directions.

2. Mix the concrete. Follow the manufacturer's directions. The wet mixture should have the consistency of soft cookie dough.

3. Cut a piece of old screening or hardware cloth about 1 inch smaller than your mold, and set it aside.

4. Start spooning your concrete mix into the mold. Fill the mold to the halfway point and smooth it down.

5. Lay your cut piece of screening or hardware cloth into the mold and then finish scooping the cement into the mold until full.

6. Gently tap around the outside of your mold to help remove any air bubbles and to even out the surface.

7. Now leave your stepping stone to set for 30 to 60 minutes before adding handprints or other decorations to the concrete.

8. Once the concrete has had some time to set, you can make prints in it. Children might also enjoy adding decorative rocks, beads, shells, or other materials to their stones.

9. Be sure to wash hands, feet, or paws immediately afterward to remove concrete. It's probably best to use an outdoor hose for this, as concrete should not be washed down a drain.

10. Your stepping stone must now sit for two to three days without being disturbed—do not move it. Once it is dry, you can gently pop it out of the mold. At this point, children can use paint to add personal touches to their stones. Let the stepping stones sit for another week before putting them outside.

❏ 7. Attend Story Hour

Want to make books come alive? Nothing can do that like story time at your local library, where character voices, sound effects, and a live audience of children and parents draw you and your children into well-loved stories.

Today, libraries around the country are dedicated to offering programs that nurture a child's love for books. But that wasn't always the case. Before 1854, children weren't even allowed in libraries! And once they were, they had to be at least 14 to be admitted. It wasn't until the start of the 20th century that children's literature assumed the valued place it holds today, thanks to the pioneer of children's story time, Anne Carroll Moore of the New York Public Library. So pull up some tiny chairs for the kids (and for you too!), and lend your ears to some timeless tales. To find a story time near you, check with your local library.

❏ 8. Vote!

It's never too early to start teaching your child about civic responsibility. And perhaps the best way to teach this particular lesson is by setting a good example. Stand up and be counted!

To make the voting experience fun and interactive for your child, consider these ideas:

- Hold a mock election at home and vote on what game to play, what TV show to watch, or what kind of pizza to order.

- Make special campaign buttons using markers declaring the years that each of your children will be old enough to vote.

- Get a sample ballot and go through it with your child, explaining why you are voting for the candidate of your choice. (Note: This works best with older children, perhaps beginning around age nine or ten.)

- Before going to the voting booth, be sure to check the rules for bringing your child with you.

- Allow older children to watch election night coverage with you; this provides a good opportunity to explain the voting process.

- After the election has been held and the winners have been announced, follow through with another look at the sample ballot to see if your candidates won.

❏ 9. Make Time Stand Still

Have you ever wished you could preserve these precious childhood days? Stuffing a time capsule is an opportunity to do just that!

Help children select special objects (but be sure they don't mind parting with the items—this isn't the place for that special blankie or beloved stuffed animal!) that represent what is important to them. They might even draw pictures of items that are special to them. Include mementos from favorite places and trips. Postcards, napkins from a favorite ice-cream parlor, paper hats from an especially fun birthday party—anything that is special to your child and will evoke treasured memories has a place in your time capsule. Include the front page of a newspaper from the day to remind yourself (or whomever finds your time capsule in the future!) of the news at the time.

Other ideas include:

- a scrap of fabric from a beloved blankie
- an item of outgrown clothing (a favorite T-shirt, for example)
- a letter from your child to the finder of the time capsule (even if that person is your child 25 years in the future!)
- your child's report card
- ticket stubs from movies or events you've attended as a family
- art projects
- greeting cards from special birthdays or holidays

Be sure to choose a waterproof container for your time capsule so that items inside aren't ruined by water or the elements. Discuss with your child when the time capsule should be unearthed. Do you want to open it as a family five years in the future? Ten years in the future? Do you want to leave it for some other family to find 25 or 50 years down the road? Either way, be sure to draw a map of your time capsule's location so it can be located later.

❑ 10. Listen to Music Under the Stars

As summer approaches, outdoor concerts begin to spring up everywhere. It's great fun to listen to music under the stars, plus these concerts are usually free! What could be a better recipe for summertime fun?

Be prepared to picnic, and don't forget the lawn chairs, a blanket, bug spray, sunscreen, and a camera. Encourage your kids to dance to the music, clap their hands to the rhythm, and applaud at the end of a song. If your children are too little to sit still for long, consider bringing along some additional entertainment. Crayons and coloring books can be a fun (and quiet!) way to keep a little one occupied.

❏ 11. Gaze Up at the Starry Night

The sky's the limit when it comes to finding planets and stars on a dark night. Check the library for an easy stargazing guide with pictures of constellations such as Ursa Major (which includes the Big Dipper), Ursa Minor (which includes the Little Dipper), and Orion. Then spread a blanket on the lawn, lie on your back, and find Polaris at the end of the curved handle in the Little Dipper. Polaris is the North Star, which is almost exactly above the earth's North Pole. If you can find the North Star, you'll always be able to tell which direction is north. Stargazing reminds us that we live in a world of limitless possibilities. Remind your kids to hitch their wagons to a star, not a lamppost, and they'll go far in life.

THE CONSTELLATIONS

While there are 88 constellations in the Northern and Southern hemispheres, the constellations of the Zodiac receive the most fanfare in literature. Here are their names and when they can best be seen:

Capricornus (the sea goat)
January 20
Aquarius (the water bearer)
February 17
Pisces (the fish)
March 12
Aries (the ram)
April 19
Taurus (the bull)
May 15
Gemini (the twins)
June 21

Cancer (the crab)
July 21
Leo (the lion)
August 11
Virgo (the maiden)
September 17
Libra (the scales)
November 1
Scorpius (the scorpion)
November 24
Sagittarius (the archer)
December 18

❏ 12. Teach Money Matters

The more your kids know and understand about money—earning it, saving it, spending it—the better off they'll be when they're no longer on your payroll. Opening a bank account is one way to nurture the habit of saving for things.

Kids often begin receiving money from the second they are born. You, the parent or guardian, should control gifts given at birth. But money received for birthdays, holidays, jobs, and allowance is perfect for teaching your child how to budget.

How do you find a kid-friendly bank—one that won't charge fees or require a minimum deposit or balance? You'll have to ask, and it's wise to compare programs among different banks. Most offer a no-fee, no-minimum option for minors, but they don't advertise that fact. When you ask, you may even be surprised to find that there are special prizes or higher interest rates for kids who save. Shop around and find a bank that will make your child's account one that is fun to add to—an account they can be proud to call their own.

❏ 13. Amuse Yourself at an Amusement Park

A visit to an amusement park is almost a rite of passage. The chance to experience a favorite amusement park or ride through your child's delighted eyes is priceless. This is definitely something you'll want to do with your kids at least once—if not many, many times!

Of course, the larger amusement parks can come with a hefty price tag. But with careful planning and a little flexibility, you can save a bundle.

Here are some ways to make your amusement park visit more affordable:

- Keep an eye out for discount tickets, good deals on hotels or motels, and package deals to the park of your choice.

- Plan your trip for the off-season. Parks often have better rates when the crowds are down, and airfares and hotels follow suit with their pricing.

- Budget ahead for souvenir spending. Include your kids in the budget discussion so all agree ahead of time on the ground rules.

- Eat before you enter the theme park or pack a lunch and snacks. (Be sure to check the individual amusement park's Web site for information regarding outside food and drink. Some parks do not allow food to be brought in from the outside.)

- Book a hotel or motel that offers a full breakfast.

- Use the convenient free shuttles to the park that many hotels and motels offer—that way, you won't have to rent a car.

- Take your own pictures to save money on expensive photos taken by theme park photographers.

❏ 14. Make a Sick-of-Being-Sick Emergency Fun Kit

There's nothing fun about being sick . . . or is there? Beat the boredom with some stay-in-bed activities that take the patient's mind off the problem.

- Make a cheer-up pillowcase. Provide the patient with a bed tray for a work surface, a plain white pillowcase, and fabric markers. Suggest drawing smiley faces, polka-dotted chicken pox faces, or anything else that brings a smile to your child's face.

- Contagious patients still need to communicate. Make paper airplanes and send messages written on the wings from bed to doorway.

- Keep a Sick-of-Being-Sick Journal—here's the perfect place to write down all the complaints about that scratchy throat or stuffy nose. Moan, groan, pout—get it all out in this little notebook.

- Play Slam Dunk Tissue Target Practice. Toss tissues into a waste-basket that is positioned slightly out of reach.

- Keep a cooler full of popsicles and ginger ale next to the bed.

❏ 15. Canoe—and Kayak Too!

There's no better way to get to know our rivers and lakes than in a canoe or a kayak. Arms and paddles become the motor for your human-powered boat as you glide along the water. Be on the look-out for local wildlife—is that a turtle over there on that log? Maybe you can get closer—and take in the scenery together. Bring along a picnic and find a place to pull off and eat a quiet lunch together under a shade tree, or eat on the go if you can't stop exploring. As always, don't forget your cameras!

For the more adventurous among you, learn to whitewater kayak on some light rapids and get in touch with your inner need for speed. Or, take a sea-kayak trip and paddle with the dolphins. Visit your local outfitters or park district for information on kayaking and canoeing in your area.

❏ 16. Go Snorkeling

Do your kids think straws are just for blowing bubbles in a glass of milk? When you go snorkeling, you can show them that straws are for breathing, too! You'll put on swim fins, a diving mask, and a breathing straw—a snorkel—and swim around just below the ocean's surface where you can see schools of fabulously colored fish, coral reefs catching the sunlight through the water, and anemo-nes waving their tentacles at you as you pass. Snorkeling can be done in just about any body of water, but the most beautiful sites tend to be found in tropical locations. Happily, snorkeling adven-tures are offered at most family vacation spots along the ocean, so grab an underwater camera and dive in together. Even if you don't get any good pictures of real fish, you'll all look a little fishy in your swim fins and diving masks!

❑ 17. Learn to Carve a Spook-tacular Pumpkin

There was a time when a carved pumpkin, better known as a Jack-o'-Lantern, was limited to a jagged smile, triangular eyes, and a matching nose. That was then, this is now. With new tools, fantastic patterns, and easy instructions, pumpkin carving has become an art form. In no time at all, you can turn an ordinary pumpkin into an extraordinary one.

First things first. Be sure to select a pumpkin that is flat enough on the bottom to stand on your porch or steps. And don't carve your pumpkin any sooner than two days before you plan on putting it outside. Ready to get started? Check out the following carving tips:

- Spread newspaper on your work surface to collect the pumpkin's pulp and seeds.

- Using a water-based marking pen, draw your design on the pumpkin. Older kids might enjoy drawing the design themselves; younger kids can help by instructing the drawer: Should the face be happy or sad? Scary or silly? Have two eyes or one?

BAKED PUMPKIN SEEDS

Baked pumpkin seeds are quick and easy, and they make a tasty, healthy snack for the kids. Here's how to make them:

1. Preheat oven to 350°F.

2. Separate the pumpkin seeds from the fibers. Wash, drain, and dry the seeds on paper towels. Coat 1½ cups seeds with 1 teaspoon vegetable oil. Toss the seeds with salt (or omit salt and toss seeds with any of the suggested seasonings below), and spread them in a single layer on a baking sheet.

3. Bake, stirring occasionally, 12 to 15 minutes or until golden brown.

For an extra twist, trying coating pumpkin seeds in chili pepper or sugar and cinnamon. Yum!

- Cut the stemmed lid out of the top using a sharp, straight-edge knife. (Grown-ups only!)

- Scoop out the seeds and pulp. Use a big metal spoon, or let your kids use their hands. Sort the seeds into a colander if you'd like to bake pumpkin seeds later.

- When your pumpkin is cleaned out and you're ready to start carving, do not stab the pumpkin. Instead, keep a portion of the blade in the pumpkin and use a slow and steady sawing motion.

- Carve from the center outward—eyes and nose first, larger features last.

- To remove the carved pieces, push them into or out of the pumpkin.

- Place a candle inside on the bottom of the pumpkin. Replace the lid. Happy Halloween!

❑ 18. Experience Ethnic Foods

You know the saying "You are what you eat"? Well, get ready to transform yourself. There are lots of ways to experience different backgrounds, but one of the tastiest is to cook and eat popular dishes from other cultures. You can find ethnic recipes online or at your local library. Add to the fun by researching other details about the region—popular styles of dress, music, customs, and so forth. Encourage your children to pretend they are walking through tomato fields as you select the perfect tomatoes for ravioli and marinara sauce. Or they can imagine themselves in India, wandering through the markets in search of the perfect spices with which to make Chicken Tikka Masala. Or maybe they are on the island of Jamaica enjoying the sun on the beach when you prepare Jamaican Jerk Pork. Choose different places all over the

FUN TIP

For added fun, listen to music from the region as you prepare your ethnic meal.

world and find out what foods they are known for. You and your children will love learning about new peoples and places—and your taste buds will thank you!

❑ 19. Chill Out–Go Ice-Skating!

There was a time when ice-skating was limited to frozen ponds, lakes, and streams. If the weather didn't cooperate by blowing in some cold temperatures, ice-skating was not an option. But the advent of indoor

FUN FACT

Frank Zamboni invented the Zamboni ice resurfacing machine in the early 1940s.

ice-skating rinks has made the sport a year-round activity. Rental skates solve the problem of fast-growing feet and give your whole family the chance to try before you buy. Check your phone book for local rinks, then call or stop by for information regarding open skate times, lessons, and special skating sessions for families with younger kids. When it's time to skate, make sure you're familiar with the rink's rules and pay attention to the direction of skate traffic. Remember: The safest spot on the rink is in the middle where traffic doesn't flow. Dress warmly. Even indoors, the ice keeps things cool, and little hands and feet need to stay warm and flexible for safe skating.

Take a break for a cup of hot chocolate while the big Zamboni ice resurfacing machine clears the ice and smoothes it out again. Then get back out there and skate. Practice makes perfect, and ice-skating makes perfect family fun.

❑ 20. Shake Your Family Tree

How much do your children know about their grandparents? Their great-grandparents? For that matter, how much do *you* know about the history of your ancestors? You might be surprised by what you'll discover if you just do some digging. And what better way to spend time together as a family than by tracing your roots? The knowledge you uncover becomes a gift for your children and your children's children—not to mention older members of your family who might learn a thing or two themselves!

Start with oral histories. Interview grandparents and great-grandparents to find out what they might know about *their* parents and grandparents. Dig through photo albums and personal papers. From there, take your search to the Internet and see what else you can uncover. Before you know it, your family tree will branch out to other countries. Maybe you'll even find out you are related to royalty or to a famous scientist, artist, or explorer.

❑ 21. Go Fish...Really!

You may not have to fish for your food these days, but a fishing trip is a guaranteed source of memories and family fun. There are many types of fishing to try depending on where you are. If you're up in the mountains, strap on some waders and grab some tackle for fly-fishing in majestic mountain streams and rivers. If you're near the ocean and have an appetite for the big ones, try deep-sea fishing. Join a trip out into the deep waters and go after marlins and bar-racuda. Lakes and wide rivers are great places to fish for bass, those large-mouth fish you see in professional sport fishing competitions. Rent a boat and head out with the sunrise; fish like a hearty break-fast just like the rest of us. Or you can keep it simple—this is your safest bet when taking little ones fishing for the first time. Dig up some earthworms in the backyard, grab a pole, and take a quick trip to the local fishing hole. That creek, canal, or pond might just have a monster fish that's been hiding there for years. Who knows, your family could become legendary!

▲　▲　▲　▲　▲

"Give a man a fish and you feed him for a day.
Teach him how to fish and you feed him for a lifetime."
—Lao Tzu

▼　▼　▼　▼　▼

❏ 22. Coauthor a Book Starring Your Child

Once upon a time…who wouldn't want to star in his or her own book? Take your children's favorite hobbies and begin to build a story. Include their friends and their families too! Ask your children to draw some pictures to illustrate their stories. Then type it up, scan in the pictures, and have the book printed and bound at your local copier or office supply store. Invent a new story for every birthday, and you'll have a nice family history of imagination to turn to every year.

Not sure how to write a story? It's not so hard. Just break it up into four parts: 1. Introduce the characters (your kids!). 2. Give them an obstacle to overcome, whether it's something difficult they have to learn, a place they have to get to, or a villain they have to outsmart. 3. Explain the actions your children take to successfully solve the problem. 4. Tie it up nicely with a happy ending at home. If you don't want to try an original work, you can take an existing story and change the hero or heroine's name to that of your child.

❏ 23. Experience Different Religions

Understanding the world in which we all live is easier if we understand and acknowledge that each religion is unique. Religious and spiritual traditions are one way of explaining the mysteries of life—how and why the world was created, why people live and die. Introduce children to different faiths, including their worship ceremonies, rituals, celebrations, and holy days. Discuss the traditions other people honor and how those traditions and beliefs compare with your family's own traditions. Older children may enjoy attending the service of another faith—Christmas Eve mass at a local Catholic church, for instance.

❏ 24. Eat with Chopsticks

Fork? Easy. Spoon? Easier. Chopsticks? Well... sure, why not? Let's try it!

Step 1: How to hold chopsticks

- Position the first chopstick so that the thicker part rests at the base of your thumb. The thinner part should rest on the lower side of your middle fingertip.

- Move your thumb forward so that it holds the stick firmly in place. Be sure that two or three inches of chopstick extend beyond your fingertip.

- Hold the second chopstick the way you would hold a pencil. Position it against the side of your index finger using the end of your thumb.

CHOPSTICK ETIQUETTE

- DON'T spear food with the tip of a chopstick.
- DON'T lick the ends of the chopsticks.
- DO use your chopsticks to cut up pieces of food too large to eat in one bite.
- DO replace your chopsticks on the chopstick rest. If a rest has not been provided, fold the chopstick wrapper and use it as a rest.

- Holding the chopsticks at a slight angle, press the ends of both sticks on your plate. Let them slide through your fingers a little so that the ends line up.

Step 2: Moving the top chopstick

- Slightly press on the top chopstick. It will pivot or move on your index finger and thumb.

- Your index and middle fingers are used to move the top chopstick.

- The bottom chopstick always stays steady.

- Your thumb almost always stays steady.
- The tip of the top chopstick will move toward the tip of the bottom.
- Hold the tips together firmly enough to grasp a piece of food and lift it off the plate.
- Put the food into your mouth.
- Practice, practice, practice!

❏ 25. Attend a Civil War Reenactment

History comes alive as men and women dress in authentic Civil War costumes and soldiers set up their tents with genuine equipment from the days of the war. Then they begin the serious business of reenacting battles, medical response, cooking in old camp style, and telling stories from the time when the United States of America was at war with itself. How could a country be so divided that it would have a War Between the States? What was the outcome and how did this Civil War shape our country and change the way its people think, behave, and govern?

People of all ages—yes, minors too—can participate in Civil War reenactments. Enactors speak in the language of the 1860s and provide detailed stories and demonstrations. Costumes are made exactly like clothing worn during the Civil War. Even the stitching on the costumes is faithful to that era. Find a Civil War reenactment near you online and put your family on the road to an historic adventure!

❏ 26. Create a Family Emergency Plan

Do you know what to do in an emergency? Do your kids? If an emergency should strike your family, you definitely don't want to waste valuable seconds trying to figure out a plan of action. That's why it's a good idea to take some time to prepare emergency plans for a variety of situations, including fire; a natural disaster, such as a tornado or hurricane; or a national emergency on the scale of 9/11. The mere thought of such crisis situations may seem frightening, but you'll feel better knowing you're prepared to handle whatever may come your way.

As your prepare your emergency plans, try to think the situations through from a child's perspective. For instance, keep in mind that a young child's first instinct in the event of a fire may be to hide. Make certain your children know what the fire alarm sounds like, and be sure to outline some basic fire safety rules so that they'll know how to exit the house safely. Remember, too, that a firefighter can look and sound pretty scary when dressed in full gear. That's why it's a good idea to introduce children to firefighters and police officers when you have the opportunity. Knowing what to expect can make all the difference in a scary emergency situation.

> Get your emergency plan off to a good start by visiting www.ready.gov/ america/_downloads/familyemergency plan.pdf.
>
> This government-sponsored Web site includes printable forms and emergency contact cards to fill out and distribute to all family members.

Every emergency plan should include:

- Safe places to meet; for instance, if there is a fire in the house, where should everyone meet after safely exiting the house?

- Contact information so that family members know how to get in touch with each other if an emergency occurs while they are separated. Keep in mind that in times of local crisis, it may be easier to place a call to a relative in another state than it will be to reach one another on cell phones. Make sure everyone has a single contact person to get in touch with if necessary.

- Information about where supplies such as first aid, extra water/ food, extra clothing, and so forth are stored.

Hopefully, you'll never need your emergency plan. But if you do, you'll definitely be glad you planned ahead!

❑ 27. Adopt an Animal

Play a part in the effort to save and preserve endangered species. The Worldwide Wildlife Fund (WWF) has identified 90 extinct, endangered, and near-threatened species for a symbolic adoption program. Donate to WWF, and choose an animal adoption to represent your commitment to conservation. Depending on the level of your contribution, the Adoption Kits may contain a certificate and a photo, plush toys, pillows, mugs, books, and a variety of other premium items to represent your chosen adopted species.

Be sure to take the time to browse the WWF's Web site, which is chock-full of interesting facts about all the species in the program. Children will enjoy learning more about their adopted "pet"—what it eats, where it lives, whether it's warm-blooded or cold-blooded, and so forth. And just think: The extra bonus for adopting a wild animal is that you don't have to walk it!

❑ 28. Get Lost in a Corn Maze

Looking for an a-MAZE-ing autumn activity? Spend a day picking your way through a corn maze. You'll find these attractions in the fall—after all the corn has been harvested. These labyrinths come in all shapes, sizes, and levels of difficulty, so you're sure to find one near you that is perfect for your family's level of interest.

To add to the corny fun, some mazes feature multiple-choice quizzes to help visitors navigate the twists and turns. But, of course, a wrong answer means incorrect twists and turns, which could leave you lost and disoriented. Other mazes include scavenger hunts for the kids, complete with a candy prize at the end. Any way you slice it, a corn maze is an activity the whole family can really lose itself in! But have no fear, most mazes have Corn Cops stationed throughout to make sure no one gets *too* stuck or lost.

❑ 29. Start a Cool Collection

Collections of any kind add an extra purpose to travel, whether it is near or far. Plus, when kids become passionate about collecting things, they may also learn history, money management, and the importance of taking care of things. Collections don't have to consist of stamps, coins, baseball cards, or other things that might cost a lot of money. It's free—and fun—to collect shells, rocks, beach glass, or other items found in nature. Inexpensive collection items might also be found at flea markets and antique stores. Consider, for example, old toys, salt and pepper shakers, buttons, postcards, a particular animal (bunnies, frogs, kittens, puppies—all made of glass or ceramic, of course!). The only limit is your imagination. Help your kids identify something to collect, and then make a day of going to garage sales. You might also enlist the help of relatives and friends, who can search out items for your child's collection while traveling. You have your own collections—let your kids have theirs. When the collections start to grow, have fun creating neat displays and showing them to others.

❑ 30. Host a Masquerade Party

Themed parties are fun because they involve the invitees as much as the host. Decide on your theme—Victorian ball gowns and dress attire, pirate costumes, or Mardi Gras costumes, for instance—and plan accordingly. You're likely to find neat ideas for handmade, themed invitations online, and your children are sure to delight in helping you make them. If you'd like guests to dress a certain way, be sure to include this information in the invitation. Make the party a family affair, and invite several families to dress up, wear masks to hide their identities, and come prepared for a costume contest, games, and food for a crowd.

Be sure to let the kids help you decide on food and games for the event. This is a great opportunity to get those creative juices flowing!

❏ 31. Take a Harbor Tour

If you visit a city or town with a harbor, it's a pretty safe bet that guided tours of the waterfront will be available. Depending on the location, the sightseeing tour might include whale watching, wildlife preserves, historic war stations, islands, and sites of sunken ships. Simply seeing the shoreline from out on the harbor gives you a different view, and the tour guide will fill you in on the historical significance of the buildings and sites, what role the harbor may have played in the founding of the city, and anecdotes about the original settlers of the town. Check out the local tourist center wherever you are to find out the schedules for harbor or sightseeing tours.

❏ 32. Let the Kids Help Plan the Family Vacation

When it's time to plan a vacation, a better time will be had by all if the kids are involved right from the start. Giving your children a say in where the family will go for summer vacation, spring break, or the holidays is insurance against later hearing, "Why did we come here? When are we going home? This is such a drag."

To begin, it's best to choose a select number of destinations/trips that you are willing to finance. Present the options to your children, then search the Internet together for information about accommodations, activities, restaurants, and sights in the area. Take a vote; majority rules. Think outside the box—instead of always going to the beach, why not try a lake house or mountain cabin? Instead of staying in your own state, why not drive across the border to the next state and see what it has got to offer? Exposing your kids to more of the world and different ways to have fun broadens their experience and their tolerance for others.

Make the next family vacation a real family decision!

❏ 33. Create a Family Recipe Book

Whether it's Grandma's secret meatballs or Dad's French toast, everyone in the family has a specialty or two. Bring them all together in a family recipe book that you can pass down from generation to generation.

Let your children play a role in deciding what the recipe book will look like. If you'd like yours to have a more personal touch, you can buy ready-made books just for recipes, embellish or decorate the covers, and have the chefs write their recipes in their own handwriting. Or you can type up your recipes on the computer and have the book bound by a local printer. If you're especially computer-savvy you can even create a Web site to share with all of your family and friends.

FUN TIP

As you make each meal, take a picture of it looking tasty on the plate and add the photo to the book to tempt you every time you open it. And if you're really daring, invent a few meals of your own and add them to the book as you try them out.

❏ 34. Learn How to Ski or Snowboard

When the air starts to get crisper and the skies grow heavier, don't despair that winter is just around the corner. Embrace the season by playing in the snow! What could possibly be more fun than skiing or snowboarding down a mountain? The thrill of speeding down the hill, negotiating the moguls, and swooshing by your friends and family will stay with you even as you warm yourselves in the lodge afterward with hot chocolate and marshmallows. There are several levels of difficulty at every mountain resort, ranging from the bunny hills to the black diamonds, so don't be intimidated if you've never skied before. No matter how old (or young!) you are, there's a suitable slope and instructor for you.

If you find that downhill skiing or snowboarding are simply not for you, check out the wonderful world of cross-country skiing, where you can trek across the countryside and enjoy the winter scenery and wildlife at a slower pace.

☐ 35. Save Some Dough—Make Your Own Play Dough

Touch and smell are great senses to explore when you play with play dough! Make models of animals and insects, people or places. Anything you can imagine can be made fun with play dough. And it's even more fun when you make it yourself.

Here is a simple, nontoxic recipe for making your own:

Mix together 3 cups flour, ⅓ cup salt, 2 tablespoons vegetable oil, 1 cup water, and food coloring to desired color. If you want to make several different colors, separate the dough before adding food coloring. Or try adding a Kool-Aid packet instead of the food coloring; Kool-Aid offers the added bonus of scent. Store your dough in an air-tight bag in the refrigerator when not in use. If you want to preserve your sculptures, simply let them air-dry.

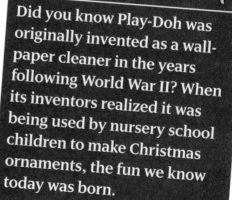

FAST FACT

Did you know Play-Doh was originally invented as a wallpaper cleaner in the years following World War II? When its inventors realized it was being used by nursery school children to make Christmas ornaments, the fun we know today was born.

❑ 36. Use Your Noodles

Do you have oodles of noodles? Then we have a recipe for rainy-day fun! Making macaroni jewelry is easy. All you need is a 12-inch length of yarn, uncooked macaroni, and a piece of tape to wrap around the end of the yarn to make threading easier. Go for the natural macaroni color or give the noodles a quick dip in a mixture of water and food coloring. Mix and match all kinds of noodles with holes in the middle. Embellish your necklaces with real beads, shells, or other things found around the house. Make a bracelet to match. A more perfect Mother's Day gift was never made!

❑ 37. Discover an Elder's Wisdom

When's the last time your family visited Great Aunt Betty or Great Grandpa Joe? It's an opportunity to make an elderly relative smile—and it's a chance for your children to gain an appreciation for the elder's wisdom. To make the most of the visit, prepare your kids with a little bit of history about the person's younger life. For example: "Aunt Betty used to make her famous butterscotch candy every holiday and send it to everyone in the family. She said the recipe was a secret, but I'll bet she'll tell *you* the secret if you ask!" Or: "Great Grandpa Joe was a great inventor! He used to go around the house inventing new gadgets for every chore that needed to be done. Maybe he'll help *you* invent something to make cleaning your room go faster. Why don't you ask him?"

Teaching your kids to engage elderly people in conversations that call on them to remember their strengths can turn an obligatory visit into one that is interesting, fun, meaningful for everyone, and something to look forward to doing again. And remember, it's a two-way street. Arming your kids with pictures they've drawn, stories about their sports team's win (or loss), and funny things that happened at school or at home will brighten the elder's day and make the visit a true sharing experience.

❏ 38. Splash at a Water Park

Arrive early or late but never in between. That's the best advice when it comes to a family trip to a water park. With more than 1,000 water parks to choose from in North America, it's almost certain you'll find one within driving distance of your home. A day at a water park is very different from a day at the beach. Water parks are set up with many different water features, including slides, chutes, ladders, caves, tunnels, waterfalls, showers, and more. There are pools for babies, toddlers, teens, and adults. Lockers are available for a fee. Some parks have a picnic area if you plan to bring your own food. When you spend a day at a water park, remember these handy tips:

- Wear a well-fitting bathing suit that will stay on when worn on all the different kinds of water features. Two-piece suits are not advisable.

- Wear water shoes so you can walk from one feature to the next without having to take shoes on and off.

- Slather on sunscreen often.

- Warn kids against swallowing park water.

- Follow age and height restrictions.

- Keep toddlers in the shallow pools.

- Watch your children at all times! Lifeguards have an important role to play at a water park, but you have the best opportunity to safeguard your own child's well-being.

- Leave valuables, rafts and floats, water wings, and cut-off jeans at home.

❏ 39. Make Music Together

If your family is fortunate enough to own and play musical instruments, you can create some of the most memorable evenings of your children's lives. A family music hour spent singing around a piano, learning duets, or forming a trio or quartet shows that you are not just a spectator of the arts but a participant.

Learn songs you can all sing and play. Compose a song together and play it when the grandparents visit. Having musical talent that you can all share gives added value to the lessons and practice sessions to which students of music devote so much of their time. Don't wait for the recital to allow your children to showcase what they've learned. Show an interest in hearing their pieces as they're learning. A family that plays together . . . well, you know the rest!

❏ 40. Have a Snowball Fight

Put on your gloves, don your hat, and pull your collar tight—it's time to head outside for a snowball fight! This classic winter activity is the perfect way for a family to spend a long winter day. There's nothing like molding fresh snow in your own two hands and hurling it through the frosty winter air. Increase the stakes and involve some other families from the neighborhood. Split up into teams, build snow forts, and play capture-the-flag. Bring the family dog outside for even more fun, as every snowball thrown is something for him to chase. Then, when the games are over, invite everyone in for warm apple cider and cookies.

WHITE IS OUT!

Here's another fun snowy-day activity: Add a little color to your life by painting the snow! All you'll need are food coloring and water. Add about 10 drops of food coloring to 3 teaspoons water in a bowl that's okay to get dirty (use one color per bowl). You can also mix your colors in empty spray bottles. Pack a four-foot-by-four-foot section of snow hard and firm. Use paintbrushes to add color to your snowy canvas. Be sure to wear older clothes that can get dirty—food coloring doesn't wash out of most fabrics.

❑ 41. Pop Some Corn for the Birds

Popcorn is perfect for stringing and hanging outside as a snack for the birds. Simply thread a needle, pop a bowl of popcorn, and start making garlands. Even if your kids aren't ready to work with a needle, they'll have fun hanging your garlands in the trees when you lift them up high enough to reach. Watching the birds peck at your popcorn string will give you all a close-up view of your winged visitors enjoying a very POP-ular treat!

❑ 42. Tour a Fun Factory

"Made in the U.S.A." takes on a whole new meaning when you take the time to go on a factory tour. Factories have played an important part in the history of our industrial nation and continue to do so today. Chances are if something is made in a factory, that factory is open for tours. The Hershey chocolate factory in Hershey, Pennsylvania, offers a tour that explains how chocolate is processed from cacao beans to Kisses. The Jelly Belly factory, which has locations in Fairfield, California, and Kenosha, Wisconsin, offers a 40-minute walking tour with guides showing why it takes a week to make a single jelly bean. The Cape Cod Potato Chip Factory in Hyannis, Massachusetts, fills visitors with fun facts about the potato chip then ends in the factory store, where free samples are distributed. These are just a few of the hundreds of kinds of factories open to you and your family. Kids are fascinated by how things are made, and seeing how everyday items are created makes that Hershey's Kiss, jelly bean, or potato chip taste that much better.

❑ 43. Bag a Peak

You may not be Sir Edmund Hillary or Tenzing Norgay, who in 1953 became the first men to reach the summit of Mount Everest, but that doesn't mean a mountain peak is out of your reach. There are several large mountain ranges across North America and many accessible mountains for you to climb, from the Appalachians in the east, to the Rockies in the middle, to the temperamental Mount St. Helens in the Northwest. You can even climb some of these mountains in your car. Maybe you have seen the bumper stickers: "This car climbed Mt. Such and Such." As convenient as that sounds, and as beautiful as the views may be from your air-conditioned auto, nothing can compare to the satisfaction your family will get from hiking up to a summit under an encouraging sun and looking out over the vast expanse of land in all directions. If you're not up for a hike from the bottom to the top—and who can blame you?—you can drive your car to various parking lots at different elevations and follow the trails up from there. However far you hike, the effort may test you at times, but it will bring you closer as a family as well, knowing that you accomplished the feat together and earned the spectacular view.

❏ 44. Explore a Tide Pool

To plan the best time to visit tide pools, get a tide table from a local sporting goods store. Arrive at the tide pools an hour or two before low tide to begin looking as the tide is going out. Sit near the edge of a large pool to observe animals. The longer you look, the more you will see. While actual species will vary at each shoreline, here are some types of animals you're likely to see:

Sea Anemones: These simple animals have tentacles around their mouths to attract food. If you touch a tentacle, it will feel sticky. This sensation is caused by tiny stingers too small to pierce your skin but able to sting small prey.

Sea Stars: Get flat and watch a sea star in the water. Can you see the tube feet moving? Sea stars eat mussels, clams, and other shellfish. If you see one with its arms pulled in close and its middle hunched, it's probably eating.

Sea Urchins: These close relatives of sea stars look like colorful pin-cushions. Urchins use their spines for defense as well as to scrape rocks to make round holes in which to hide. Can you see long tube feet sticking out between the spines? The urchin uses these to move and to pass food to the mouth on the bottom of the animal.

Crabs: Most tide pool crabs are scavengers. Watch them using their claws to feed. Crabs are usually shy, so be patient and watch for them.

Use a notebook to record what you see and approximately where you see it. You'll notice that some animals live in certain areas of the tidal shore. A guidebook to tide pool animals will help you identify actual species. Be sure to take photos to include with your notes!

❏ 45. Ride a Duck

It's one thing to tour a city by land, another to tour it by water, but it's really special to tour it both ways in the same vehicle. That's what you'll be doing if you take a Duck Tour, a sightseeing adventure that showcases the streets and waterways of most major cities. Don't let the silly name fool you, though. These amphibious vehicles were originally used in World War II when the Allies were faced with the problem of transporting cargo and men from their ships to land. The first "DUKW" was actually a GMC truck in a watertight shell, and it got its name from GMC's model terminology—*D* for a vehicle designed in 1942, *U* for utility, *K* for all-wheel drive, and *W* for two powered rear axles. In some cities, such as Boston, the original vehicles are still used alongside some newer Duck boats, so there's a good chance you'll be seeing the sites on an authentic piece of WWII machinery.

To find a Duck tour, check out the visitor's guides to the city you're visiting or search online ahead of time. These tours can be popular, so it's best to plan ahead.

Some major cities with Duck tours include: Washington, D.C.; Boston, Massachusetts; Miami, Florida; Philadelphia, Pennsylvania; San Francisco, California; Portland, Maine; Portland, Oregon; Austin, Texas; Seattle, Washington; Baltimore, Maryland; and Nashville, Tennessee.

❑ 46. Grow a Salad Garden

The first sign of a sprout in a homegrown garden makes smiles grow. You and your kids can work together to grow everything you need for your own salad bar at home. Advice is free at your local garden center, and asking questions with your kids present makes them part of the experience right from the start.

To begin, you'll need seeds or starter plants, stakes, string, gardening tools, and a 10-by-10-foot plot of ground in a sunny location. Draw a garden plan that shows where you will grow lettuce, cucumbers, tomatoes, and whatever else you choose, leaving space between the rows so you can walk through to weed, water, and harvest your produce. Then prepare the plot with good soil, and plant according to the directions on the seed packets or starter plants. Water your plants early in the day, providing about one inch of water per week.

Record the family gardening experience with pictures and captions saved in a Family Salad Garden Album. The family that grows together…well, grows together!

❑ 47. Pick an Apple— or Two or Three!

Apples grow in all 50 of the United States to the tune of an amazing 2,500 varieties! So it's likely that no matter where you live, there's a place to pick apples near you. This is a great autumn activity that can be enjoyed by children of all ages.

Finding a pick-your-own orchard is as easy as looking in the phone book or doing a quick search on the Internet. As you compare orchards near you, remember that dwarf trees make it easier for little hands to reach up and pluck apples off branches. Some apple orchards also feature entertainment—pony rides, play areas, corn mazes, train rides—which will definitely be a hit if you have little ones in your family.

Apples ripen from the outside to the center of the tree. So, when you pick apples, take them from the outside branches first. You can't always tell by color whether or not they are ripe, but the farmer will let you know which trees are ready. Carefully place picked apples into a basket or bag so they won't bruise. To prevent them from going bad too soon, don't wash them until you're ready to eat or use them. Pick enough to make a pie, caramel apples, apple crisp, or applesauce. Involve the kids in these culinary adventures so they can experience the joy of cooking with fresh fruit.

❑ 48. Celebrate First Night

For many years, cities and towns across the United States have been ringing in the new year with a First Night New Year's Eve celebration. First Night programs vary in size and content. Many include food, entertainment, fireworks, and singing and dancing. The tradition offers a safe, nonalcoholic, fun family celebration for which the theme is "out with the old and in with the new." Community businesses, local bands, art groups, and local government officials work together to make First Night the best night of the new year.

Spending New Year's Eve out with the whole family introduces the healthy and wholesome concept of celebrating without alcohol. Make this a family tradition to look forward to each year.

❑ 49. Ride a Ferry

There's much excitement to be found on the ferry: the blast of the horn, the grind of the bay doors, the scent of the sea air. As the anticipation mounts in your children, take them for a tour around the boat. Visit the decks, and look out over the water where the seagulls are fishing and the sailboats are gliding underneath a warm sun. Some ferry rides, such as that from Woods Hole to Martha's Vineyard in Massachusetts, have long, fascinating histories. Take some time to learn about them with your family so you can appreciate your place in history, taking the same route as so many have before you.

❑ 50. Tour Some Colleges

A college tour? But my kid's just a kid! As true as that may be, chances are you're saving for college already, so why not see where your money might go? College campuses often offer beautiful grounds, musical concerts, art exhibits, poetry readings, plays, lectures, festivals, sporting events, and open houses. Whether or not you're planning on sending your child to the college in your town, taking advantage of what colleges have to offer for free is an opportunity for a great family outing. Visiting colleges also gives you a preview of what to look for when your child does reach application age. And when your child is a sophomore or junior in high school (It really does go so fast!), the real college tour won't be such a scary experience. In fact, it will be just another family outing.

❑ 51. Work on a Crossword Puzzle

As the King often said in *The King and I*, "Is a puzzlement!" And that's exactly what crossword puzzles are until you get good at solving them. Crossword puzzles increase vocabulary, improve spelling skills and memory, and—when solved—give the puzzle solver a feeling of accomplishment. Teach your child how to work a crossword puzzle. Show how the clues relate to the puzzle grid, and introduce the concept of "cross words"—how the letters in one word also work in another word.

Crossword puzzles created specifically for kids may be found on the kids' page in a newspaper, on the Internet as a printable puzzle, and in puzzle books and magazines at the newsstand or the bookstore. Sitting together as you both work your own puzzles will lend a feeling of coziness to this quiet activity. Ask your child for help on your puzzle, and she or he will feel better about asking you for help with theirs. "What's a three-letter word for puzzle solving?"

F-U-N!

❑ 52. Take an "I Spy" Hike

A hike with an I Spy purpose takes the whines and woes out of a walk through the woods. A little preparation goes a long way toward making this type of family outing memorable. Bring along a notebook, a pen, a field guide, a camera, water, and snacks. The game starts the moment you set foot on the trail. Who can spy a bird's nest? A chipmunk? Bark peeling off a tree? Animal tracks? An animal den? Leaves of all kinds? Wild flowers? And bugs of all kinds? Use the field guide to help you identify animals, trees, insects, and flowers you might encounter. Make a game of who saw what first. Stop often and take water and snack breaks to keep energy levels high. Take this opportunity to explain that there are three important mottos to remember when you hike in the wilderness: Leave only footprints. Take only memories (or pictures!). Kill only time.

TIPS FOR THE UNEXPECTED:

If you ever get lost,

- Hug a tree.
- Make your whereabouts known by whistling, shouting, and waving.
- Stay calm.

HIKING SAFETY TIPS:

- Stay together.
- Walk, don't run—roots can trip even the most nimble-footed hiker.
- Bring plenty of water.
- Rest often.
- Maintain a safe distance from wild animals.
- Identify and avoid poison ivy, oak, and sumac.
- Seek shelter away from trees if lightning strikes.

❏ 53. Put the "Family" in Movie Night

Nobody will appreciate your home movies as much as the people who star in them. What could be more entertaining than the gasps of horror at Mom's hairdo gone terribly wrong, the laughs at Dad's shorts gone terribly plaid, and the squeals of delight at baby's face gone terribly pudding-covered? An evening spent sharing popcorn, home movies, and memories is sure to bring the whole family closer together.

❏ 54. Go to a Renaissance Festival

Kings and queens, princes and princesses, knights and fair maidens may be the stuff of legend and history, but legend and history come alive at Renaissance festivals. Costumed actors and elaborate village sets re-create (and embellish) life in Elizabethan England to the delight of young and old alike. Sample Elizabethan-era food and customs; cheer on your favorite knight in the joust; take in some Shakespearean drama or a comedy act; watch live performances of early music or Morris dancing. Give archery and axe-throwing a try, ride horses, and see falconry exhibitions. It's a county fair and a theme park all in one. This is a great escapist activity, and all of you will surely leave with a new appreciation for our modern times.

❏ 55. Visit an Art Museum

The soul of a culture lives on in its art. School art programs are constantly in danger of losing funding, so it is more important than ever to make art a part of your family's everyday life. Pay a visit to a local art museum and appreciate the paintings and sculptures, installations and photographs. There are works of beauty and works of cleverness, works that draw a sense of reverence and works that shock. Take some time to learn about and discuss the artists who created the pieces you see at the museum. By making art a part of your family's life, you take an important step toward making your family's life a work of art.

❏ 56. Got Milk?

It's time for the kids to learn how that milk ends up in your refrigerator. Dairy farms often invite visitors to come by and see what life on a working farm is like. Check the phonebook for a farm near you and call to find out their milking hours. Watching a farmer milk a cow isn't at all what it used to be. The dairy industry is industrialized, and the sight of the cows lined up with their udders attached to mechanical milking machines is truly moo-ving! Cows are milked 365 days a year, so the chances of having an udder-ly fantastic dairy farm experience are very good!

❏ 57. Visit the Smithsonian Museums in D.C.

Washington, D.C., may arguably have more free sites than any other city in the United States. It's a city of monuments, memorials, and museums. The Smithsonian Institution Museums are supported by endowments and by the federal government, which means the museums are open to the public without charge for admission. Most of the Smithsonian's 19 museums, zoo, and 9 research centers are located in Washington, D.C., but also include sites in New York City, Virginia, Panama, and elsewhere. The most popular Smithsonian museums in D.C. are the National Air and Space Museum, the National Museum of American History, and the National Museum of Natural History. Each museum offers more than a day's worth of things to see and learn about. And if you just want to be able to say you visited all of the ones located in D.C., you can walk along the Mall and stop in at most of them. Before you leave home, visit the Smithsonian Web site for a closer look at all they have to offer.

❑ 58. Instill Six Good Homework Habits

Homework is a part of being a kid, and life is easier for everyone when good homework habits are taught early. You can help make your child's homework time productive and pain-free by following these tips:

1. Let them unwind with a snack immediately after school. This will give kids a chance to relax and decompress after a long, busy day.

2. Set up a comfortable work environment where the temperature is right, the noise level is low, and there are no distractions.

3. Make sure your child gathers all the books and materials needed before they start working. That way they won't have to stop and get up again and again.

4. Teach your child to write down all assignments and check them off as they are completed.

5. Let your child take a ten-minute break while working on homework. This will help keep his mind fresh.

6. Make sure all assignments are put back into notebooks and backpacks so they aren't forgotten the next day.

❑ 59. Attend an Air Show

The Experimental Aircraft Association's annual AirVenture in Oshkosh, Wisconsin, is perhaps the most elaborate aviation celebration in the United States. It takes place in late July/early August and features vintage aircraft, the newest in aviation, and some of the finest air performers in the world. Every year, tens of thousands of people flock to the Wittman Regional Airport to witness stunt flying at its best, concerts by headliner stars, evening entertainment, workshops, and tours. If your family is just plane crazy, AirVenture is for you! If Oshkosh is a little too out of your way, check your local airports and Air Force bases for air shows coming to a sky near you.

❏ 60. Sled Down a Hill

When winter's magic turns the whole world white and school is canceled, there's no better family activity than sledding. Bundle up, grab your sled and saucers, and head to your nearest hill! Have fun racing each other to the bottom of the hill. See how many people you can fit in one saucer. Pack the snow into a jump and see who can fly the highest and the farthest. The snow's the limit in this wintertime activity. Don't forget to take a few breaks to warm up over a nice cup of hot chocolate. And when the day is over and your snow pants and jackets are hung up still dripping with melted snow, gather around the fire and recount the best runs of the day.

❏ 61. Play Miniature Golf

The game of miniature golf began in 1916 on the private estate of James Barber in Pinehurst, North Carolina. Garnet Carter patented the game, which he called Tom Thumb Golf, in 1927, and ever since, miniature golf courses have popped up at amusement parks, in tourist towns, and everywhere else where there are kids and families looking for fun. Play for fun, don't worry about the score, and be a family who putt-putts together.

❏ 62. Create a Tool Kit

It's no secret that little kids love tools. If your children are old enough and mature enough, consider making them a tool kit of real tools, including such things as a hammer, a screwdriver, and a tape measure. Teach children the responsibility and safety measures that each tool requires, and involve them in some of your household projects. The gift of tools can be a right of passage, so don't be afraid to make your kids earn them by showing that they can handle that responsibility. No matter how mature your children are, be sure to supervise them with the tools, and always remind them that tools aren't toys—no matter how excited Dad gets over them.

❏ 63. Ride a Canal Barge

Before railroads, canals were an important form of transportation for goods and people. Though some might seem so natural, canals are actually artificial waterways that connect existing lakes, rivers, or oceans. The Chesapeake and Ohio Canal, for example, ran alongside the Potomac River to bypass all the waterfalls and allowed transportation by barges along a route from Cumberland, Maryland, to Washington, D.C. If you and your children have read *The Wind in the Willows*, you may remember that Mr. Toad, after escaping from jail, flees on a canal barge. Today, many canals have barge rides on which a family can get a sense of how life used to be before the Industrial Revolution really took hold. These barges are usually pulled by one or two mules, but they can also be pushed along with large poles. Your family will enjoy the slow pace of the ride while listening to historic anecdotes and learning about navigation on North America's watery highways.

❏ 64. Put the "Wonder" Back in Winter Wonderland

Everyone loves making snowmen, but it's always a little sad to disturb pristine blankets of snow. So why not turn the chore of shoveling snow from the driveway into an adventure of *gathering* snow to make a snowman? With all the snow you'll have at your disposal, you could even make an entire family of snowpeople! Work together to clear the driveway and gain the satisfaction of a job well done. Then have some fun creating your army of snowpeople. Line the driveway with one for each member of the family, and you'll have the coolest house on the block. Be sure to get a picture, though, because unlike your real family, your snow family won't last forever.

❑ 65. Bake a Pie

Pies are synonymous with the holidays. The rich, warm aroma filling your home embodies the love found in those special family gatherings. But you don't have to wait for the holidays to have this feeling. You can bake a pie with your family any day of the year. So gather everyone together this evening, and put them to work on this tasty task. Or, if you want to make a day of it, visit a pick-your-own farm and gather some bushels of apples. When you get home, try this easy and delicious recipe:

Apple Crumble Pie:

INGREDIENTS:

- 1 9-inch, deep pie crust
- ½ cup white sugar, plus ⅓ cup
- ¾ teaspoon ground cinnamon
- 5 cups apples, peeled, cored, and thinly sliced
- ¾ cup all-purpose flour
- 6 tablespoons butter

1. Preheat oven to 400 degrees Fahrenheit.

2. Arrange apple slices in unbaked pie shell. Mix ½ cup sugar and cinnamon; sprinkle over apples.

3. Mix ⅓ cup sugar with flour; cut in butter until crumbly. Spoon mixture over apples.

4. Bake in preheated oven for 35 to 45 minutes, or until apples are soft and top is lightly browned.

❑ 66. Visit Your Hometown

Kids are naturally very curious about their moms and dads. They're especially interested in what you were like when you were a kid. A trip back to your home town, with a tour of the place where you grew up, can be a warm and meaningful experience for everyone. Seeing your town through your children's eyes can also be a surprising experience. Was your house really that small? Is that really the school where you won all those trophies? Did you really meet Mom at that church? How old is that movie theater anyway? Is that the tree you fell out of after Grandma told you not to climb it?

Connecting you to a specific place brings your childhood stories to life for your kids. It also gives them a connection to their own family history. Eat dinner at a restaurant that's still there after all these years. Walk along Main Street and talk about what's changed or stayed the same. You'll enjoy sharing a piece of your childhood with your children, and they'll appreciate the fact that you were once a kid too!

▲　▲　▲　▲　▲

"A good laugh is sunshine in the house."
—William Makepeace Thackery

▼　▼　▼　▼　▼

❏ 67. Record Your Child's Voice

Most of us are pretty good about capturing the important moments of our children's lives on film. But a picture isn't worth a thousand words when it comes to hearing your child's voice. A portable mini-tape recorder kept close at hand allows you to record the silly sounds the baby makes, the funny words she says from where she sits in the car seat, the songs he sings, the stories they tell to you and to each other, and the change in the level of sophistication in their language as they mature. Once the changes occur, it's impossible to go back and recapture those moments in sound that will mean so much to them, to you, and to relatives who may have missed them. As important as a photo album, a recording album fills in the blanks left by photographs.

Mark each tape clearly with the date, your child's name and age, and where they were when the recording took place. What a fun time you'll have even one year later when you let your child hear how he or she used to sound!

❑ 68. Create a Set of "Things to Do" Note Cards

"But there's nothing to do!" We've all been there—it's too rainy or too snowy or too hot, and the kids are bored. Arm yourself for the next wave of boredom blues by creating a note card file of fun activities. Arrange the cards in categories for easy reference. For example, you might include crafts for rainy days, snowy days, or sick days; card games; easy recipes; and so forth.

Have your child help think of activities to write on the cards. They might enjoy helping to decorate the cards too. Make extra sets to give as presents. It's the gift that keeps on giving!

❑ 69. Every Bunny Loves Coloring Easter Eggs

While Easter is a Christian holiday, Easter eggs, Easter egg hunts, the Easter Bunny, and all the tales that go along with it can be symbols of spring and new growth to be enjoyed by all. Coloring eggs is something that the whole family can do together. To start, you'll need hard-boiled eggs. Then simply buy the coloring tablets available in grocery stores, or make your own colors by mixing 2 drops food coloring, 1 teaspoon white vinegar, and ½ cup hot water, using a separate glass bowl or mug for each color. Lower the egg into the colored mixture and let it soak until it has reached the desired shade. Then lift each egg out and place in the egg carton cups to dry. Cool your eggs in the refrigerator, then hide them around the house or in the backyard nested in Easter grass. Assign a separate area for each child to hunt in. Provide a basket for collecting the eggs and candy you may have added to each nest. When all the eggs have been gathered, make egg salad sandwiches.

❏ 70. Make a Sand Castle

Planning to spend a day at the beach? Why not build a little monument to your family while you're there? You can do it as a spur-of-the-moment activity, using just your hands, or you can plan ahead and bring buckets, plastic knives and spoons, and even specially designed molds. More than anything else, though, the two keys to sand castles are sand and water. Without water, the sand can't be compacted, and without compaction, you can't have a sand castle. So make sure to get your sand good and wet from the water's edge, and pack it tightly. First use your hands to mold the general shape you want to make your castle, then simply carve away until you have the castle of your dreams. Add some seashells for the windows or a bird feather for a flag to top it all off. Don't forget to capture your creations with a photo before the tide takes them out!

❏ 71. Make Snow Angels

No childhood is complete without the invigorating experience of making snow angels. When the first snow falls, it's time for your kids to fall too—flat on their backs and into the freshly fallen blanket of snow. It's simple. All you do is lie flat on your back, spread your arms and legs out, and move them back and forth to make an angel shape. Make one, make a few, or fill your entire yard with angels of all sizes. For extra fun, use pebbles, pinecones, and berries to give your angels faces. When you're all finished, be a real angel and take a picture of your little angels standing behind their creations!

❏ 72. Collect Shells and Make a Shell Lamp

Wandering along the beach searching for the most interesting and beautiful shells is fun by itself, but did you ever wonder what to do with the shells afterward? Why not make a shell lamp? It will serve as a wonderful memento of your vacation.

Here are nine simple steps to making a shell lamp:

1. Collect the best shells that you can find!

2. Rinse the shells in water and let them dry completely.

3. Go to a craft store and buy a glass or clear plastic container with a secure top through which you can drill a hole.

4. Go to a local home improvement store and buy a lamp kit, a lamp shade, a lightbulb, and play sand. (Note: Do not use sand from the beach just in case there are little critters in it.)

5. Drill a hole in the top of the container and secure the lamp kit to the top.

6. Fill your container with shells and add some sand as filler.

7. Attach the top to the container with the shells in it.

8. Put the lamp shade on the lamp.

9. Plug the lamp in, and enjoy it for years to come! When the light shines, you'll always remember your beach vacation.

❑ 73. Make Music with Homemade Instruments

Look around your house. Did you know that almost everything you see can be used to make music? Here are a few examples:

Maracas: Take an old water bottle or soda can and put a handful of beans inside. Close up the opening, and you have a maraca! The number and size of the beans will change the sound, so experiment until you have it just as you like it.

Drums: Turn over a pot, a bucket, or a trash can and hit it with a wooden spoon. You have a drum! Try out different size containers and different materials to see how the sounds change.

Wine Glass Orchestra: Take a set of wine glasses and fill them with different amounts of water. Wet your fingers and run them along the rims to produce a warm tone.

Of course, this is just the tip of the iceberg. Once you've got your musical mind working, you'll be amazed at all the things around your house that make great musical instruments.

☐ 74. Recycle!

There's no denying the importance of preserving our environment. Your family can make a significant impact by following the three Rs: Reduce, Reuse, and Recycle. Even very young children can begin learning about the earth and the everyday steps we can take to help protect our planet.

Engage your children in the process of deciding what to recycle and what to reuse. Help them decorate recycling bins. Children can also play an important role in sorting the recyclables if this is something your community recycling program requires of you. Just make sure to supervise their efforts, as aluminum cans and glass bottles may have sharp edges.

If possible, pay a visit to the recycling plant in your town or county so your child can experience the process in action. Emphasize that even a little bit of effort goes a long way when it comes to protecting Mother Earth!

▲　▲　▲　▲　▲

"Parents lend children their experience and
a vicarious memory; children endow
their parents with a vicarious immortality."
—George Santayana

▼　▼　▼　▼　▼

☐ 75. Make a Halloween Costume Together

Carving a pumpkin, bobbing for apples, and telling ghost stories are part of the festivities on Halloween, but trick-or-treating just wouldn't be as much fun without the costumes! After all, what other day of the year can you spot groups of witches, pirates, bunnies, ghosts, and mummies roaming the streets? It's one thing to go to the store for costumes, but how about making some together with your children? Crafting a creative Halloween costume is really not as difficult as it might seem!

With cardboard boxes you can make dice, milk cartons, presents, robots, refrigerators, televisions, and cameras—just to name a few. All you need is some paint and markers to decorate, some scissors to cut holes for arms, and some string to make straps to hold the costume up.

Want to make a mummy? No need to embalm your child. Just wrap him or her in a few rolls of gauze or cloth bandages, and leave room for the nose and eyes.

Care for something of the animal variety, such as a bunny, a puppy, or a kitten? Start with tights, a leotard, or a sweat suit. Get some fabric paint and paint on the animal's coat, or cut out felt in the right pattern and sew it on. Use face paint for the whiskers, and add some felt ears to a winter cap to complete the look.

See, there's nothing scary about making a cool Halloween costume! And your kids will have a blast helping with the creations.

❏ 76. Pick Some Berries

Berry picking is a great activity for kids both big and small. Berries grow on bushes and plants close to the ground, so even the youngest tots can take part in the fun. And who doesn't love the sweet taste of strawberries, blackberries, blueberries, and raspberries? This is a summer activity that has sweet rewards—berry pies, berry crisps, berry shortcake, berries and cream, berries on ice cream, berries on cereal—the list goes on and on. Find a farm near you by checking the phone book, your local newspaper, or the Internet. The farmer will supply berry baskets and will charge you by the pint or quart.

❏ 77. Go Roller-Skating

The first time a child puts on a pair of roller skates may be a little bit scary. After all, it wasn't that long ago that he or she got the hang of walking! But once the wheels start rolling, the breeze starts blowing through the hair, and the realization hits that rolling is faster than walking, fears quickly turn to fun. With the proper knee pads, elbow pads, and helmet, roller-skating is a childhood rite that brings with it a new sense of power—the power to move swiftly. Roller-skating provides a complete aerobic workout and involves all the body's muscles, especially the heart. Plus, like ice-skating, roller-skating is an indoor and outdoor sport, which means it can be enjoyed year-round. Roller rinks dot the landscape all over the United States. Plan a roller-skating party, a family day at the rink, or just take the skates to the park and skate on the paths provided.

❏ 78. Visit Amish Country

Modern-day life is a flurry of activity. Families rush here, there, and everywhere. So why not slow down with a visit to Amish Country?

The Amish don't use power-line electricity. They ride in horse-drawn buggies instead of automobiles, limit the use of telephones, and dress in a distinctive style. As of 2008, the Amish population in the United States numbered 231,000. You can find Amish communities in 21 states, with Pennsylvania having the largest population, followed by Ohio and Indiana.

A visit to Amish Country often includes demonstrations of such skills as furniture making and candle making. Find a store backed by a farm to get fresh milk and dry goods and to discover eggs and cheese in their natural colors. You might also find farmers' markets where fresh pies, jams, sausage, handmade quilts, and hand-whittled wooden toys are just some of the wares offered for sale and sampling. This peek back to the time when all people lived by their talents, hard work, and independence from modern conveniences will give you and your children an appreciation for a simpler life.

❑ 79. Build a Bonfire on the Beach and Make S'mores

Nothing says summer like a bonfire on the beach, songs sung around the fire, and marshmallows toasted on the end of a long stick.

Whether your local beach is on a lake or ocean, you can dig a shallow hole in the sand, stack kindling and driftwood in the middle of the hole, and enjoy a crackling fire by the shoreline (if local laws permit!). When the marshmallows are toasted, the best is yet to come—s'mores! Sandwich a marshmallow and four squares of a chocolate bar in between two graham crackers and eat. Why are they called s'mores? Because everyone is sure to want s'more!

❑ 80. Fun Is in the Cards

Card games provide more than just a fun way to spend time together. They're entertaining and educational, plus games provide a forum for teaching good sportsmanship: how to be a good winner and a good loser. Beginner games such as Go Fish, Old Maid, and Slap Jack are fun for all ages and easy enough for kids to learn without too much practice. Play a couple of practice hands that "don't count" before playing to win. Learning by demonstration is a great way to teach cards. Once playing cards becomes a pastime your family looks forward to, you can move on to more difficult games that match the interest level of all players. Play cards with the whole family. You can't lose!

❑ 81. Bake a Cake

There's no better way to say "Happy Birthday!" than with a home-made birthday cake. And making the cake with your child's help becomes a part of the birthday tradition as you divide up the cake-making steps—getting out the mixing bowls, measuring cups, ingredients, and pans—then mixing the ingredients, pouring the batter into the cake pans, and popping the pans into the oven. When the cake is cooked and cooled, icing and decorating it can be as much fun as eating it. Let your child add the finishing touches and don't worry about perfection. Take pictures of the cake-making process, and spend time reviewing photos from previous years as part of the fun.

❏ 82. Write the Perfect Thank-You Note

E-mail and telephones have made handwritten thank-you notes a lost art. But it doesn't have to be that way! Good manners mean writing good thank-you notes. After all, it's the least you can do after someone has taken the time and thought to give your child a gift. A well-written thank-you note includes a mention of the gift, a thank you for it, a compliment to the gift-giver's choice, and a warm sign off. If your child can't write yet, a drawing with your child's name on it makes a thoughtful addition to a thank-you note.

❏ 83. Take a Ride on a Glass-Bottom Boat

There's a wonderful world under the sea, and you don't necessarily have to get all wet to visit it. Get up close and personal with some of nature's underwater spectacles with a tour on a glass-bottom boat. These tourist vessels will give you such clear views of underwater flora and fauna, you'll feel like you just moved in! Your kids will be amazed by coral reefs, anemones, schools of colorful fish, sand sharks, and many other natural wonders of the deep. Keep your eyes out for treasure! You never know what you might find. Most seaside destinations offer glass-bottom boat tours, so the next time you're on vacation by the water, look one up—or down!

❏ 84. Create "Experience Albums"

You may not realize it as you go through your days together, but when you look back, you'll know there's a story to be told about almost everything you've done. Why not bring it all together in an experience album? The next time you and your family have a special outing planned, stop at the supermarket and purchase a disposable camera for each person. Then fill up each of your cameras with pictures. When the day is over, drop the cameras off to be developed. When you get your photos back, gather together to discuss them and put them in an album. Not only will you all have fun snapping whatever pictures strike your fancy, you'll also learn how each of you sees the same events and get to know each other a little better by understanding your unique points of view.

Not sure what to do? Almost any activity in this book would make the perfect subject for your experience album. So get out there, and make it snappy!

▲   ▲   ▲   ▲   ▲

Like mile markers on a map,
memories connect me to my past
and guide me to the future.

▼   ▼   ▼   ▼   ▼

❑ 85. Start Family Traditions

Every family has its own special traditions. Maybe when you were a child, that tradition was pork chop night or the big family holiday party or an annual vacation. Maybe you still do those things with your family now, just like your parents did with you. Those are your traditions, and they are a big part of who you are today. It's wonderful to pass traditions from one generation to the next, but that doesn't mean you can't start one for your own family—a tradition you and your children can start to pass on to future generations. Your own new tradition can be as simple as a weekend waffle breakfast where everyone plays a role. Maybe certain ingredients in or on your waffles will become special to you—cottage cheese, strawberries, and chocolate chips anyone? Or you can go big and start a new tradition around the holidays with a special dinner—lobster on New Year's Day, perhaps. Whatever you choose, you'll be strengthening the bond between you and your kids.

❑ 86. Play Board Games

Board games are back—and bigger than ever. Put away the video games and play these original interactive games instead! How many of us remember marathon Monopoly games played with our siblings? Or wars of checkers and chess waged with our parents? Family game nights or afternoons will be real quality time spent together. Game playing introduces kids to the concept of taking turns, playing by the rules, and being good losers and winners. Start young with games such as Chutes and Ladders, Candy Land, Cooties, and Mousetrap. As the game players become more adept, move on to Clue, Monopoly Junior, and Risk. Garage sales are a great source for games on the cheap. Just be sure all the pieces are there before you make your purchases. Pop a little popcorn and let the games begin!

❑ 87. Love Bugs

Believe it or not, bugs can be fun. At some point in our lives, bugs may become icky, but fearing them is a learned reaction, not something innate. Before your kids learn to run at the sight of them, look at bugs as something to learn from instead. Share the excitement of capturing fireflies in a jar, watching them blink on and off, and then releasing them back into the night air.

Ant farms are another option for studying what goes on underground where the ants build their colonies. Worker ants can live for about a year from birth, so ant farms provide educational entertainment for a good amount of time.

If watching bugs doesn't suit your fancy, try listening to them. The cricket's song on summer evenings, the sound of a cicada's tymbal muscles vibrating, and the warning sound of approaching mosquitoes, wasps, and bees are all sounds worth listening for. Bugs are a valuable part of our ecosystem, and learning to live with them is a good lesson for your kids.

❑ 88. Visit a Dinosaur Site

Dinosaurs capture the imaginations of boys and girls alike. It's almost as if they existed in an entirely made-up world. It might surprise you to know that there were dinosaurs all over the world, even right in our own backyards! There were far more than 100 different dinosaurs that roamed North America alone, including the famous *Stegosaurus* and *Triceratops,* the fearsome *Tyrannosaurus rex,* and the hard-to-pronounce *Pachycephalosaurus.* You can start your journey back into their world by visiting one of the many dinosaur sites in North America, where you'll see reconstructed skeletons and life-size reproductions. If you howl loud enough and do your best *Corythosaurus* impression, you might even be able to take part in a dig. So check out a dino site. It's guaranteed to be dino-mite!

❑ 89. Go Camping

Spending a weekend in a tent with your family may not be for everyone, but if you're patient, good-natured, go-with-the-flow types, setting up camp in a safe place can be a lot of fun. Kids will learn that there's more to life than television, video games, and fast-food restaurants. Communing with nature, building a fire, cooking freshly caught and cleaned fish, singing songs and telling stories around the campfire by night add up to a memorable experience, which, if well-planned, will be one everyone wants to repeat. Equipping yourselves with the right size tent, proper utensils for outdoor cooking, sleeping bags, bug spray, maps of the area, field guides for wildflowers and birds, and proper hiking shoes, ensures a good time. Checking out the campsite ahead of time removes the possibility of bad surprises and disappointment. Arriving at your campsite with plenty of daylight left for setting up camp and relaxing after a long drive is an essential ingredient in making a good time better. If roughing it with only a lake for bathing and the woods for a toilet is a deterrent, look for a campground park complete with showers, toilets, and concession stands. How does one find the perfect campground park? The phone book, recommendations from friends who've camped out before, and the campground parks' Web sites are all good sources of information. Create a checklist of supplies, what to pack for comfort in and out of the tent, games and books, and food, drinks, and snacks. If kids have favorite blankets or stuffed animals they sleep with, be sure to bring that little bit of comfort from home. Camping is a very popular family activity in the United States and around the world. Each time you go camping, you learn something new about the outdoors, about your kids, and about yourselves.

❑ 90. Fond of Fondue

The word *fondue* comes from the French word *fondre*, which means "to melt." Your kids will have a blast dipping bite-size pieces of food into pots of melted cheese, chocolate, or hot oil. For supper, try a Swiss cheese fondue recipe with French bread cut into bite-size cubes and raw carrots, broc-

FAST FACT

The Melting Pot is a fondue franchise restaurant with more than 129 locations from coast to coast in the United States. If you want the fondue experience without the mess, check your local restaurant guide for a location near you.

coli florets, and green and red peppers cut up for dipping. For dessert, try a chocolate fondue recipe with angel-food cake cut into cubes and strawberries hulled and ready for spearing and dipping. Whether you use an electric fondue pot, a fondue pot that's heated with a sterno flame, or a regular cooking pot placed over medium heat on the stove, fondue turns meal time into a party.

❑ 91. Tell Ghost Stories

Ever wonder why we love to scare each other so much? It's because a good scare brings us closer together. Remember the ghost stories around the campfire? If it was a really good tale, no one wanted to leave the fire or the group. That's where they felt safe. When you think of ghost stories this way, they're not that scary after all. They're just plain fun. So turn off the lights, gather around a candle or flashlight, and get your scariest voices ready. Let everyone in the family have a turn trying to outdo each other's last scare. Just remember, it's not only about scaring each other. It's about getting closer as a family.

BOO! Did that scare you?

❑ 92. Eat Dinner by Candlelight

Date nights for Mom and Dad may not be as common anymore with a growing family, but that doesn't mean you can't still have special evenings together. Include the whole family in a date at home with a candlelight dinner. What could be better than having the people you love most gathered around the table, sharing the quiet warmth of the flames dancing among you? It's the perfect way to step outside the world together. Let the kids light the candles and blow them out at the end (for young kids, it might even feel like a birthday) to really include them in the evening. Combine the candlelight with a meal, drink, or dessert only served on these occasions, and your whole family will look forward to candlelight dinners with growing anticipation.

❑ 93. Go to a Parade

Arrive early and stay late! There's a parade happening on Main Street, and you want a front-row seat (or at least a place to stand!). Whether it's Thanksgiving, Fourth of July, St. Patrick's Day, Mardi Gras, Oktoberfest, or a special day in your town's history, parades are great opportunities for the whole community to turn out and watch marching bands, floats, people in uniform, local leaders, firefighters, cheerleaders, scouts, and more. Make the parade even more entertaining by searching out the less obvious sights. See if you can find where the driver of the float is hidden. Pick out your favorite instrument in the band. Wave at the celebrities, police officers, and firefighters and try to get them to wave back. Get your picture taken with the mascot, the chief of police, the leader of the band, or a politician. Try to get on television if cameras are around. Whatever the occasion for the parade, teach your child the history behind it. Check your local government's Web site for the parade schedule in your city or town.

❏ 94. Make Puppets and Have a Puppet Show

Puppets can be as simple or as complicated as you wish, but perhaps the easiest puppet to make is a bag puppet. Here's how:

YOU WILL NEED:
Paper lunch bag
Construction paper
Scissors
Markers
Glue

1. Take a new, flat paper bag. This is the body of your puppet. One side of the bag is all smooth. That's the back of your puppet. On the other side, there's a flap folded over. That flap is going to be your puppet's head. Lay the bag down with the flap facing up.

2. On the construction paper, draw the eyes, nose, and tongue. Cut these pieces out with scissors.

3. Attach the eyes. Remember that the flap on the bag is the puppet's head. Glue the eyes to the bag just above the middle of that flap.

4. Next attach the nose. Put the nose just slightly over the bottom of the eyes, and glue it down. Your puppet's face is almost ready!

5. The final step is to attach the tongue. Remember the flap on the bag? Take the tongue oval and slide half of it under the flap. Glue it in place, and you've got your mouth. Slip your hand into the bag, curling your fingers into the flap. Move your fingers to make the mouth talk.

Now you know how to make a bag puppet. Just repeat these instructions until each family member has made his or her own puppet, and you'll be ready for a show!

❏ 95. Practice the Perfect Handshake and Introduction

We teach our kids all kinds of valuable lessons, and here's another one that lasts a lifetime: handshake, eye contact, and the perfect words of introduction. Good manners generate immediate respect from others. First impressions last. Knowing how to present a firm handshake and a proper introduction fosters a level of confidence that will benefit your child throughout his or her life. Practice at home, then take it out to the public and test it. Results are guaranteed.

❏ 96. Make a Music Video

Not everyone was born a pop star or a singing sensation, but that doesn't mean we don't like to play at it sometimes. Your children, no matter what their ages, probably have favorite bands or musicians, just like you did when you were their age. Get to know their tastes and direct their creative energy by making a music video. For younger kids, the video can be as simple as filming them in costume, dancing and singing along with their favorite songs. Older kids, especially if they're musicians, might be making their own videos and writing their own songs, but that doesn't mean you can't be involved. Assist them by editing the video or operating the camera for them as they play their instruments. This will show your kids that you take their interests seriously and support them in what they do, especially in their teenage years. Many computers already come with video editing software installed, and it's pretty easy to use. Even the most basic software can enable you to produce a high-quality video. No matter what age your children are, they'll appreciate your earnest involvement—especially when they see the results!

❏ 97. Play Car Games

I Spy

"Are we there yet?" Cut down on the frequency of that question with "I Spy." This guessing game helps familiarize young kids with the alphabet and increases observation skills. It's also fun! Make your rules in advance—will things inside the car be included? The game starts with one person selecting something such as a truck and saying "I spy with my little eye, something beginning with *T*." Other passengers in the car try to guess what it might be—"tunnel," "train," "telephone pole," "truck." Reply with "Yes! Truck is the thing my little eye spied." The person who guessed correctly chooses the next object. Clues may be given to help those who are guessing, and you can play for points or just for fun. If your kids are too young to know their alphabet well, you can play the game by color instead.

The License Plate Game

The License Plate Game keeps kids' eyes open as they search the cars on the road for plates from different states. Depending on how many people you have in the car, divide up into teams or play as individuals. Check off each state as you find it. The first to check off the most states wins. A variation of this game is to make anagrams using the consonants in each license plate; you can add vowels for free to help make words. Everyone is a winner as you brainstorm and compete to make the most interesting anagrams.

❏ 98. Learn to Juggle

Juggling is a very impressive skill. Practiced jugglers make it look effortless as they begin first with two balls, then add another and another and another until the air is filled with balls going round and round in a circle above the juggler's head. But can *you* learn to juggle and teach your kids how to do it too? You bet you can! The Internet is filled with instructions accompanied by step-by-step video demonstrations. It's recommended that beginners start with beanbags rather than balls.

▲ ▲ ▲ ▲ ▲

The life of a family centers not on its members but on the love and support that fill the spaces in between.

▼ ▼ ▼ ▼ ▼

❏ 99. Make a Bird Feeder

Feeding birds accomplishes two things—you feed the birds and you feed your children's curiosity about other living things. Of course, you could just put food out in a store-bought bird feeder, but it's so much more fun to make your own, hang it up, and watch from your window as the birds stop by for a bite to eat. Here are a few ideas for homemade bird feeders that will have these feathered friends flocking to your yard:

• Pinecones covered in peanut butter and dipped in birdseed—tie an 18-inch string to the end of each pinecone and hang it on a branch where the squirrels won't get it.

• Cheerio to the Birds—tie the end of a fishing line to a large button. Then thread Cheerios onto the line until it's filled. Hang a bunch of them on the branches of your trees.

• Make an egg carton feeder. Poke a hole in each corner, then tie strings through the holes. Fill the cups with seed, cereal, or bread cubes. Hang the feeder and watch the bird buffet!

❏ 100. Count to Ten in Five Different Languages

What fun it is to learn something new along with your kids! How about making some foreign languages less foreign? Counting to ten is a great way to start, and as the world grows smaller, the more you know about other cultures, countries, and languages, the better! Start with the easy one—your own language.

Spanish

Uno (OO-no)
Dos (dose)
Tres (trace)
Cuatro (KWA-tro)
Cinco (SINK-o)
Sies (seis)
Siete (see-YET-ay)
Ocho (OH-cho)
Nueve (new-AY-vay)
Dias (dee-ACE)

German

Eins (AH-eens)
Zwei (TSVAH-ee)
Drei (DRAH-ee)
Vier (FEE-er)
Fuenf (fuenf)
Sechs (zehks)
Sieben (ZEE-ben)
Acht (AHHHH-t)
    (HHHH=heavy-sounding *H*)
Neun (NOH-een)
Zehn (tsane)

Greek

Ena (EH-na)
Dyo (THEE-oh)
Tria (TREE-ah)
Tessera (TEH-sse-ra)
Pente (PEHN-de)
Exi (EH-ksi)
Efta (ef-TAH)
Okto (ok-TOH)
Ennea (en-NEH-a)
Deka (THEH-ka)

French

Un (unh)
Deux (deuh)
Trois (Trwa)
Quatre (CAT-ra)
Cinq (sank)
Six (sees)
Sept (Set)
Huit (weet)
Neuf (noof)
Dix (dees)

❏ 101. Pretend You're Royalty– Visit a Castle

You don't have to go to Europe to see a castle (although if you can afford a trip to Europe, all the better!). Believe it or not, the United States has its fair share of medieval-style homes, follies resembling those built on castle grounds in Europe, and châteauesque homes like those in France. But how does one find these architectural monuments to pseudo-royalty? And are they open to the public? Of the hundreds of Gothic Revival–era structures labeled "castle" in North America, many have been turned into bed-and-breakfasts, hotels, and museums. However, there are just as many open for sightseeing, complete with tour guides and gift shops. To find a castle that may loom large on a travel pathway you're taking, check online.

▲ ▲ ▲ ▲ ▲

Like a glacier the first five years crawl by.
The next ten years like a jet plane fly.
The last three of childhood—in the blink of an eye.

▼ ▼ ▼ ▼ ▼

❏ 102. Build a Racetrack out of Blocks and Toy Race Cars

Kids have a lot of fun zooming their toy cars through the air on invisible racetracks, but when Dad or Mom sits down on the floor with them and breaks out the building blocks, that's when the real fun begins. Those wooden blocks that used to be toddler toys become something quite extraordinary when they're laid out like a roadway system on the flat floor. Build walls on both sides of the roadway so cars won't spin out and off the road. Prop up blocks on piles of books or on top of other blocks and race the cars downhill.

Create a "pit stop" station for "refueling" and refuel yourselves with a snack and a drink between races. Compete for best roadway patterns, the longest straight run, and the fastest cars.

❑ 103. Make "It's the Thought that Counts" Gifts for Holiday Giving

Coupons are easy to make and even easier to give. In fact, a coupon that promises the gift of one's time, a service, or a homemade specialty, is not only thoughtful, it's inexpensive and invaluable. When a gift-giving event arises, teach your kids not to hop in the car and run to the store. Instead, ask them to put on their thinking caps and come up with a truly thoughtful gift idea.

Here are some ideas for coupons that count:

• Serve breakfast in bed

• Load the dishwasher

• Water the plants

• Sort the socks

• Empty wastebaskets for a week

Such gifts are sure to be received with great pleasure. Making gifts by hand is also a good lesson in valuing talents and skills more than store-bought items. Bake cookies, frame artwork and class pictures, play a piece on the piano, write a poem, make a booklet of a hundred smiles. The idea is to teach your children that it is better to give than to receive—and that giving from the heart is the best gift of all!

❑ 104. Join a Gym as a Family

A family gym membership is a great way to stay fit, teach your kids the importance of exercise, and set the example for a physically healthy lifestyle. Gym clubs offer all kinds of programming for kids and adults. While babysitting may be provided so that parents can take classes or work out, there are also parent/child classes, one-on-one personal training sessions, and exercise equipment, including floor mats, balls, and weights. Pick a day for Family Gym Day, dress in workout clothes and shoes, pack a bottle of water for each family member, and head for the gym. Stave off childhood obesity by getting your kids off on the right track. Healthy habits started early are the easiest ones to keep!

☐ 105. Go on a Family Yoga Retreat

In Sanskrit, the language of ancient India, where yoga began, *yoga* means union. It is a practice of physical postures that help unite the mind, body, and spirit. Yoga is more than just stretching. It's about creating balance throughout the body. A family yoga retreat encourages families to spend quality time together while reducing stress and time pressure on parents. When you are less stressed, you are more relaxed and are able to listen with all of your attention. Family yoga retreats are set up with the purpose of creating a greater bond within the family. There are family yoga retreat centers all over the world. Usually they are located in beautiful, pristine places with much to offer in addition to yoga classes. To find a vacation that suits your budget and desires, search "family yoga retreats" on the Internet.

☐ 106. Visit a Reptile Park

Television wildlife programs have generated an interest in all kinds of species that might once have been considered totally yucky. That's cool news because reptiles are valuable to humans in many ways. For one thing, they eat the bugs and rodents that annoy us. Seeing reptiles—snakes, komodo dragons, alligators, crocodiles, and more—in their natural habitats is an awe-inspiring experience. There are reptile parks all over the country. Tourism books, the Internet, the phone book, and the "things to do" section of the newspaper are good sources of information for locating a park near you or on your next vacation route. Visit www.reptilechannel.com to learn more about reptiles before you go. It's a cool site that has games as well as fun photos and lots of information.

❑ 107. Invent Something Together

Got a problem? Invent something that will solve it! Necessity is indeed the mother of many inventions, and teaching your kids to problem-solve is fun when it involves creativity. Inventions may be inspired by something as simple as creating a better way to display a collection, a new carryall for school books, an innovative invention for watering the garden, or even a new way to wash the dog. Start the inventive process with this Invention Ice Breaker game— give each of your kids a paper bag with the same items inside. Items could include: a toilet paper roll, a roll of tape, a length of string, a few puzzle pieces, a feather, and some cotton balls. Set a time limit of ten minutes. On "Go," each team or person opens their bag and begins to create something. At the end of the time limit, the inventors show what they've made and explain its use. This gets a lot of laughs and definitely gets the inventive juices flowing.

❑ 108. Read the Newspaper Together

Newspapers often offer kids' pages in the hopes of getting kids into the newspaper habit so they'll become future customers. Your reason for introducing your kids to the newspaper is different. You are showing your children an alternate method of getting news— through reading rather than viewing. Just as our interests fall into different categories, so do the sections of the newspaper. Find a section that has a story of mutual interest, read it together, and then talk about the main points of the story. What was the most interesting part of the article? Why was the story important enough to be in the newspaper? Whose life does it affect; does it affect yours? Did the story answer the five questions of journalism: Who, what, when, where, and how? Listening to your child's opinions, thoughts, and level of understanding gives you some insight into their views and thought process. And reading the newspaper together gives both of you some well-spent, quality time.

❑ 109. Go Antiquing

When you visit an antique store, treasures wait on every shelf, in every corner, under every table, and inside each display case. Antiquing truly is a treasure hunt as well as a lesson in history. While you may be looking for a specific piece of furniture, your kids will stick with you through your search if they have a specific mission—something special to be on the lookout for. Antique stores are filled with collectibles. Your antiquing days are the perfect opportunity for starting or adding to collections. For example, you might look for things with a bunny motif, or toy soldiers, or costume jewelry for dress up. Talk to the store owners to gather stories and information about the treasures you find. To ward off boredom or crankiness, make frequent rest stops, eat lunch, run around in a park, and leave before everyone is too tired. Knowing when to end the perfect day keeps it perfect.

❑ 110. Learn How Things Work

Nobody is suggesting that you take apart the plasma television and put it back together again just to see how it works. Chances are if you do that, it *won't* work at all! But, on a smaller scale, with simple machines, taking them apart for repairs is a great lesson in self-sufficiency and in how things work. You can do something as simple as lifting the top of the toilet tank to get a look at how the ballcock rises and falls when the flusher handle is pressed or take on a more complicated project like replacing a belt in a vacuum cleaner. Learning how things work and how to fix them when they don't is empowering and leads to money savings. It also can involve a fun trip to a hardware store, and that's the cherry on this how-things-work sundae: When your kids see all the nuts, bolts, screws, tubes, batteries, bulbs, and everything else a hardware store has to offer, you've opened up a whole new world of discovery. Fix it instead of throwing it away—that's a lesson that saves the environment in addition to saving money!

❑ 111. Play Video Games Together

You thought your days of playing video games were over? Not if you're smart enough to stay in touch with the new technology and the latest messages that are constantly thrown your kids' way. What better way to stay informed about what's new, what's good, and what's not so good in the video game industry?

Chances are it's your cash being laid on the counter when the games are being purchased. It's good to know what you're buying, and it can be a lot of fun to play the games with your kids. Plus, kids who are allowed to play video games often revere them less than kids who've been forbidden. When you take the time to play the games together, you can also start the habit of putting the games aside after a while and going outside for a walk, to throw a ball, or to play at the park. Accepting video games into your home can prevent your child from being the one who goes to someone else's house and only wants to play video games. So play, and then you can be the one to say "game over."

❑ 112. Play Lawn Games

Croquet, badminton, horseshoes, bocce, lawn bowling—don't let these time-honored games become a thing of the past. Some of the games have a history that reaches back to ancient Greece and the Middle Ages, and they've survived the test of time because they are competitive and fun. Did you know that badminton was originally called Battledore and Shuttlecock? Or that croquet was the forerunner of billiards and that family of games? Lawn games are fun for the whole family and provide great entertainment for outdoor family gatherings. Badminton, anyone?

❏ 113. Get Cool in the Pool

You don't need a fancy pool membership to cool off on a hot day. All you need is a blow-up pool big enough for you and your youngsters to sit and splash around in together. Inflate the pool, set up beach chairs around it, spread out towels, pack a picnic basket, and enjoy pool time without leaving home. Keep the hose handy to freshen the pool water and to elicit squeals of delight as the hose water rains down. Take a Popsicle break and then resume the splash time. Even with a little pool, it's the thought that counts, and the thought is: "Let's get cool in the pool!"

▲ ▲ ▲ ▲ ▲

"The most wasted day of all is that on which we have not laughed."
—Sebastien Roch Nicolas Chamfort

▼ ▼ ▼ ▼ ▼

❏ 114. Stop and Smell the Flowers

A pretty day, a lovely basket, a pair of scissors, and a garden full of flowers that may be picked are the perfect ingredients for a wonderful time with your kids. Whether you have a big garden or a small one, the flowers picked can be arranged and placed throughout your home. Choose your flowers with an arrangement and vase or container in mind. Use a sharp knife (YOU, not your child!) or scissors to cut the flowers. Remember to cut the stem long enough to reach the bottom of your container. Take this opportunity to talk with your children about the colors, the types of flowers, and the fragrances. Engage all your senses, and teach your kids how to engage theirs. Once you've picked your flowers, look for containers that suit the blooms. One big flower in a small bowl, teacup, or vase is just as beautiful as a group arrangement. Pick colors that complement one another. Small groups of flowers can fill a room with their fragrance. Keep the water fresh and clear, and keep your arrangements in cool places rather than in direct sunlight. Flowers add life to a room, and picking them together adds quality to your life.

▲ ▲ ▲ ▲ ▲

"The happiest moments of my life have been the few which I have passed at home in the bosom of my family."
—Thomas Jefferson

▼ ▼ ▼ ▼ ▼

❑ 115. Set Confidence-Building Goals and Work Together to Reach Them

The unconditional love you give your child is the foundation on which your child's confidence is built. Knowing that they will have your love and support whether they win a race or lose it, get the A or the C, spill the milk or pour it perfectly on the first try can make all the difference in the risks children are willing to take. You can start building confidence in your child from a very young age. Make a goal chart and set easy goals to start: put dirty clothes in the hamper without being told, put toys away, set the table. Keep track of progress on the chart, and when goals are reached, reward your kids with a compliment and a hug. Positive feedback on a job well done and encouraging words on tasks that are in progress remind your children that you are involved, you are aware, you are pleased, and you are always there to support them. The self-esteem and confidence these steps instill will lead to greater success and independence. As the goals become greater, so will the confidence needed to reach them.

❑ 116. Send Away for Free Stuff

Who doesn't love free stuff? Believe it or not, there are many Web sites listing companies that are giving away free samples of all kinds of things. In addition to coupons for groceries and other items, there are actual freebies in the form of books, videos, toys, crayons, safety kits, and a whole lot more. Kids who have not yet been inundated with junk mail are thrilled to receive mail addressed solely to them, and if the mail just happens to have a free coloring book, stickers, badges, and more, then that mail is even better.

Here are some Web sites that offer free stuff for kids. You may even find something for yourself!

- www.actualfreestuff.com/kidfreebies.htm
- www.freestuffchannel.com/kid.html
- www.dailynewfreestuff.com/kid.htm
- www.fema.gov/kids/freebie.htm

❑ 117. Write a Letter Together to Express Your Opinion

Every voice counts, and that's no more apparent than when a letter from you or your child receives a response from a member of Congress, the White House, or a local government official. All letters are answered, and that very fact is a good lesson—that everyone is entitled to express an opinion, hopefully influencing a policy, practice, or vote by doing so. Choose a topic of interest or benefit to your family; to others less fortunate; to animals; or to the town, city, or state in which you live. The right and ability to express an opinion is a powerful freedom. Get your child involved early!

❑ 118. Cheer Them On

Participating in sports teaches kids teamwork—how each individual fits in to make a whole team and to contribute to the overall effort. After many hours spent practicing a sport, kids finally have a chance to show off their skills on game day. Your cheers and support matter whether your child is the star player or the last one sent in to the game. No matter how well (or how poorly) your child plays, hearing you say, "Nice try," "Good job," "Great catch," or "You almost had him," can make the difference between a good game and a bad one. Make those days special no matter what the outcome of the game. That's what gives kids the courage to go out next week and try again.

▲　▲　▲　▲　▲

"A baby is God's opinion that the world should go on."
—Carl Sandburg

▼　▼　▼　▼　▼

❑ 119. Visit the Country of Your Ancestors

Where did your family come from before they lived in the country you live in now? Most people have an idea of their ancestry and the mix of cultures that exist within their family tree. And if you're fortunate enough to have fairly complete records of the country, town, or village from which your family originated, planning your trip to "the old country" will be that much easier. Even if you don't know details, visiting your ancestral country provides a good backdrop for understanding certain traits, features, and traditions that carry over into your life today. If it's not possible to actually visit the country, take the time to learn about the traditional dress, music, art, foods, industry, and history of the country.

Set aside a day to celebrate your origins with a special dinner and a travel film showing the sights.

❑ 120. Go to a Garage Sale

A dollar can go a long way when you take it to a garage sale. Garage sales offer great deals on very usable stuff, and teaching the value of recycling goods instead of buying new is another opportunity for a lesson in planet-saving. Toys, books, CDs, DVDs, bicycles, skates, and sports equipment are all things that show up at neighborhood garage sales. Demonstrate the thrill of getting a deal by proposing a contest. Who can get the most stuff for a dollar? Or five dollars? It might also be fun to have a garage sale of your own to make money and room for your new deals!

❑ 121. Visit a Beekeeper and Buy Fresh Honey

Honey is one of the oldest foods known to humans. In fact, honey was found in King Tut's tomb and was still edible! There are more than 211,000 beekeepers in the United States. A worker bee can only produce $\frac{1}{12}$ teaspoon in her lifetime, so beekeepers must raise hundreds—even thousands—of honeybees to produce large amounts of honey. Visiting a beekeeper and watching the colonies of honeybees at work is fascinating. The beekeeper will explain what is required to keep bees and may even share some fun facts with you. For example, did you know that honeybees are the only insects that produce food for humans? Or that fresh honey never goes bad?

FAST FACT

A worker bee visits between 50 and 100 flowers on each trip away from the hive. It takes two million visits to make one pound of honey.

In addition to using honey as a replacement for sugar (it's 25 percent sweeter than sugar), you can also use it on cuts and burns instead of over-the-counter remedies. It's good for the skin, good for the diet, and fun to watch being made. Have a honey of a day at your local beekeeper's place!

▲ ▲ ▲ ▲ ▲

"The rules for parents are but three . . . love, limit, and let them be."
—Elaine M. Ward

▼ ▼ ▼ ▼ ▼

❏ 122. Celebrate a Special Occasion at a Dinner Theater

Are your children old enough to sit quietly through a show? If so, the dinner theater experience is one you don't want to miss! The atmosphere is lively and fun for the whole family. Waitstaff are often members of the cast, and kids will love seeing them costumed and performing at show time. Typically, doors open at 6 P.M., dinner is served at 6:30, and the curtain goes up at 8:00. Theaters that welcome children often offer a reduced rate for them. In addition to a served meal or a buffet, you'll be treated to a musical evening, a murder mystery involving audience members, a play, or a review. Check the newspaper listings or online movie Web sites before you go to make sure what you're going to see is suitable for families, then dress up and have a night out to celebrate a birthday, Mother's Day, Father's Day, or a Just-Because Day.

❏ 123. Go Caroling

The tradition of Christmas caroling is alive and well in many neighborhoods. If it isn't a tradition in your neck of the woods, why not start one? The excitement of Christmas Eve can begin right after dinner. Post notices in the neighborhood asking others to meet at a particular corner or house for caroling. Print out multiple copies of song sheets, bring flashlights for easy reading, dress warmly, and go from door to door. Ring the doorbell and then start singing. End the caroling with hot chocolate, hang up the stockings, leave cookies out for Santa, and then it's off to bed for the little ones.

❏ 124. Conquer Fears Together

Maybe it's the dark. Maybe it's the boogeyman under the bed. Or maybe it's a fear of getting on the new two-wheeler, facing a bully at school, or trying a new food. Fears, no matter how big or how small, can be paralyzing. But facing those fears and overcoming them can be liberating and empowering. While some fears are healthy because they protect us and make us more cautious—fear of crossing a busy street, fear of walking alone at night, fear of handling a weapon—other fears are unhealthy because they prevent us from doing things that may be fun, enlightening, new, and exciting.

Helping your children look fear in the eye and overcome it may start with remembering this acronym for FEAR: **F**alse **E**vidence **A**ppearing **R**eal. For example, the dark appears to be frightening. You turn on the light and the dark disappears, revealing that there was nothing scary hiding in the dark. Talking about your own fears helps your children talk about their fears. Walking them through the fear, analyzing it logically, and revealing it as false evidence appearing real will give your child the tools to conquer fears alone.

❏ 125. Play "I Remember When..."

Next time there's a gathering of family members sitting around the dining room table, bring out the photo albums and get the "Remember When?" conversation going. Let the kids start with their memories of a great day at school, the first realization of what being a "big sister" meant, great times at the lake, or a fun time with the whole family. Each family member can take a turn remembering when something funny, wonderful, amazing, or silly happened. For extra fun, make a guessing game of it. Hold up a photograph and give each person three chances to guess the event. Or number photographs, put them up around the room, give each person a paper and pencil, and have them quietly write down their guesses. No matter how you play it, "Remember When?" is sure to elicit giggles, smiles, and more memories.

❑ 126. Keep Your Eyes on Supplies

Make a Surprise Supplies Box for rainy-day craft projects. You'll never be at a loss for something to do when you've got a box filled with everything necessary for all kinds of handicrafts. A well-stocked box might have:

- Scissors
- Glue
- Clear tape
- Stapler
- Felt-tipped markers and pens
- Crayons, colored pencils
- Construction paper
- Shirt cardboard
- Ruler, tape measure
- Glitter
- Feathers
- Beads
- Cardboard tubes from paper towels or gift wrap rolls
- Yarn, ribbons, embroidery thread

- Old greeting cards
- Small boxes, egg cartons, and empty cardboard food boxes

No matter what crafts you choose to make, you'll have what you need to spend a creative day together with your kids. Let their imaginations lead the way. Then all you have to do is follow along.

❑ 127. Make a Gingerbread House

There's no place like home—especially when that home is made of graham crackers and decorated with all kinds of candies. Your kids will love being the architects of an edible house, but beware: They may end up eating you out of houses and homes!

While traditional gingerbread houses are made of real ginger-bread, you can take the easy way out by using eight to ten graham crackers, a Styrofoam tray, white frosting, gumdrops, M&Ms, sprinkles, and tubes of colored frosting. Use the tray as your base, and cover it with frosting. To make the house, stand up four squares of graham crackers in the frosting on the base. Add frosting at the seams to hold the crackers together. Ice the top rim of the square house and lay a square of graham cracker over the top. To make a peaked roof, lean two crackers against each other and seal along the top with frosting. Frost the entire house. Use the colored frosting to draw windows and a door. While the frosting is still "wet," decorate the house with candies. This is a fun and yummy afternoon activity, and the finished houses make great gifts for grandparents, too!

❑ 128. Plant a Tree and Grow a Relationship

How does your garden grow? Very well, if you bring your kids into the planting process so they can experience the joy of watching a tree grow from sapling to maturity. If you need an excuse to plant a tree, make Arbor Day your reason. Arbor Day is celebrated at the end of April and inspires community beautification efforts, classroom celebrations, and tree plantings on college campuses and public parks across the nation. You and your kids can have your own Arbor Day celebration and beautify your yard at the same time. Choose a space, a tree, and the right tools and soil for preparing the hole for your tree's root-ball. Let the kids help with the digging, the soil spreading, and the watering of the hole before the tree is lowered into it. Stand the tree in the hole and fill with soil. The kids will like stamping and tamping the dirt, followed by a healthy watering. Share the watering duties in the days to come, and take pictures of the kids standing next to the tree. Measure their growth with that of the tree. A tree is a gift that keeps on growing.

For more information on selecting the right tree and for planting tips, take a look at the Arbor Day Web site: www.arborday.org/trees/video/howtoplant.cfm.

❏ 129. Paint a Mural Together

Does your family want to express itself in a *big* way? Why not dedicate a wall in the garage or rec room to a family mural?

To begin, decide on a theme. A family of animal lovers might want to try a jungle scene or an underwater scene. A family of athletes might want to pay homage to their favorite sports. Anything goes!

To plan your mural, start with a piece of graph paper, and draw lines dividing it into eight equal parts. Then sketch out your design. Prepare your wall by cleaning it and giving it a fresh coat of latex paint. When the base has dried, divide your painting space into eight equal parts that correspond to your paper drawing. Then transfer each part of the drawing to the corresponding section on the wall. Switch to acrylic paints for the actual mural painting—it dries faster and is water-soluble for easy cleanup. Acrylics come in smaller sizes and are available at craft stores. Make the mural painting a long-range project to make the fun last longer. When the mural is exactly as you want it, save the work of art with a coat of clear varnish. Take a picture of your family and the mural, and send it to a local newspaper. You just might make the news: Family of Artists Right Here in Our Town!

❑ 130. Visit the Grand Canyon

At 277 miles long, up to 18 miles wide, and 5,000 feet deep, the Grand Canyon definitely lives up to its name. Grand Canyon National Park includes 1,904 square miles and offers well-maintained hiking trails, campgrounds, and waterfalls. Guided tours are offered by airplane, helicopter, bus, and even by donkey! The Grand Canyon boasts a large variety of wildlife—not to mention countless fun family activities, including bird-watching, fishing, horseback riding, houseboating, hot-air balloon rides, and so much more. This is a great vacation destination for families with kids of all ages and a definite must-see. Just be sure to book your accommodations well in advance!

FAST FACT

The Grand Canyon is home to five Native American tribes: the Hopi, Navajo, Havasupai, Paiute, and Hualapai.

❑ 131. Take a Class Together

As your children mature, the happy side of seeing them grow up is that their interests may begin to coincide with yours. Building on one or more of those interests can produce surprising results as well as new talents and skills for both of you. The library and Internet are full of instructional books and videos that can teach beginner to advanced skills in just about everything, including knitting, crocheting, drawing, painting, writing, and more. Taking a class together gives you a shared experience that continues after the class, through the "homework" period, and into the next class.

Some possibilities might include piano lessons, a pottery class, photography, quilting, knitting, sewing, tai chi, tennis, or sailing. Whatever class you take together, you'll find yourselves talking about what you're learning, helping each other develop skills, and sharing ideas for the next thing to make, draw, write, and create. Check with your local community center, community college, or creative center to see what classes are available. Sign up and start learning something new!

❏ 132. Learn to Tie Sailors' Knots

Okay, so they've mastered the art of tying their shoes. Now it's time to move on to the knots that will knock their socks off once they've learned how to tie them. Teach your kids that knots are not limited to the simple left over right, right over left, under, over, around, and through. Scouts and sailors have made knot tying an art form that is not only beautiful but also useful in any and all situations. Learn to tie some new knots together and maybe watch your kids pick up a badge or two in scouts because of it. Check out this Internet site for instructions for how to tie more than 50 knots! We kid you *knot!* www.troop7.org/knots/.

▲ ▲ ▲ ▲ ▲

"I came from a race of fishers; trout streams gurgled about the roots of my family tree."
—John Burroughs

▼ ▼ ▼ ▼ ▼

❏ 133. Offer a Lesson in Balancing a Checkbook and Writing a Check

"Why do I have to learn *this?*" A lot of kids may feel that way when they're struggling with math problems that don't seem to relate at all to anything they're doing in real life. Enter the checkbook! Suddenly math matters! Assuming you have introduced your kids to banks and bank accounts, a checking account is the first step toward money management. Filling out a deposit slip, keeping the receipt in a safe place, and checking those deposit receipts against the paper bank statement are lessons that last a lifetime. Writing checks, recording the checks, subtracting the amount from the balance, and keeping track of interest earned and fees charged gives the checking account owner a clear sense of how money is earned and spent. For step-by-step instructions on how to balance a checkbook, ask your bank for their printed materials or check the Internet for answers.

❑ 134. Make a Growth Chart

Measuring your child against a wall in the kitchen and drawing a pencil line to mark their height is a great idea—until it's time to repaint or move to a new house! You don't need to risk losing those precious measurements and milestones if you create a growth chart that can move with you. Start with a 6-foot length of wainscoting, paint it with a high-gloss paint, drill a hole for hanging ½ inch from the top, and decorate it with any designs you choose. Hang it on a nail placed 72½ inches from the floor (to accommodate the ½ inch you allowed for the nail hole). Have your child stand with their back to the board and measure at the top of their head. Use a marker to write the height, date, age, and name if you're measuring more than one child. Measure on every birthday and any time in between. When a growth spurt takes place, blame it on the vegetables and healthy snacks!

❑ 135. Have a Pajama Party

Goodie bags, flashlight tag, and sleeping bags spread out in a circle on the family room floor set the scene for a party that's the cat's pajamas! Make invitations in the shape of bedroom slippers or take a snapshot of the party girl or boy wearing pajamas and use the picture for the front of the invitation. Depending on the ages of the kids, offer the option of staying overnight or leaving at a specified time (after the movie, perhaps). Be sure to extend an invitation to teddy bears, special blankets, or other sleepy-time necessities. Plan games such as Pin the Nose on the Teddy Bear (you draw the teddy bear and the noses); flashlight tag; Start-a-Story-Keep-It-Going, and Musical Sleeping Bags (instead of chairs). Show a movie or cartoons and serve popcorn. Hand out goodie bags filled with a toothbrush, toothpaste, soap, and a wash cloth. End the night with a bedtime story and maybe some songs. Plan a good breakfast for morning, and be sure to make pick-up time early so you can get your house back together and let your sleepyhead kids chill out and take a recovery nap. Take lots of pictures!

❑ 136. Volunteer at the Animal Shelter

The *purr*-fect opportunity to be together and make a positive difference in your community might be waiting for you and your family at your local animal shelter. Every year, thousands of animals turn up at shelters. These organizations then work to care for the animals until they are adopted. The cutest and the littlest are the first to go, but often there are more animals than homes, and that's where you and your family can be very useful. Volunteers might walk the dogs, play with the cats, feed the animals and help to bathe and groom them, stuff envelopes to help publicize an event, and spread the word about the animals that need homes. Volunteering with your kids introduces all of you to the warm and fuzzy feelings of helping others. It also brings you into contact with a new group of friends with a common interest. For teens, volunteering provides necessary community service hours and new skills to list on college and job applications. Whether you can spare many hours or just one, animal shelters are grateful, and the rewards are well worth the time spent. Check the phonebook or Internet for an animal shelter near you. Find out what jobs need doing, and sign up for ones your family can do best.

❏ 137. Play Sidewalk Games

For generations, sidewalks have served as the playing fields for such classic children's games as hopscotch, skelly, nickel hits, tic-tac-toe, sidewalk mini-golf, bicycle mazes, sidewalk jacks, and marbles. If you've got a piece of chalk, a sidewalk, and a flat rock or bottle cap, you've got everything you need to get your kids playing some of these time-tested games. All

SAFETY TIPS

- Wear rubber-soled shoes to avoid slipping.
- Pick a sidewalk or driveway that is not near a busy traffic area.
- Clear the playing field of rocks, twigs, and leaves.
- Don't play after dark!

you need are some tips for safe playing, a couple of ideas for choosing the playing order, and a source for the names and rules of some of the most popular games.

WHO GOES FIRST?

- Flip a coin and call heads or tails.
- Draw straws—longest straw goes first.
- Do "eeny-meeny-miney-moe."

SOURCES FOR GAMES AND RULES:

- Your local library
- Your local park district or summer kids' camp
- The Internet

Get up, get out, and get into the fun outdoors. Your kids will like the big outdoors all the better if you're out there with them!

❑ 138. Make Some Cool Lists

Don't limit your list-making to a grocery list. Sit down with your kids and create some lists that can be added to on a daily basis. Pick a specific time, such as dinner time, to share what's been added to each family member's list and to help each other add more items. Here are some possible lists. If these don't work for you and yours, add some of your own lists to the list!

- Things That Make Me Happy
- Things for Which I Am Thankful
- Things I'd Like to Learn How to Do or Make
- Things I Wish I Could Do for the World
- Things I'd Like to Do for Vacation
- Things I'd Like to Do by Myself
- Things I'd Like to Do with a Friend or My Family
- Things I Saw Today that Made Me Laugh
- Things I Wish I Never Had to Eat Again…EVER

❑ 139. Get Fishy at the Aquarium

The sight of undersea creatures swimming in huge tanks is awe-inspiring to kids of all ages. Aquariums are safe aquatic environments created for viewing otherwise elusive sea creatures—stingrays, seahorses, whales, sharks, sea anemones, and fish of all kinds and colors. Exposing your children to an up-close view of marine life encourages a sense of responsibility for the oceans and all aquatic life. For the protection of the fish and enhanced viewing pleasure, aquariums can be very dark. For very young children, the darkness can be scary. Be sure to explain the reason for the darkness, and hold onto your child's hand as you move along the walls of tanks and displays. Make a game of finding the biggest, smallest, most colorful, funniest, and fastest fish in the tanks.

The Association of Zoos and Aquariums (AZA) is America's leading accrediting organization for zoos and aquariums. The AZA logo assures you that the aquarium you are visiting is dedicated to providing excellent care for animals, a positive experience for visitors, and a better future for all living things.

❏ 140. Visit a Christmas Tree Farm and Cut Your Own Tree

Ever since Christmas tree lots began selling precut, perfectly shaped trees, the ritual of looking through many trees to find just the right one has lost its appeal because all the trees look pretty much the same. Christmas tree farms offer an alternative that can quickly become a tradition in your family. Choosing the perfect tree is a family affair that includes a drive to the farm, hot cocoa at the farm stand, a hike through the rows of trees, and maybe a snowball fight on the way. You can cut your own tree or have the farm staff cut it for you. Either way, the fun is in the family effort and the tradition you establish.

▲ ▲ ▲ ▲ ▲

"All happy families resemble one another,
but each unhappy family is unhappy in its own way."
—Leo Tolstoy

▼ ▼ ▼ ▼ ▼

❏ 141. Visit an Animal Shelter and Adopt an Animal

You've discussed it as a family. You've made a checklist of the pros and cons of adding a pet to your family. You've checked into the real costs of owning a pet: food, vet bills, and boarding when you go on vacation. You've done some research on the kinds of pets that fit into your environment, won't cause an allergic reaction, and are compatible with children. You've done all that, and now you're ready to visit an animal shelter to find the perfect pet. Good for you! There are thousands of homeless animals in need of a good family. Shelters and rescue operations do their best to care for all of them, but they do need your help. To find out more about what adoption entails, visit http://www.adoptapet.com/ and go into the adoption as an educated consumer.

❑ 142. Create a Model Train Set

The train cars, the real smoke puffing out of the steam engine, and the sound of the train whistle blowing as the engine moves through the tunnel and into the station—they're just the tip of the iceberg when it comes to all the fun you and your children can have with model trains. Model training is a group-oriented hobby that can involve even the youngest family members.

Model trains come in a variety of scales, and the miniature railroad setup you choose can include yards of track surrounded by towns and topography all created by you. Once you discover the world of model trains, you'll find a whole network of fairs, model railroad exhibitions, hobby shops, and contests. To get started, go to www. nmra.org/ for free information on how to begin. You're in for some fun if you choo-choose to give trains a try!

❑ 143. Start a Pillow Fight

Mom and Dad would never let us have a pillow fight! Or would they? Loosen up a little, and show your kids your fun side. Pillow fights engage kids in harmless physical conflict that lets them blow off plenty of steam. Believe it or not, this informal game, which is most often played at sleepovers, has a couple of rules. Start the game by hiding the pillows and sending the "fighters" on a pillow hunt. Make a rule that limits hitting to the area below the neck. It's trickier than it looks as players must defend themselves while trying to wallop the opponent. The idea is not to knock anyone down, but really just to fight to the finish—when everyone is exhausted and ready to go to sleep. And that may be the best advertisement for this game: Sleep is the prize that everyone wins.

❏ 144. Give Your Regards to Broadway

Broadway is a street in New York City that is famous for being the theater capital of the world. Located in the midtown section of the city, Broadway, also known as the Great White Way, is lit with neon billboards, theater marquees, and advertisements that are the best free show in town. But the real shows are the musicals and plays that open on Broadway, sticking around for a long time if they are good and closing quickly if they are not. Broadway audiences are considered to be the toughest critics, so as the song says, "If I can make it there, I'll make it anywhere! New York! New York!" If you make a trip to the Big Apple, a Broadway show can be the highlight of your visit. The best shows sell out well in advance, so book ahead of your trip through Ticketmaster or Telecharge or the theater's box office. Half-price tickets may be purchased for same-day performances at three TKTS locations: Times Square, South Street Seaport, and downtown Brooklyn. When the show is over, try to get autographs from the stars. Stand outside the stage door with program and pen in hand. Sometimes the autograph is the best souvenir of all!

❏ 145. Camp Out in the Backyard

The kids will think it's cool, and you'll think it's a hoot to see the looks of excitement on their faces as you set up a tent in the backyard or on the deck. Experience all the fun of camping with a fraction of the hassle. No need to worry about what to pack—it's all inside the house and just steps away from your "campground." Make the experience as authentic as possible with flashlights, marshmallows toasted over the grill, ghost stories told around the flashlight "campfire," and some stargazing before eyes close for the night.

In the morning, serve pancakes in the great outdoors and share thoughts on the experience of sleeping outside. What was the best part, the worst part, and the funniest part? As always, take pictures to preserve the memories.

❑ 146. Take Me out to the Ball Game!

Seeing a baseball game live and in person gives kids a better sense of what makes baseball the great American pastime that it is. Televised games may show the action, but they don't offer the smell of hotdogs and popcorn that's in the air at the ballpark. They don't provide the excitement of a fly ball coming your way and being caught by YOU! And televised games don't really show the beauty of the well-manicured field or the larger-than-life presence of the heroes of the game. Soak in all the hoopla that goes with cheering the teams on with the help of stadium staff who toss out free T-shirts, swing the camera in your direction so the kids can see themselves on the big screen, and introduce your kids to the mascot for a photo op. Being there is where it's at when it comes to parent-kid bonding. Give your kids a play-by-play explanation of the rules of the game, and take time out for peanuts delivered right to your seat. Watch for special bat, cap, and pennant days, and you'll come home with some super-sharp team souvenirs!

If you don't happen to live anywhere near a professional baseball stadium, look for spring training camps and local high school and college teams. Minor league play is also a fun experience—and comes with a much cheaper price tag than the big leagues.

❑ 147. Hike a Civil War Trail

The Civil War began in 1861 with the secession of 11 states from the union. Mississippi, Florida, Alabama, Georgia, Louisiana, Texas, Virginia, Arkansas, Tennessee, North Carolina, and South Carolina eventually formed the Confederate States of America. The war did not officially end until May 1865. This devastating conflict pitted American against American as soldiers from 23 Northern states wore the blue uniform and soldiers from 11 Southern states wore gray. Many of the trails marched in Civil War days have been marked and notated with historical signage describing what took place on each particular spot. Hiking these trails is educational, good exercise, and provides an extra chance of a thrill if someone in your party discovers an old relic from the Civil War. Use your hike as an opportunity to talk about the main characters of the war, the reasons for it, and the consequences. To find Civil War trails in your area, search "Civil War trails" on the Internet.

❑ 148. Make Jam or Can Fruit

It might sound like something your great-grandmother used to do, but if you have a sweet tooth for natural treats, try learning how to make homemade jam. It can be a tasty adventure for the whole family to enjoy together. And it's even better when you pay a visit to a local pick-your-own farm to harvest some fresh fruit right off the bush, the vine, or the tree. Your kids will love working from bush to tasty bush, filling their mouths and their buckets with berries. Different fruits ripen at different times of year, so this is something you can do in almost any season. Bring your bushels of fruit home and get ready to jam. Easy recipes can be found online.

❑ 149. Head to the Fair

County fairs spotlight real people showcasing their best efforts in agriculture, animal, and fowl raising—not to mention the blue-ribbon-winning goods that are made by hand from homegrown ingredients. Barns and stalls are filled with prize hogs, sheep, dairy and beef cows, horses, chickens of all breeds, goats, and lots of baby animals. Scheduled events may include tractor pulls; judging of the livestock; and judging of the fresh harvest, which may include ears of corn and prepared foods such as jams and jellies, pies, cakes, chili, ribs, sausage, cheese, and a whole lot more. For a nominal entry fee, families can walk through the barns and watch the babies feeding, see the cows being milked, touch the piglets, and talk to the farmers and ranchers who bring them out.

Often, there is a carnival on the site, with rides and games, cotton candy, sno-cones, pretzels, kettle corn, and ice cream. Unlike a craft fair, this kind of fair focuses mainly on working farms, the animals raised on them, and the goods and services provided by them. Going to the fair is a good day for all, and you can feel free to skip the carnival part and just take in the sights, sounds, and smells of real farm animals.

❏ 150. Visit a Natural Bridge

We are all familiar with the Golden Gate Bridge in San Francisco or the Brooklyn Bridge in New York—two truly impressive and iconic works of engineering. But sometimes the most impressive engineer of all is nature. Pay a visit to one of North America's many natural bridges, and you will discover just how amazing Mother Nature can be. A natural bridge is a rock arch formation with a natural passageway underneath, but that simple definition doesn't do it justice. There are natural bridges in Alabama, New York, Virginia, Texas, Kentucky, Massachusetts, Wisconsin, Utah, Wyoming, Florida, Arizona, Missouri, and California, and, of course, all over Arches National Park. But the most famous natural bridge is known as— drum roll please—Natural Bridge! It's located in Virginia, and it's so famous that in the 19th and early 20th centuries it was included on many lists of the Seven Wonders of the World. Believe it or not, at 215 feet tall and 90 feet long, it's taller than Niagara Falls! During the 18th and 19th centuries, visitors found the bridge's origin absolutely mysterious. In fact, there was a miraculous origin story among the Monacan Indians, whose legend explains that the bridge appeared just as they were escaping from an advancing army. You may not be in such dire straits when you go to visit one of the natural bridges today, but you cannot help but feel a touch of the miraculous yourself when you see these wonders in person.

❏ 151. Host a Family Talent Show

Everyone in your family has a secret talent. Your kids may share their talents easily, coming home every day with a new trick or skill, whether it is a beautiful piece of artwork or the newfound ability to flip their eyelids inside out. However, you may not be so free with *your* talents. Maybe it's time to let your kids in on all the amazing things you can do. Hold a family talent show. It's a great way to get to know each other by sharing and celebrating each other's abilities. Don't worry if your talents are silly. Sharing silliness helps build trust and confidence and will help your children overcome shyness or insecurity. Plus, it's great motivation to learn new things. As you and your children get older, you can scale back on the show, but keep the talent sharing in place by supporting each other in all of your endeavors, bearing witness to success and comforting each other in times of difficulty. Having a talent show now can lay the groundwork for continued closeness throughout your family's life.

▲　▲　▲　▲　▲

"If you look deeply into the palm of your hand, you will see your parents and all generations of your ancestors. All of them are alive in this moment. Each is present in your body. You are the continuation of each of these people."
—Thich Nhat Hanh

▼　▼　▼　▼　▼

❏ 152. Tour Your Town as a Tourist

No matter how big or how small, your town didn't just pop up out of nowhere. It has a history. And introducing your kids to the town in which they live creates a sense of belonging—a connection and pride in your town. If at first glance you look around and see nothing of great interest, look again. There may be sights to see that you don't think of as "tourist spots." There may be parks to visit, museums, a library, notable buildings, historic homes, cemeteries, a railroad station, and a whole lot more. Check out your local government's Web site for cultural events, festivals, parades, and celebrations. When money is tight and gas prices are high, why not take a "staycation" right in your own backyard?

❑ 153. Score a Touchdown with a Day at the Stadium

When football season starts, bundle up and head out to a professional or college football stadium. Start with a tailgate party in the parking lot of the stadium—sandwiches, drinks, and picnic fare prepare you all to cheer for your team once inside. Make posterboard signs to wave at the TV cameras, and speaking of waving, try to start the wave in your row of the bleachers. Teach the kids how to applaud, cheer, stomp, and stand loyally for the team of their choice.

The players look bigger, the field looks longer, the plays look more intense, and you'll look like a hero for taking the kids to the game. The excitement of seeing the cheerleaders leading the crowds in team cheers gives kids something to watch when the game slows down. Share the joys of real team spirit. After the game, toss a football around in the yard and reminisce about what you saw at the stadium. What a day, what a moment, what a fabulous time it was!

❑ 154. Bowl Them over at the Bowling Alley!

Now here's a sport that offers fun for almost all ages. Bowling parties have been popular with kids for years, and bowling alleys have built their industry by accommodating a variety of ages with lighter balls and inflatable or flip-up gutter guards that prevent gutter balls. If you've got a substantial age spread between your children, adjust the rules for the youngest so he or she doesn't get discouraged. Your kids will thrill to the sight of the ball popping out of the automatic return and the sound of the pins toppling loudly down the lane. Two or three games per visit are just about right for most ages. Learning to keep score, aim the ball, and find the perfect stance and style make each trip to the bowling alley better. For extra fun, get together with another family and have a team tournament. Winner buys pizza for all!

❑ 155. Make a Movie

Stars are born every day thanks to lightweight video cameras that are easy to operate. Sure you've been recording every move, smile, wave, and wiggle since your kids were born, but as they start talking sense, start making The Movie.

Work together to create a plot for the movie and turn it into a written script, then decide who will play which role and design the costumes. Make cue cards with the lines written on them. Rehearse and videotape every move of the movie making. When you've decided that "it's a wrap," play the movie for family and friends and follow it up with a red-carpet awards ceremony in which everyone receives an award. See you at the movies … and *in* them too!

❑ 156. Paint Faces with Meaning

It seems wherever there's a fun festival, carnival, or party, face painting is on the agenda of activities. You can take it a step further by adding a little bit of information to the paint pot. For example, Native American tribes each have their own designs, and individuals paint their faces with colors and images to reflect a spiritual or personal message. Native Americans use red, black, green, white, and yellow. Each color has a meaning: White stands for peace, black is the color of the living, red stands for war, green is believed to sharpen the wearer's night vision, and yellow stands for death. Make your face painting more than just a brush with fun. Assign a meaning to each color you use and create a design that communicates a message. Instead of using random brushstrokes, add symbols of nature—a sun, a moon, a feather, a cloud, a rainbow. Look up information about Native Americans and find face paintings that will inspire new ideas. Create a message and express it in color!

❏ 157. See Government in Action

Journalist H. L. Mencken once said "A politician is an animal which can sit on a fence and yet keep both ears to the ground." But there is more to politics than banter and argument. Politics is, at heart, a civil service. For every politician like the one Mencken described, there are plenty more who have your best interests at heart. See for yourself with a family trip to watch your local, state, or national government in action. Find out online when your local legislature is in session and how you can visit. There you can witness what really happens on the floor and see how your interests are represented. There will be plenty for you and your family to talk about and debate afterward. If you don't like what you hear, gather your family to write a letter to your local representative or volunteer during the next election cycle and let your voice be heard.

❏ 158. Say It with Flowers— at the Botanical Gardens

Just about every major city in the United States has an arboretum and/or botanical gardens open to the public. These are places where art and science unite with beautiful exhibits featuring flowers, butterflies, aviaries, waterfalls, and rainforest replicas. The visit includes much more than just a walk through a pretty garden. It's an experience that includes all kinds of information about plants, flowers, and natural environments all around the world. Take advantage of the guided tours of individual exhibits so you can walk away with more than just beautiful memories. You and your kids will gain real knowledge about the important role every species plays in the ecosystem we all hope to preserve and nurture. Plan ahead and make a game of finding specific exhibits, birds, flowers, and other displays. Setting a goal for discoveries makes the trip more fun for kids.

When traveling to another country such as Canada or Mexico, make a point of finding out where the botanical gardens or arboretum are so you can compare their exhibits to the ones at home.

❑ 159. Create Headstone Rubbings

For years, student groups and history majors have visited cemeteries with the purpose of exploring history—the history of the town and the people who lived and died in it; the medical history of the town and what diseases or plagues might have reduced the population; and the history of the headstone artists of the time. Spooky tales have capitalized on the eerie aspect, with ghosts and skeletons being the main focus. But if you're more interested in the history and design of the cemetery, come equipped to capture impressions of headstone art by taking rubbings of them. There are specific rubbing materials required to make impressions that are clear and, more important, do not damage the stone. You must also ask permission from the historical society, town government, or church with jurisdiction over the cemetery. The end result is usually a beautiful impression of a design created by fine artists of the time. If cemeteries are not your first choice for taking a rubbing, cathedrals sometimes offer one-day classes for kids that include a little bit of history and a metal or tile plate from which to do a rubbing. The National Cathedral in Washington, D.C., is one such cathedral. Check your local area for others.

❑ 160. Sail Away!

What could be better than navigating through deep blue waters with the wind whipping through your hair and the sun shining overhead? Sailing is a peaceful yet exhilarating way to spend your day. And it's the perfect family activity—a way to get everyone on board and working together as you pilot your little craft through the open waters. Take turns at the helm, manning the sails, navigating, and being on the lookout. There's plenty for each of you to do, and each of you is equally important to the journey.

If you don't already know how to sail, it's not too hard to learn. Many marinas have sailing schools where you can learn the basics of sailboat technique and etiquette—from getting your boat ready, to the different points of sail, to docking, to simple racing strategies. After you successfully pass a marina's class, you can rent sailboats from them anytime. Make sure to get an early start and pack your lunch, along with lots of water and sunscreen. You'll want all the time you can get on the water. So hoist the mainsail, matey: It's time to sail away!

❏ 161. Go on a Picnic…Indoors!

Don't let a little rain dampen your kids' enthusiasm when it comes to following through on a planned picnic! Look on the bright side— no ants, no bees, and no skinned knees! Stake out the perfect indoor picnic ground and cover it with the same blanket you would have used outdoors. Pack a picnic basket with all the fixings— drinks, sandwiches, fried chicken, salads, chips, raw veggies, and cupcakes and fruit for dessert. Pretend you're on Picnic Island and make a rule that no one can let any body part extend beyond the blanket or they'll fall into the water! Keep a towel handy in case someone "gets wet," then dry them off when they're pulled back onto the island. When the eating is done, clear the blanket and play tug-o'-war, with everyone trying not to fall into the "water." Rainy day? Who cares? A little imagination saves the day every time!

❏ 162. Go on a Scavenger Hunt

When the water's too cold, the clouds are blocking the sun, and cries of "now what do we do?" threaten to dampen the mood, it's time to take out the scavenger hunt lists you made before you headed for the beach. Scavenger hunts train eyes to see things they may not have noticed before, and they provide an activity for one, two, a few, or more. Each person or team gets a list and collecting pail or bag. The first to find the most on the list wins the hunt!

Here's a sample list of things to hunt for:

1. Shark's teeth
2. Crab shell
3. Seaweed
4. Seagull feather
5. Clam shell
6. Beach glass
7. Driftwood
8. Buoy
9. Fishing bobber
10. Coins

❏ 163. Chill Out and Grill Out!

Why does Dad always get to be the Grill Master? Well guess what, kids, today Dad is turning the grill tools over to you! Let them in on the cooking right from the start—yes, even the youngest ones in the bunch. Make patty-cake hamburger patties, foil-wrapped corn on the cob, and a tossed salad on the side with you-know-who doing the peeling, placing the food in the bowl, and tossing the salad when the dressing has been added. When everyone's involved from start to finish, cleanup becomes part of the whole family affair, too.

❏ 164. Ride Bikes

With the equipment available today, family bike rides can start as soon as the baby can securely sit up, wear a helmet, and express herself well enough to say, "Wheeeee!" Bike riding with the baby in a safe bike seat behind one parent, the other kids on their own bikes, and one parent leading with the other bringing up the rear is a lovely way to get exercise, fresh air, see the scenery, and introduce the joy of people-powered mobility. Stay off the roads and find the bike trails in your town, in a park, or around a lake. Lead by example and wear helmets. Take the opportunity to practice and share safety tips. Don't know them? Don't worry. Here they are!

SAFETY TIPS

- Wear a helmet.
- Tie your shoes and make sure pants aren't so baggy they'll get caught in the chain.
- Wear elbow, knee, or any other padding.
- Don't ride after dark.
- Always ride with the flow of traffic and stay close to the curb when you ride in the street.
- Watch out for potholes, parked cars, sewer grates, and anything else that will get in your way.
- Obey traffic signals and signs.
- Before you cross the street, look left, then right. If you can't get across the street without injuring yourself, then don't go.
- Always walk your bike across streets.
- Keep both hands on the handlebar so you don't lose control.

❑ 165. Become a Card-Carrying Member of the Library

The pride that comes with getting a first library card is only matched by getting a driver's license. Both give kids a privilege they'll value—especially if you make sure to play it up as an important milestone. Make the day of library card sign-up a special one—a rite-of-passage day that impresses upon your child what a privilege it is to be able to walk into the library, find a great book, and borrow it. The money-saving factor of checking out books rather than buying them is a great lesson in and of itself. Why buy when you can borrow? The experience of selecting books, checking them out, reading them, and returning them on time is a valuable lesson in responsibility that can be a baby step toward greater social responsibility later on. The world of books, videos, and other publications is wide open to the curious and made available for free to all. Learning how to use the library is a lesson that follows your child through all of his or her schooling and into adult life as well. Libraries are a privilege. Take advantage of them.

❑ 166. Go Bird-Watching

It's a bird! It's a plane! No, it's just a bird. Wait, *just* a bird?! That's the wrong attitude. Birds are fantastic, beautiful creatures; they're inspiration for human flight and closely related to dinosaurs. When you go bird-watching, or birding, as it is sometimes called, you'll get to observe birds in all of their habitats—in the trees and in the bushes, making their nests, and feeding their young. Since birds are most easily distinguished by their unique calls, those sweet-sounding trills, you'll have to keep your ears peeled. Beyond the fun of getting to know birds as more than just the charming little noisemakers that flap around your yard, you'll also have the chance to spend the day in the peaceful outdoors with your family. With younger children, this is a great opportunity to share their excitement with every noise, while with older kids, it may be a chance to have some quiet bonding time without the pressure of conversation. Sometimes an effortless outing like this can bring you closer together than all the questions you may have about your kids' lives. So get out your binoculars and open your ears to these flighty little creatures.

❑ 167. Run Through the Sprinkler...Yes, You Too!

You may not have a membership to a swim club or a community pool, but if you've got a hose, you've got a way to cool off on a hot summer day. If the point is to fend off the heat and have a blast doing it, running through sprinklers is every bit as fun as jumping into a pool. The sprinkler does double duty as it waters the grass and cools off the kids and *you,* too. Bathing suits on, sprinkler on, and the fun starts now! Play sprinkler games such as Jump the Sprinkler, where everyone anticipates each rotation the sprinkler makes and jumps over the stream of water when it comes around, or Dancing in the Rain, where each person takes a turn to dance, twirl, or do gymnastics in the sprinkler's spray. Can't stand the heat? Get into the sprinkler!

❑ 168. Plant a Butterfly Garden

Butterflies are among the most beautiful and graceful members of the insect family. But did you know that the butterfly has many symbolic meanings around the world? In Chinese culture, two butterflies flying together symbolize love. In ancient Greek, the word *butterfly* means "soul" or "mind." And let's not forget the well-known superstition that it's good luck if a butterfly lands on you! So why not attract these lovely sentiments and all the luck you can get by planting a butterfly garden? A butterfly garden draws butterflies at each

PLANTS FOR YOUR BUTTERFLY GARDEN

Bee balm
Butterfly bush
Butterfly weed
Columbine
Marigold
Milkweed
Poppies
Purple coneflower
Shasta daisy
Sunflowers
Sweet pea
Yarrow

lifecycle (egg, larva, pupa, and butterfly) so that the population of butterflies is naturally and continually abundant. Butterflies are attracted to the nectar of many flowers, so not only are these gardens stunning with their insect inhabitants, but they are also quite beautiful with their flowering plants. There are hundreds of plants that attract butterflies, so depending on your planting zone you will have many choices. For more information on butterfly gardening, check your local zoo or botanical gardens, look for books at your local library, or search the Internet.

Planting a garden is a great family activity. You'll all enjoy selecting the plants, planting them in the ground, and watching them grow. Just as the insects you're attracting will metamorphose from pupa to butterfly, your garden will transform from empty ground to blooming, vibrant beauty.

❏ 169. Someone's in the Kitchen with . . . *You!*

"Just like Grandma used to make" is a phrase that automatically makes a meal sound better. Recipes that carry on generation after generation just can't be beat. Share the experience of re-creating a special recipe and take the time to explain how your own mother or grandmother taught you all the steps for making it. Choose a recipe that requires some good hands-on work. Meatloaf is a great choice. With freshly washed hands, your kids will love squishing the ingredients between their fingers to mix the ground meat, egg, milk, onions, breadcrumbs, and whatever secret ingredients the family recipe includes. Serve the dish up on special plates and make one night a week a family recipe night. You'll connect your kids to their own family history and give them something delicious to carry into the future.

❏ 170. Visit Chinatown

You don't have to hop on a plane to experience a foreign land. Many large cities have Chinatowns—areas where the population is made up of people who have emigrated from China. The Chinese traditions, arts, flavors, foods, and festivals make a visit to Chinatown a colorful, educational, and fun experience. In cities such as New York, San Francisco, and Chicago, Chinatown has become a tourist attraction, offering walking/talking tours detailing the history of the area and the people who live there. There are tourist maps detailing all the restaurants, specialty shops, museums, and entertainment venues. The kids will be awed by the colors, energy, and cultural sights. Plan to eat in Chinatown—refer to a restaurant guide to find the best and most authentic eateries. Visit the shops and markets to experience the cultural richness of the country. Make a game of finding the most unusual food for sale, the most beautiful parasol, the best souvenir toy, and the most creatively packaged rice candy. When you get the little parasols in your drinks or desserts, peel the white hub off and unroll it. What a surprise to find a tiny piece of a Chinese newspaper inside!

▲　▲　▲　▲　▲

"Other things may change us,
but we start and end with family."
—Anthony Brandt

▼　▼　▼　▼　▼

❑ 171. Make a Memory Quilt

Quilting has always been a social activity—something for people from the whole community to do together. Quilters gather around tables to work on their community quilt and talk. So much time and love goes into these quilts that quite often they become beautiful family heirlooms. A memory quilt can become the most precious of your family heirlooms because when you pass it down from generation to generation, it will contain your family's stories. To start your own family's memory quilt, collect clothing or material that is important to each of you from different times in your lives. This is perfect for youngsters who are particularly attached to a favorite

T-shirt that doesn't even fit over their head anymore or to a beloved blankie that has become torn and tattered: It can live on forever in the family quilt! So get everyone involved in selecting the pieces, and gather them around the table to share why each one is important. Each piece that you add brings back memories and stories to tell to your future grandchildren and great-grandchildren and will bind your family together for generations to come.

❏ 172. Pick a Family Vacation Spot

Variety may be the spice of life, but when it comes to traditions, repetition is a very good thing. Find a favorite family vacation spot—a lake, a beach, a mountain cabin, or Grandma's house—and plan a trip there every summer. The kids will make new friends, who may become pen pals or e-mail pals during the year, and they'll look forward to seeing each other after a year's worth of growth. Seek out the best ice-cream shop, a favorite pizza place, the wildlife habitat, a bird sanctuary, a bike path, a school playground, and anything else that makes your special vacation spot memorable. Having this to look forward to all year is a shared anticipation that will be the source for many conversations, reminiscences, and plans. The place isn't the main point. It's the fact of being together as a family at the same time every year. Save special board games, recipes, and activities just for summer vacation. And don't forget to take plenty of photos to record your trips forever.

❏ 173. Learn to Knit

Do you think knitting is an old-fashioned activity for grandmothers and great-grandmothers? Well, think again! A knitting revolution has swept the world, transforming what was once a waning pastime into a hip and cool needle art. Embrace the colors and textures of different yarns by making scarves, hats, and clothing of all kinds.

There are so many great ways to learn how to knit. There are books and classes at yarn stores or park districts. You can also seek help online or from a knitter that you already know. Learning as a family can be fun! Did you know that men were the first to knit for an occupation? In fact, entire families in the Scottish Isles were once involved in making knit sweaters, socks, stockings, and accessories. Knitting can truly be a family endeavor. Don't be shy, fathers and sons, give knitting a try!

❏ 174. Master a "New Tongue"

Okay, so maybe your family isn't bilingual. But you can still have great fun speaking in a coded language—called Pig Latin—that gives kids the feeling that their secrets will *stay* secret. It's easy, it's funny, and it's o-say illy-say (so silly!). Here are simple rules for mastering Pig Latin:

1. Words that begin with a consonant or double consonant have all the consonants before the first vowel shifted to the end of the word, followed by *ay*. Example: Pig = igPay, Latin = atinLay, Shout = out-Shay.

2. If a word begins with a vowel, simply add *ay* to the end of the word. Example: I=I-ay, All=All-ay, Every=Every-ay.

Try it at dinner tonight by shouting: "inners-Day eady-Ray!"

❏ 175. Build Something Together

The tap, tap, tapping of a hammer, the whirring of a saw, and the smell of freshly cut wood are all sure signs that something is being built. Show your children how a stack of wood can be transformed into something magical—a birdhouse, a shelf, a spice rack. Teach them how to measure twice and cut once, hammer nails, and screw screws. This is a great time to go over tool safety, so be sure to set a good example by wearing your safety glasses. Tackling a project together teaches kids the process of building and gives them a sense of pride when the project is completed. It is also a great way to spend quality time together with a common goal at hand.

Whatever your project, make sure to take some time to add the finishing touches and embellish it. Let your kids pitch in by choosing the colors, painting the finished project, and helping you decide where to place or hang it.

❑ 176. Attend a Poetry Reading

Poetry is as much a verbal art as a written one. Only when a poem is read aloud can you truly appreciate the rhythm of language. Poetry readings are a great way to get your family connected to the arts and to expose your children to sides of themselves they didn't know they had. Most local poetry groups are more than happy to welcome new people, especially young ones, into the artistic community. Visit your local bookstore for more information or check the events listings in your local paper. Who knows—attending a poetry reading might even inspire the poet in you and your kids!

▲　▲　▲　▲　▲

"You don't really understand human nature unless you know why a child on a merry-go-round will wave at his parents every time around—and why his parents will always wave back."
—William D. Tammeus

▼　▼　▼　▼　▼

❑ 177. Experience Another Era

When you take the family to visit Grandma and Grandpa, it's not just a chance for your kids to be spoiled rotten by the adoring older generation; it's also a chance for a game of dress up with a twist. Instead of putting on Mom's and Dad's clothes like they usually do, have them dress up like Grandma and Grandpa. Ask Grandma and Grandpa to go through their closets and pick out their oldest, most out-of-fashion attire and let your kids try them on. The old clothes are just an entry point, though. This is really an opportunity for your children to get to know their grandparents a little better. Encourage Grandma and Grandpa to tell stories about those old outfits and what times were like when they wore them. What phrases and slang were popular when they were young? What did they like to do for fun when they were the same age as your kids? This is a fun, immersive way to help your children understand their origins. And we're willing to bet that Grandma and Grandpa will enjoy it too!

❑ 178. Host an Invention Convention

The world's greatest inventions were once nothing more than crazy ideas. So why not try your own hand at creating the next best thing? Encourage your children's creative spirit by working on an invention together. This is a great way to learn and share each other's thought processes, develop creative and critical thinking skills, and—most important of all—have fun as a family.

If a bright idea doesn't just come to your group out of the blue, think of all the things you do over the course of a day. Maybe something could be done better with a new invention. Talk about it with the whole family. Coming up with ideas is the most exciting part. Once you have your idea, help your children draw it or even build it!

MARKET YOUR INVENTION!

Developing your invention is only half the job. After all, you still have to market it! Guide your children through thinking about how you would sell your new product. Come up with an inventive tagline that captures how important your invention is. Not only will this whole process get you dreaming, it will also get you thinking about why you use the things you do, what you want, and what you need.

❑ 179. Learn How to Eat an Artichoke

Artichokes might be the world's funniest looking vegetable. But they're also a lot of fun to eat—especially for little kids who like to eat with their hands! Here's what you need to know:

HOW TO COOK AN ARTICHOKE:

1. Using a kitchen scissors, cut the sharp tips off all the leaves.

2. Pull off the smaller leaves at the base and on the stem. Then trim the stem, leaving only an inch of it.

3. Rinse the artichoke in cold water.

4. Cook the artichoke in a steamer basket placed inside a large pot with a few inches of water at the bottom. Cover and bring to a boil before leaving it to simmer for 25–45 minutes (cook time will depend on the size of the artichoke).

5. When the artichoke is done, you'll be able to pull off the outer leaves easily.

THE FUN PART—EATING THE ARTICHOKE:

Artichokes are typically served with a dipping sauce such as hollandaise, lemon butter, or mayonnaise flavored with balsamic vinegar. And we all know how much kids like foods they can dip! Pull off the leaves, one at a time, and dip the bottom of the leaf—the white fleshy part—into the sauce. Place the leaf in your mouth with the dipped side down, and pull it through your teeth to scrape off the soft, dipped part. Throw out the rest of the leaf. When all the leaves have been eaten, you'll reach the artichoke heart. Use a fork or spoon to scrape out the "choke," or fuzzy part. Underneath this fuzz is the artichoke heart. Cut it up, dip it in the sauce, and eat it. Yum!

> **DID YOU KNOW...?**
> Believe it or not, the artichoke is actually a flower bud. And a healthy flower at that—a medium-size artichoke has only 60 calories!

❑ 180. Tell the Story of Your Family Heirlooms

Most of us have treasured items that have been passed down from generation to generation: Great-Grandma's sewing machine or Great-Grandpa's tools. Maybe a dresser or a mirror, a ring or a necklace. These heirlooms aren't just part of your life, they're part of your family's long tradition. More than that, they offer the perfect opportunity to share the story of your family—to look back and talk about the lives of your ancestors and reinforce for your children the history that makes them who they are. Telling these stories is not only beneficial to your children but will also enrich the understanding between you and your spouse and strengthen the sense of family you have created together.

❑ 181. Learn to Sew Together

With all of our modern conveniences, sewing just doesn't seem as common in the home as it once was. Despite the many talents of the modern mother and father, the ability to pull thread with a needle tends to elude most of us. Fortunately, it's easy to learn how to sew, and the hobby is a great, inexpensive way to work with your children to customize their rooms. Curtains are the perfect project for the amateur because you only need to know how to sew straight lines. With today's sewing machines, this is even simpler than threading a needle.

To make simple curtains for your child's room:

1. Measure the window opening and figure out how much fabric you need to buy. Fabric is sold in yards, and it is better to overestimate rather than run out of fabric before you are done.

2. Go to the fabric store and have your child choose the fabric he or she likes best. Buy thread to match as well as curtain rings with clips attached.

3. Clear off a big table, and set up the sewing machine, ironing board, and iron.

4. Iron the curtain fabric.

5. Fold the top and bottom of the curtain fabric over about 3 inches, and pin it in place.

6. Iron the folded ends of the fabric to form a nice, clean edge.

7. Sew the folded ends in a straight line.

8. Clip the curtain rings to the top of the curtain panel and hang your curtain on the rod.

9. Pull the curtains shut, and gaze in wonder at a family project well done!

❑ 182. Attend a Classical Music Concert

With so much going on around us all the time, it's easy to be overwhelmed by distraction. Take a time-out with some quiet time spent listening to music together. Chamber music players gather to perform in a variety of places, including schools, churches, theaters, and museums, so you're likely to have an easy time finding a concert near you. Hearing classical music played live is an awe-inspiring experience. Prepare your children ahead of time by listening to classical music at home. For fun, listen to the music with your eyes closed. It may seem strange at first, but visualize the music—do you hear a color, a shape? Does it have a texture? You will hear things you never noticed before. Some families are more talkative than others and are more interested in discussing their inner experiences, but don't feel pressure to do so. In this case, it might be best to simply share the space while enjoying the music, to feel each other's presence, and to say nothing about it afterward. Let the music sit with all of you. Then sample a live performance for an experience you and your family will remember for years to come.

❏ 183. Create a Book Nook

Make every season bright—and make your kids brighter too—by ensuring that books are an essential part of family life. Start by sharing the stories you loved when you were a child. Then visit your local library to see what books are on display for each season, holiday, and special event. You and your

THE ORIGINAL BOOK NOOK
The original book nook was called an *inglenook*, a cozy bench most often tucked in next to a large open fireplace that would provide warmth (for you and your tea) and light for reading. Inglenooks popularized in early Arts & Crafts homes sometimes had bookshelves built in!

kids will find your own special favorites, but to make a tradition stick, set the book reading scene so it's pleasurable in and of itself. Choose a comfortable spot in your home and plan ahead for your Book Nook time by making snacks that relate to the story you're reading. For example, if you're reading *Stuart Little* by E. B. White, make everything you serve tiny—dime-size cookies and demitasse cups of milk. As your children grow and become ready to read on their own, keep the Book Nook tradition going and spend time reading together, whether you all read the same book or different books. Sharing books, sharing time, and sharing ideas all make family bonds stronger. Boredom never strikes when books are around!

❏ 184. Rock the Climbing Wall

Being a family is all about trusting and supporting each other no matter what. No sport assigns more importance to that trust than rock climbing, where you are literally supporting each other with rope and belay at all times. One of you climbs the rocks, the other holds the rope. It's an obvious metaphor for parenting— encouraging your children to scale great heights and always being there to catch them if they fall—but your kids don't have to know that. It's also an apt metaphor for aging, as your kids may one day catch you as you fall, but they don't need to know that yet either. They'll just enjoy the activity and the challenge. Some outdoor outfitters have rock walls where you can try the sport out for the first time. If your family enjoys it, consider visiting—or even joining—an indoor rock gym where you can take classes together to learn all of the safety and climbing techniques required to have a great time. When you're comfortable inside, sign up for an outdoor climbing adventure through the gym or go on your own. As a bonus to you, rock climbing works out every muscle in your body, so if you keep at it, you'll soon be in the best shape of your life.

▲　▲　▲　▲　▲

"The only rock I know that stays steady, the only institution I know that works, is the family."

—Lee Iacocca

▼　▼　▼　▼　▼

❑ 185. Take Something Apart and Put It Back Together

Whether it's your toaster, your car, or your children's action figures, many of the things you take for granted in life are little mechanical marvels. These things may not pique your curiosity so much now, but there's a good chance your children have already let theirs run away with them—as evidenced by all the things they break or bang. Tap into this natural inquisitiveness by channeling it into a worthwhile goal. Choose an object from around your home and try to figure out how it works by taking it apart and putting it back together. Ask questions of each other, and use family teamwork to work out the puzzle. Not only will you learn the inner workings of objects, you'll also gain a new appreciation for the way each of you thinks about problems.

❏ 186. Watch a Foreign Film and Learn About Another Culture

Your family may already get together to watch movies, and there are certainly plenty to keep you occupied. But as your children mature, consider introducing an occasional foreign film into your plans. This will provide a change of pace along with insight into other cultures. Consider how the films differ from the ones you usually watch together. What do these differences reveal about the culture that produced the film? How do the characters behave, what do they care about, what do they eat? What do the films you usually watch reveal about your own tastes and culture? Make the whole evening special by replacing popcorn with a tasty treat from the country of the film. Who knows, these films may even inspire you to take a different kind of vacation!

❏ 187. Collect Postcards from Around Your World

Call yourself a deltiologist and everyone will say, "Huh?" But this ten-dollar word is a fancy way of referring to someone who collects postcards. Serious collectors are interested in antique postcards from all over the place. You and your kids can be serious too—serious about collecting cards that remind you of the wonderful, fun, interesting places you've visited. Postcards are often the least expensive souvenir and sometimes they're even free, plus they don't take up a lot of luggage space. Make a postcard file box out of a shoebox, start a scrapbook, or keep them in photo albums. Write the date you found the card, the best thing about the place from where it came, and perhaps an anecdote about something funny said or done by one of your family members. Postcard collecting is a hobby that can last a lifetime. Start with cards from your own town's sights and build your collection every time you go to a restaurant, museum, or park.

❏ 188. Start a Family Journal

Remembering what happened and when is not always easy, unless you've kept a journal of family events, special times, shared conversations, discoveries, and all things worth remembering. Family journaling often starts with a baby book in which every first is recorded, funny antics are relayed, and poignant moments are preserved in writing and photos. Initially, it's the parents' job to do all the writing, and as the kids grow, schedules become fuller and finding the time to sit down and write seems impossible. But it doesn't have to be that way if you make the choice to continue what you started the day they were born—recording the times of your lives together. Make journaling a family affair and share the effort it takes to keep the book current. Select a journal with lined pages for easy writing. Keep a pen or pencil attached to the book. Start the first pages with some quotes from each family member about why a family journal is a good idea. Choose a time when everyone is together— perhaps over dessert after dinner—and pass the book around for each one to add something or just read what others have written. Something as simple as "Audrey said her brother's name for the first time today," might be an entry from the big brother in the family. Whether short and sweet or more detailed, a family journal will add up to a keepsake for all to enjoy for generations to come.

❏ 189. Adopt a Grandparent

Not everyone is fortunate enough to have living parents. If you have lost your parents, your children have lost grandparents. A relationship with grandparents is very special to children. It offers a window into another time. Fortunately, Adopt-a-Grandparent programs have popped up all around the country. Whether or not you have an official Adopt-a-Grandparent program in your area, you and your family can share your joy with senior citizens from your church, neighborhood, or a local assisted-living community. Sharing your family's love and attention with an elderly person who has no family gives your children an extended family and the mutual benefits that come from intergenerational activities. Start with a visit to an assisted-living facility and ask the social worker there to match you and your child up with someone who would enjoy a visit. Plan to visit often to build a relationship. Or perhaps there's someone in your neighborhood who has known your children since their birth and now finds him or herself alone and without family. Include your adopted grandparent at holiday dinners, birthdays, class plays, piano recitals, team sports demonstrations, and family photos. Everyone can have a Grandma and Grandpa and all the joys that come with the relationship.

❑ 190. Visit a Frank Lloyd Wright Home

Frank Lloyd Wright was responsible for some iconic American buildings, including the Guggenheim Museum in New York and Fallingwater in Pennsylvania. Wright had such a profound impact on the development of American architecture that in 1991 the American Institute of Architects recognized him as "the greatest American architect of all time." He was known for using local materials and the local landscape to inspire his particular projects, so while there are some unifying visual themes to his work, there are also many notable differences among his projects. Take your family to visit some of his houses or to his studio homes, such as his Home and Studio in Oak Park, Illinois; Taliesin in Spring Green, Wisconsin; and Taliesin West in Scottsdale, Arizona, and be inspired by the work of this master architect. Even if you have young children, this can be a rewarding trip. Exposure to beautiful works of art can leave a lasting impression and awaken talents in children they may not have otherwise known.

❏ 191. Take Your Sons and Daughters to Work

Did you know there is an official day each year that has been identified by a national organization as the day to take your kids to your workplace and show them what you do? Take Our Daughters and Sons to Work Day always falls on the fourth Thursday in April. The recommended age range for this program is 8 to 18. The purpose goes beyond just visiting the workplace; it introduces your child to the value of education, skill-building, communications, and the socialization necessary for success in the workplace. Is your place of business included in the program? If not, maybe you'd like to be the one to start it. The program is sponsored by businesses, schools, and corporations across the country.

❏ 192. Change the World

Kids may be small, but that doesn't mean they can't make a difference in the world. Start in your own home, where chores that benefit the whole family can be divided up according to one's ability. Laundry folding, taking out the trash, feeding the family pet, putting clothes in the hamper or hanging them up—such household responsibilities teach the idea of caring about the environment, the comfort of others, and the role each of us plays in the success of a group. What's learned at home is carried over to school, relationships with friends, and eventually to the greater world in which your children exist.

▲ ▲ ▲ ▲ ▲

"A person's a person,
no matter how small."

—Dr. Seuss, *Horton Hears a Who*

▼ ▼ ▼ ▼ ▼

❏ 193. Go to a Book Fair

Favorite books serve as reminders of wonderful, meaningful moments. And a book fair is a great place to collect new treasures. There are all kinds of book fairs—school book fairs, where new books are available at full price; library book fairs, where used books are sold at a steep discount as the library tries to make room for new books; and fundraiser book fairs, where, again, used books are sold at very reasonable prices. For book lovers of all ages, seeing books categorized and displayed on tables is as much fun as a trip to the candy store. Allow plenty of time for browsing. Pick up books of interest and thumb through them before making final selections to take home and share later. Book fairs advertise in local news-papers, on community bulletin boards, in church bulletins, and at schools. Keep your eye out for a book fair coming soon, and mark the date on your kids' calendars. There's always room for a good book—in the car, at home, on vacation, or anywhere, and a book fair is a great place to stock up!

❏ 194. Create a Family Coat of Arms and Motto

What do some of the greatest families of the past, universities, and nearly all nations have in common? A coat of arms and a motto! The Great Seal of the United States, with its eagle clutching an olive branch in one talon and arrows in another, is America's coat of arms, while its motto, clutched in the eagle's beak, is E Pluribus Unum, which is Latin for "Out of Many, One." Coats of arms and mottos are designed to capture the essence of a group's identity and to define that group for others to see. Take the opportunity to bring your family together and make a coat of arms and motto for yourselves. What are your family's values? What image best represents those values—is it an eagle, an oak tree, a flower, a kitten? Talk it over with your children. Find out what they think your family stands for. When it comes to dreaming up a motto, the trick is to distill all your values into one sentence. It can be a challenge, but your family is definitely up for it!

For more information, visit your local library.

❏ 195. Ride on a Double-Decker Bus

Hop-on, hop-off double-decker bus tours make sightseeing easy, relatively inexpensive, and much more fun than walking. Double-decker buses are two-level buses, sometimes open-air on top, other times enclosed. Many cities around the world feature tours on double-decker buses. Passengers buy a ticket that allows them to hop on and off along the tourist route so they can take a self-guided tour of specific attractions. The other option is to stay on the bus and listen to the guide's detailed explanation of all the sights along the way. Kids love sitting on the top and seeing it all from a bird's-eye view.

❏ 196. Set the Table

Setting the table is something kids can do to help out at dinnertime—often a very busy time of day with parents coming home from work. And teaching children the proper way to set the table can be a fun lesson in and of itself. Have a la-di-da, oh-so-sophisticated luncheon with all their favorite foods and set the table together. Here's an easy way to remember what goes where!

> **Fork is four letters—Left is four letters = Fork goes on the left.**
> **Knife is five letters—Right is five letters = Knife goes on the right.**
> **Spoon is five letters—Right is five letters = Spoon goes on the right.**

Now the fork is all alone on the left, so give it a napkin to keep it company!

❑ 197. Visit a Lighthouse

Before radar and sonar and GPS, ships relied on the ever-vigilant lighthouse keeper to look out for them, to shine his light into the night sky so they could judge their position to land. Though lighthouses don't play such a large and vital role today, they still stir up a sense of wonder, mystery, and nostalgia in all of us. Next time you're on a beach vacation, look out for the nearest lighthouse. Many have museums dedicated to their history and to the maritime livelihood of the area. Climb to the top and get the same view the solitary lighthouse keeper had all those years ago. What does the lighthouse make your family think about? What does the view mean to them? Everything else may have changed around the lighthouse, but the seemingly endless ocean horizon is the same now as it ever was.

❑ 198. Celebrate Artists at a Craft Fair

In a world filled with machine-made goods, what a joy it is to visit a craft fair and see the difference handmade makes! A craft fair is usually made up of a series of booths with artists displaying their handicrafts and sometimes demonstrating how they work. You'll find weavers, quilters, woodworkers, clothing and accessory designers, and toy makers displaying all kinds of clever handicrafts. Some crafts may even be made from recycled aluminum cans, machine parts, spools, wires, and a variety of odds and ends. As you and your child walk through rows of displays, it's interesting to talk with the artists about how they discovered their interest in a particular craft. Look for inspiration and discover a craft you and your kids might enjoy trying.

❑ 199. Visit a Planetarium

If you love astronomy, why not take your kids to the place where the stars truly are the stars of the show? A planetarium is a showcase for entertaining programs about astronomy and the night sky. Perhaps the best part of a planetarium is the large dome-shape projection screen that makes the audience feel as if they are truly outside and looking up at an endless universe. Settle down in a seat and enjoy scenes of stars, planets, and other celestial objects twinkling, sparkling, and shooting across the screen sky. A voiceover explains the explainable, but you and the kids will have a sense of wonder just realizing how big, how far, and how amazing our universe is.

▲   ▲   ▲   ▲   ▲

"A happy family is but an earlier heaven."
—Sir John Bowring

▼   ▼   ▼   ▼   ▼

❑ 200. Rock Out at a Rock Concert

Before you know it, your kids are going to be old enough to think it's totally uncool to attend a concert with their parents. So why not grab the opportunity to take your children to their first rock concert the moment they reach the age when they begin to discover teen idols, rock stars, favorite songs, CDs, and rock groups? Show your kids that you respect their taste in music. Paying attention to the listening habits your children are developing keeps you in the loop about the messages they're receiving from song lyrics and the stars who sing them. And showing support for the ones they like (those who have a healthy message), gives you another opportunity to share a piece of their world. Kids need to choose their own role models, but going to a rock concert and withholding judgment helps keep the lines of communication open. Find something you do like about a song, a singer, or a band, and share that thought.

If your kids resist the idea of going with you, allow them to invite a few friends along, too. You may be invisible to them, but they'll be visible to you.

❏ 201. Take Dictation and Listen to the Story Grow

The act of putting pen to paper can inhibit a young child's story-telling. Over time, as their small motor skills develop and they become more proficient at decoding the words in their heads and translating them to written words on paper, kids may write longer stories or papers. Still, give any child the chance to dictate while you do the writing or typing and you can be sure the story will have more details, better structure, better grammar, and a beginning, middle, and end that make sense. As soon as concern for hand-writing, spelling, and punctuation are removed from the equation, story "writing" becomes fun again. Do a little experiment of your own and see what happens. Yes, it's important that your child learn all the rules of writing, but once in a while the freedom from *physically* writing makes a child a much better "writer."

❏ 202. Build a Snow Fort

Snowmen and snowballs aren't the only things you can make when the flakes are falling. If there's enough snow on the ground, try your hand at snowchitecture—the art of building snow forts. A snow fort can take many forms, ranging from a simple wall to a more ornate structure complete with battlements just like a medieval castle. The ornaments are up to you, but one thing is required no matter how you build your snow fort: SNOW. Lots and lots of snow. To provide shelter from flying snowballs, you'll have to build a fort that's at least a few feet high, so everyone needs to grab a shovel and start piling snow to make the walls. Once you have the snow in place, pack it tightly and put on the finishing touches—use food coloring to write your family name and add carrots along the top to make it comically imposing. Take a minute to enjoy your work, then stock up on snowballs and challenge another family to a snowball fight!

❏ 203. Get Fit at Your Own Family Olympics

Every two years, the Olympics capture our imaginations and expose us to sports and feats we don't see in everyday life. The Olympics are, at heart, a celebration. According to legend, the ancient Olympics were founded by Zeus to celebrate his victory over Cronus and his ascension to

the throne of heaven. These first Olympics were a family affair, as Zeus' son Heracles defeated his brothers in a running race and was crowned with a wreath of wild olive branches. You may not have such a crown in your house, but you can certainly celebrate your family by holding your own Olympics. For added fun, invite another family to join you! Make "medals," select judges, then start with the opening ceremony—a parade of the athletes: your kids, of course!

Here are ideas for games for each season:

Summer Olympics: Water Balloon Relay, Hose Limbo, Inflatable Pool Biggest Splash

Fall Olympics: Leaf Pile Jumping, Running Race to the Finish, Pumpkin Rolling

Winter Olympics: Snowball Making, Snowball Throwing, Long Jump in Snow

Spring Olympics: Downhill Rolling, Tree Climbing, Timed Jump Rope

Whatever games you play, hand out medals and celebrate the day with a picnic, a cookout, a soup and sandwich supper, or popcorn and a movie. Competition is a healthy way for you to bond and to bring out the best in each other, but don't forget to teach your children about sportsmanship and winning or losing gracefully. After all, this is a celebration of your family.

❏ 204. Sing Songs Together

Whether you whistle while you work or sing aloud while riding in the car, everyone has a musical bone or two. Bring your family together to share their musical tastes for a weekly sing-along. Each week a different family member can bring a song for everyone to learn and sing together. Already have a musician in the family? Even better! Let him or her provide accompaniment. Every week can be a celebration of your family and their own unique voices if you take the time to learn each other's songs.

❏ 205. Power Down

Spending an evening without using electricity is a good excuse for gathering together in one room and finding sources of entertainment that don't involve the television or video games. Break out the flashlights, candles, and sleeping bags, then spread out on the family room floor and snuggle in to read stories by flashlight, play card games, and share quiet time. Living even briefly without the benefit of electricity brings a new appreciation for this modern convenience. As an added bonus, spending a night without light prepares the whole family for an emergency situation!

❏ 206. Grow an Avocado

Next time you use an avocado for something, keep the seed and let the kids in on a growth experience. An avocado is fun to watch as it grows, and all you'll need are small toothpicks, a glass, water, potting soil, and a flowerpot. Here's what to do:

1. Insert three toothpicks around the middle of the seed, equal distance from each other.

2. Set the seed into the glass so that the toothpicks are holding it up on the rim of the glass.

3. Fill the glass with water so that about an inch of the seed is covered.

4. Place the seed in a warm place with indirect light. In about a week, you'll see white roots growing in the water and a green shoot sprouting from the top.

5. Add to the water as it evaporates, keeping it at the same level.

6. When the green shoot is about six inches long, plant the avocado in a pot of damp soil. The pot must have holes in the bottom for drainage to avoid root rot.

Be sure to keep your plant watered and give it plenty of sunlight. Although it will be years until your avocado plant will produce fruit, it's still a lot of fun to tend the plant and watch it grow!

▲　▲　▲　▲　▲

"When you look at your life,
the greatest happinesses
are family happinesses."

—Joyce Brothers

▼　▼　▼　▼　▼

❏ 207. Teach Good Manners

It's no secret that good manners will take you far in life. It's also no secret that it's our job as parents to teach our children how to be polite. Here's a top ten list to get you started:

1. Say "thank you" when you are offered something.

2. Say "no thank you" if you prefer not to accept the offer.

3. Say "please" when asking for something.

4. Take turns.

5. Teach the Golden Rule—"Do unto others as you would have them do unto you." Treat others the way you would like to be treated.

6. Make eye contact when talking with another person.

7. Offer a firm handshake when meeting someone.

8. Play fair and be a good sport.

9. Say "excuse me" when appropriate.

10. Share.

❑ 208. Watch the Big Game and Party Hearty!

If you can't be at the game in person, do the next best thing—have a party! Sporting events are a great reason for a party and the perfect opportunity to show your kids that your family is number one when it comes to fun. Plan the party feast together and include favorite appetizers, a main course, and dessert. Explain the rules of the game, pick a team to root for, and choose some favorite players to watch for. Let your kids know that it's just a game and be sure to display good sportsmanship yourselves even if your team loses. Watch the commercials with an eye toward funniest, silliest, best, and worst. Invite other families over to share the team spirit. Make your house the place to be when the big games are being played. The merrier you make your home, the more your kids will want to be there.

❑ 209. Attend a Native American Powwow

A powwow is a Native American celebration during which people get together to sing, dance, renew old friendships, and meet new friends. The gatherings are a reminder of Native Americans' rich heritage and traditions. Many powwows are open to non–Native Americans as well, and the excitement of the dances and songs performed in traditional dress is a moving experience for everyone. The Red Earth Festival in Oklahoma City, Oklahoma, is the largest Native American gathering. For three days every June, members of more than 100 tribes gather to demonstrate their traditions. A highlight of this powwow is the dance competition in which both northern and southern tribes compete.

❏ 210. Visit a Wild West Town

All set for some rootin', tootin' Wild West shooting? Wild West towns are activity parks set in the 1800s when the West was wild and there were acres and acres of land between towns. Fans of horses, rodeos, cowboys, old-time blacksmith shops, general stores, saloons, and one-room schoolhouses will love to experience a visit to one of these live reenactment towns complete with country-western music, sundown cookouts, mule-drawn carriage rides, trail rides, and everything that's been glamorized about the Wild, Wild West. Where do you find such a town? Just rustle up some leads on the Internet!

❏ 211. Follow that Cat!

How do you get the kids up and off the couch when the weather is glorious and they just don't seem motivated to move? Take a walk with a mission in mind, and add an element of interest to the usual neighborhood route. Follow the neighborhood cat—or your own, if it's an outdoor cat—and find out exactly where that kitty goes once the door opens and he darts out. Let the cat's path lead you and see if it takes you a new way—through a hedge, perhaps, or over a fence, across a field, up a tree? The possibilities are endless, and you're sure to get some giggles out of trying to track the cat. Don't be surprised if you lose the cat only to find it sitting on your front porch!

❏ 212. Live in the Moment

Writer/singer/performer David Byrne partnered with Brian Eno to write a prophetic song entitled "Everything That Happens Will Happen Today." With an understanding of that statement as fact, consider taking a photograph of something in your family's life every day for a week, a month, or a year. Create a "Today in the Life of Our Family" album and fill it with photos of simple things that happened—whether big or small. Your kids brushing their teeth, feeding the cat or dog, trying a new food, playing with other kids, eating dinner with the family, doing homework, talking on the phone to Grandma, greeting Mom or Dad when they come home from work—these are the moments that make up the days that make up the weeks, months, and years of your children's lives. Your photographic record will be a welcome reminder some day of everything that happened today.

❏ 213. Blow Bubbles

Bubbles. Even the word sounds fun! But forget about the bottles of ready-made bubble solution you have sitting around. Add to the fun by letting your kids help you make the bubble solution. Simply mix ¼ cup liquid dish detergent with 3¾ cups water (filtered water works best). To make your own bubble wand, bend and twist a wire coat hanger into a small loop. Dip the loop in the bubble solution and wave it in the air or blow softly into it. Little children love to chase the bubbles and even bigger kids find something magical in bubbles floating until they pop! Keep a supply of bubble solution in a clean mayonnaise jar and bring it out whenever your kids are looking for some good, clean fun.

❏ 214. Celebrate Summer Solstice

FAST FACT

In Latin the word *sol* means "sun" and the word *stice* means "to stand still."

Many of us—especially those of us who live in cold climates—anticipate the beginning of summer all winter long. So why not give summer a proper welcome by celebrating the summer solstice? This major celestial event celebrates the longest day of the year—and the shortest night. In the northern hemisphere, summer solstice takes place in June, but for people in the Southern Hemisphere, the longest day comes in December.

Make this first day of summer extra-special by celebrating with a BBQ kickoff. Grill tasty food, dance, and play fun summer games such as croquet, badminton, and Frisbee golf. Let the little ones stay up and party until it's dark. This is the time for watermelon seed spitting contests, two-legged races, and tug-o-wars. Your summer is bound to be a blast when you welcome the solstice with fanfare!

❑ 215. Experience the Quebec Carnival

Carnival typically takes place during the last week of January and the first week of February. The whole two weeks are geared toward families with children of all ages. It's truly a winter wonderland of night parades, slides, snow rafting, ice fishing, concerts, snow sculptures, dogsled rides or horse-drawn carriage rides, ice-skating, the Maple Sugar Shack, and more. The cost of admission to the fairgrounds includes all the days of the carnival, and there are family packages offered as well.

When you're ready to take a short break from the carnival, tour the quaint streets of Old Quebec City. Both you and the kids will want to head for the giant ice slide located by the famous Chateau Frontenac. Go for a quick ride or rent a sled for a couple of hours and slide to your heart's content. You'll enjoy the feeling of being in a magical winter place.

❑ 216. Visit Little Italy

Bongiorno! That's "good day" in Italian, and rest assured that when you take the kids to Little Italy, you're sure to have a good day! Little Italys are historic districts that can be found in cities all across the country. Perhaps the most well-known is New York City's Little Italy on Mulberry Street in lower Manhattan. But San Diego, California; Cleveland, Ohio; Toronto, Canada; Baltimore, Maryland; and many other cities also have Little Italy sections, so it's pretty likely that wherever you live, you have a Little Italy near you! Soak up the sights, sounds, and smells that are reflective of the rich and delicious Italian culture. It might be fun to time your visit with the celebration of an annual festival that might include a parade, music, dancing, and samples of Italy's best foods and pastries. The Feast of San Gennaro in New York's Little Italy takes place during the last two weeks of September. The Little Italy Festa in San Diego happens in October. Italian Americans take great pride in their heritage and are eager to share it. Be on the lookout for announcements of festivals near you.

❏ 217. Make a Piñata

The time-honored Mexican tradition of hanging a piñata from a tree, blindfolding the players, and having them bop the piñata with a stick is as fun to watch as it is to participate in. Birthday parties often save the piñata game for last because the piñata is filled with wrapped candies and toys that the children gather up and take home in their goodie bags. You can buy a piñata and fill it yourself, or you and your kids can make one, fill it, and play the piñata game with or without the party.

YOU WILL NEED:
2 cups flour
3 cups water
1 balloon
Newspaper
Paint, crayons, or markers
Colored crepe paper
String

INSTRUCTIONS:

1. Blow up a large balloon and tie the end shut.
2. Mix the flour and water together until it makes a smooth paste.
3. Cut the newspaper into 1-inch long strips and dip them into the flour mixture.
4. Place the strips on the balloon until it is covered, leaving an uncovered hole at the top.

5. Set the balloon aside and let dry.

6. Repeat steps 3 through 5 two more times.

7. When the third layer has dried, pop the balloon and pull it out through the hole at the top.

8. Paint your piñata with poster paint and decorate it with painted designs.

9. For extra decoration, hang colored crepe paper from the sides and bottom.

10. Punch two small holes in the top near the opening and thread a large piece of string through the two holes

11. Fill your piñata (through the hole you left at the top) with candy, toys, or any other fun surprises. Add strips of colored paper so the treats are not all lumped together.

12. Hang your piñata from a tree branch and let the blindfolded piñata boppers take individual turns whacking the piñata until it breaks open.

❑ 218. Host a Tag Sale

Look around the house. Do you see it? Cold, hard cash is in every room, just waiting to be earned. A family tag sale is just the way to turn what seems like trash into cash. A successful tag sale requires organization and each family member's willingness to clean up, weed out, and tag all the stuff that's sure to be someone else's treasure.

Commit to the cleanup and gather all the sale items together in one spot. Then follow these steps to tag sale success:

- Categorize everything: books, CDs, toys, sports equipment, household items, etc.

- Dust, polish, wash, and clean all the items so they are more appealing to your buyers.

- Advertise the date, time, and place—in the newspaper, on signs on street corners, and on grocery store bulletin boards.

- The day before the sale—or the morning of, if it's an outdoor yard sale—set up tables. Put things out in categories—toys together, books together, etc.

- Price and label each item. Put all items that are priced the same on one table.

- Be willing to bargain and remember: If it doesn't sell today, it will get thrown out or given away tomorrow. In other words, sometimes it pays to take what you can get.

- When it's all over, gather up what's left and donate the items to a charity.

- Add up the money earned and put it toward a family dinner out, a day trip together, or a necessity for which you've all been saving.

❑ 219. Institute Movie Night

PJs on, blankets and pillows spread out on the couch or on the floor, individual bowls of freshly popped corn, a movie in the DVD player—it's just another Friday night with the best family on the block! Show the kids how it used to be—show a cartoon first and then the main feature. Give each family member an opportunity to select the movie of the week. Add to the fun of movie night by preparing review and rate cards with the title of the movie at the top and spaces for each viewer to express an opinion about the movie you've just watched. Rate the movie from one star to four stars, with one being the lowest and four being the highest. Keep the cards in a recipe box for future reference. After all, you'll want to watch your family's favorite movies more than once!

❑ 220. Redecorate Your Child's Room Together

A change of scenery is always welcome—especially when the change is going to be in your child's room! Kids spend a lot of time in their rooms and making it a pleasant and happy space is good for their spirits. When your children are old enough to express opinions about what they would do to change their rooms, listen, take notes, and involve them in the process of the makeover. Let them choose a paint color, curtains, and bedding. Then, when the room is ready to accessorize, let the kids place their things exactly where they want them. Having the kids involved in creating the look and feel of their room may even instill in them a desire to keep it neat and tidy—but we can't make any promises!

❑ 221. Light Up the Night

Holiday light shows are a magical experience. The excitement of seeing the colors, the figures, and the shining stars lighting up the cold winter night is worth repeating year after year. But perhaps the greatest reason to love a festival of lights is the fact that someone else does all the work of hanging the lights and creating displays so that your family and others can simply drive through and say "ooo!" and "aaahh!" Sponsored by local governments, parks, businesses, and communities, light festivals often begin just after Thanksgiving and are displayed on weekends only. As the winter holidays approach, the hours of operation increase. Check your local government Web site and watch for signs around town or in the newspaper. Then pick a night, bundle up, and take a car ride through a dream scene you'll always remember.

❑ 222. Ride the Waves—Go River Rafting or Tubing

Every family feels the strain sometimes—the sense that you're all going in different directions. Take the plunge and navigate the occasionally rough waters of family life by going river rafting, where you and your family can work together to tame the rapids. No matter how confident you are, you should start by visiting a whitewater rafting outfitter, where you will join an experienced guide who can show you the ins and outs of the river. Most outfitters offer many different adventures, including full-day and half-day trips, to suit your experience level. Rapids are rated from Class 1 through Class 6, with Class 1 being the easiest, and Class 6 being the hardest. Rafting should be both safe and thrilling, so be sure to choose the trip level and length that suits your family best. You will all be wet and exhausted as the day comes to a close, but you will have memories to last a lifetime.

For a more relaxing journey down the river, try inner tubing. You can grab your own tube and float down the river at your own pace, or you can tie the tubes together and float as a group. Slather on the sunscreen, then soak up some rays while you watch the world go by for a day. However you choose to ride the river, you'll be doing it together, and you'll all be going in the same direction for once!

❑ 223. Rake the Leaves and Jump in the Piles

Autumn is in the air. The leaves are turning from green to bright orange, red, and yellow, and the wind is picking up, scattering those leaves through the air and onto the ground. To some, it's the most beautiful time of year. To others, it's days and days of hard work—an unending chore of raking and bagging leaves, only to have more fall in their place. Well, don't just leave poor Dad out there all on his own. Take the whole family out to join him. Put on your gloves and get raking. Turn it into a game. See who can clear an area the fastest or who can make the biggest pile. Then when all the leaves have been raked into neat piles, the fun can really begin—it's time for jumping! So get ready, get set, GO! Race to the pile, and take a flying flop on top. Don't worry if you scatter a few leaves; you know how to get them back together. When the fun is over, rake those leaves up one last time and help Dad bag them. But don't forget to bring in some leaves as souvenirs. Iron them between two pieces of wax paper, and put them in an album with all the photos you'll be taking of each other buried to the neck in leaves upon leaves upon leaves. And always remember, the more leaves that fall, the more piles you can make, and the more fun you can have together.

❑ 224. Tour the Local Fire Station

Open house at the local fire station is a big day for kids as well as for the firefighters and emergency medical technicians who spend a lot of time maintaining their equipment, running through practice drills, creating educational materials for their communities, and answering the alarms that call them to action. The excitement of seeing and hearing a fire truck racing by with horns honking, lights flashing, and a crew of dressed-and-ready firefighters is exciting for kids and adults of all ages. Seeing the trucks, meeting the men and women, and touring the fire station's bunk room, kitchen, dispatcher center, and equipment stations can be a fascinating and fun experience. Check with your local fire department to find out the dates of an open house, or make an appointment for a personal tour. You'll be the real hero when you introduce your kids to a behind-the-scenes look at a fire station.

❑ 225. Teach Your Teen to Drive Responsibly

Children are introduced to wheels the first time they are placed in a baby carriage or stroller. As they grow, their set of wheels changes, from tricycles to bicycles, rollerblades to skateboards, and yes, eventually to cars. They've been taught that wheels are a good way to get places, so it's no surprise that the day will come when your child *will* want to learn to drive. *Don't* panic. *Do* prepare.

The first lesson is to set a good example yourself. Obey the speed limit, require all passengers to wear seatbelts, don't multitask, and don't take risks. The Internet is full of sites that give advice for crash-proofing your kids. You'll find tips, rules to set, ideas for drawing up a contract for your teen to sign, and thoughts on curfews. But no written material replaces hands-on training provided by a trained instructor or by you. Only you will know if your teen is really ready to be responsible behind the wheel of a car. Your child's safety should always be your reason for any rules.

❑ 226. Make Ice Pops with Juice

It's another hot summer day. You've just returned from the pool, and you open up the fridge to offer your kids an ice pop. "What flavor do you want?" you ask them. "Red!" "Green!" Red? Green? Those aren't flavors. Those are colors! It's a little silly to eat an ice pop named after the color of its dye, so why not make some real juice ice pops? After all, "raspberry" sounds a while lot better than "red," doesn't it?

Making ice pops is a fun activity you can all do together. Ice pops are healthy, tasty, and easy to make. All you need are some wooden craft sticks, some paper or plastic cups (or some ready-made plastic molds), and your family's favorite juice. You can even get creative and mix your favorite juices!

INSTRUCTIONS:

1. Fill cups ¾ of the way with juice.
2. Cover cups with aluminum foil or wax paper.
3. Puncture the foil or paper in the center and slide a craft stick in until it hits the bottom of the cup and can stand on its own.
4. Place cups in the freezer.
5. Wait a few hours, and voilà! Homemade, nutritious, ice pops made with real fruit juice!
6. Eat to your heart's content.

❑ 227. Hit the Hay...

Halloween is much more than trick or treat, costumes, and candy. It's the perfect time for a family outing to a local farm to pick out the perfect pumpkin! Put on your jeans, a pair of good walking shoes or boots, and a pair of pumpkin-picking gloves, and get ready for a fun but bumpy ride in a hay wagon towed by a tractor. Seeing the farm equipment up close is a thrill, and the drivers usually take the scenic route, allowing you to get a good look at the orchards, corn fields, and other crops. You'll be dropped off in the middle of the pumpkin patch, where you can snap great photos of your kids sitting on the pumpkins and choosing the ones they'll want to take home. Once you've taken all the time you want picking out your pumpkins, the wagon will take you back to the farm stand. Don't forget to pick up some caramel apples and a jug of fresh-pressed apple cider. They'll make great snacks when you go home to carve your pumpkin!

☐ 228. Be a Guest Speaker at Your Child's Class

No matter what you do for a living, your kids will be proud to introduce you to their teacher and classmates as a guest speaker. Teachers often invite parents into the classroom to supplement textbook learning. Let your child's teacher know that you'd be interested in being a guest. Sharing the details of your career—what your interests are, how you got into your chosen field, what you like about your job, and exactly what your title and duties are—gives students insight into the field you're in and into what kind of careers they might enjoy.

☐ 229. Make Valentines for Our Troops

Handmade Valentines are the best ones of all. They're the ones we save and smile over years later. When you and your kids sit down to make Valentines for the family or for classmates, make some extra ones for military personnel stationed around the world. Far from home and often in very dangerous situations, the men and women in our armed forces love to receive positive messages from their homeland. And your kids will like the idea of doing something for their country, too.

Follow these guidelines for handmade Valentines, and you'll make someone very happy:

- Do not send candy or any other food items with the Valentine.

- Do not use glitter.

- Do include your name and address if you'd like to correspond, or you may just sign your first name along with a positive message and a thank you.

- Check out http://amillionthanks.org/ for complete guidelines. Your Valentine's Day will be better for it!

❏ 230. Join a Clean-up-the-Stream Team

Do you and your family enjoy swimming, fishing, or rafting? Would any of these be as appealing with trash and debris floating in the water or beached on the shore? Our waters are a great natural resource that we should protect and preserve. You can do your part by teaching your children about nature stewardship. Show them that they have the power to make a positive difference—to help the environment for their own generation and for generations to come. Join one of the many volunteer programs all across the country, including those sponsored by neighborhood associations, schools, and local environmental organizations. Some recognized campaigns for stream cleanup include International Coastal Cleanup, organized by Ocean Conservancy, and National River Cleanup Week, sponsored by American Outdoors. Or, if you can't find a local program, start your own! What are you waiting for? Put on your boots and gloves and get ready to pitch in.

❑ 231. Visit a National Park

With all of your responsibilities, chores, and errands, it may seem like your life is just a network of jobs and obligations. That's when it's time to step outside and go where nature can still be nature—a national park. Whether you're looking for hot springs or mountains, deserts or lakes, the National Park Service (NPS) has a park for you. There are national parks all over North America, with 391 designated areas in the United States alone covering more than 84 million acres! For more about our national parks, visit the U.S. National Park Service Web site at www.nps.gov.

As Pulitzer Prize–winning author Wallace Stegner once said, the national parks are "The best idea...They reflect us at our best, rather than our worst."

FAST FACT

President Andrew Jackson signed the first legislation by any government to set aside protected lands in 1832. This legislation created what was known as Hot Springs Reservation in Arkansas. The first official national park, however, was Yellowstone, which was established in 1872.

❑ 232. Horse Around

The horse is such a majestic, powerful, yet gentle animal that it captures the hearts of children and adults alike. You don't need to be a rancher or an equestrian champion to enjoy a day of riding. There are many stables that will rent horses and lead children on a trail ride. This is a safe and easy way to get the experience of riding a horse while enjoying a beautiful landscape as you wind your way through fields, meadows, and forests. As you clop along the trails, take some time to appreciate the landscape in silence—an under-appreciated virtue in modern life. There will be plenty of time to talk about the whole experience later. This is also an excellent chance to give your children a hint of independence as they ride their own horses and have their own experiences, all while feeling the support and comfort of a group ride. Don't forget to bring some carrots or apples to make friends with your equine companion (but be sure to ask for permission before feeding the horses). And don't be surprised if you're soon fielding requests for a pet horse!

❑ 233. Go Wild at the Zoo

Lions and tigers and bears, oh my! And giraffes and elephants and prairie dogs and lemurs and orangutans and gorillas and reptiles … There's no shortage of fascinating creatures to see at the zoo. But that's not all. There's a lot your family can learn from them, too. How do the animals show affection for each other? How do they show anger? If you watch them closely enough, you will see a range of behaviors and emotions to which the whole family can relate. You may even understand yourselves and each other a little better after the trip.

❑ 234. Go Fly a Kite

Did you know that the Wright Brothers used kites to perfect their ideas for flying machines? Besides being a fun thing to do on a windy day, kite flying provides a feel for aerodynamic forces. Toy stores and hobby shops sell paper kites and sturdier ones made of nylon and other fabrics. They also sell spools of kite string. Choose kites that are light enough for your kids to handle but sturdy enough not to get ripped apart by the wind at first flight. Then find a wide open space where trees and power lines won't get in the way. You hold the spool while your child holds a small length of string and runs with the kite behind him or her until the wind lifts it up. Once the kite is up, let more string out a little at a time. If the kite starts to dip, give a little tug on the string to lift it again. Let it rise between 50 and 100 feet. Watch it dip, dive, and soar again. When you're ready to bring it down, rewind the string slowly and try to grab the kite before it hits the ground. For even more excitement, take the kids to a kite flying festival. The American Kitefliers Association's Web site lists festivals all over the country at www.kite.org/cal.php. Check it out, then go fly a kite!

☐ 235. Make Homemade Ice Cream

I scream! You scream! We all scream for ice cream! And when it comes to ice cream, homemade is really something to scream about. Get the family involved in picking out the flavor, mixing the ingredients, and—most important of all—eating this delicious creation.

ICE CREAM IN A BAG

This recipe yields one scoop, so have each family member make his or her own.

YOU WILL NEED:

- 1 gallon-size plastic food storage bag
  Ice cubes
- 6 tablespoons rock salt
- 1 pint-size plastic food storage bag
- ½ cup milk or half & half
- ¼ teaspoon vanilla
- 1 tablespoon sugar

INSTRUCTIONS:

1. Fill the large bag halfway with ice. Add the rock salt.

2. Put milk, vanilla, and sugar into the smaller bag and seal it.

3. Place the sealed small bag inside the large bag. Seal the large bag carefully.

4. Shake for about five minutes, or until your mixture becomes ice cream.

5. Wipe off the top of the small bag and open carefully.

6. Enjoy the cold, sweet confection with your family!

❏ 236. Make a Model Together

Saturday mornings at the hobby shop can make for fun bonding time. Shelves are lined with kits geared to all levels of proficiency, from beginner to advanced, and include cars, airplanes, trains, ships, boats, and a whole lot more. Everything you need in the way of paints, glues, decals, display racks, and environments to build and place your models is available. Model-making is a pastime enjoyed by kids of all ages, and the hobby often follows them into adulthood as they perfect their model-making skills and create museum-quality pieces. Start with a favorite car or plane and teach the importance of organizing the parts, cleaning the paint brushes, following directions, and adding the finishing touches. Your child will experience the satisfaction of a job well done—not to mention the joy of spending quality time with you!

▲ ▲ ▲ ▲ ▲

"There is no doubt that it is around the family and the home that all the greatest virtues, the most dominating virtues of human society, are created, strengthened, and maintained."
—Winston Churchill

▼ ▼ ▼ ▼ ▼

❏ 237. Go to an Airport and Watch the Planes Take Off

Better than a movie! More exciting than a video game! As thrilling as a roller-coaster ride! It's a trip to the airport to watch the planes take off and land! Everybody knows that flying is one of the coolest superhero super powers, and watching planes of all sizes start their engines, taxi down the runway, and lift off the ground to soar in the air is every bit as awe-inspiring in the eyes of kids. Strike up a conversation with the owner of one of the planes and maybe you and your kids will get a tour of the cockpit. Rate the takeoffs and landings—bumpiest, smoothest, fastest, slowest—and learn about the different aircraft. Pack a lunch or eat at the airport's snack bar. Seeing the planes on the ground and in the air gives a new appreciation for aviation.

❑ 238. Work on a Jigsaw Puzzle

A jigsaw puzzle is more than a pretty picture. It's an opportunity to learn while playing, as young children sort, match, and problem-solve while having fun at the same time. Each time a piece is correctly placed in the puzzle, your child will experience success. Working on a puzzle together as a family makes those successes more meaningful as you all cheer for one another. And the best part is, you don't need much to get started. Just clear a space on a table where you can leave the puzzle out indefinitely, then find the time to sit down together as a family. Encourage everyone to stop by the puzzle table any time to add another piece until the puzzle is completed. Save it with special puzzle glue, or break it up and store it away for another puzzle-play day.

❑ 239. Make a Tire Swing or Rope Swing

The sight of a tire swing or rope swing hanging from the sturdy branch of a stately tree evokes memories of simpler times and the happy days of summer. If you've got a big tree in your yard, put it to good use with a thick and sturdy rope and an old tire (the older the tire, the better, since older tires didn't have steel belts that might poke out with age). Find a tire at a junk yard or perhaps at a gas station. Power wash it to remove dirt and to cut down on the black stuff rubbing off on kids and clothing. Use a power drill to punch holes in the bottom of the tire so that water and dirt can run out. Then tie the rope around the top of the tire, loop it over a very strong tree branch, and tie it with a double dose of classic square knots. Test it yourself before you let the kids try it. Once it's secure, let the swinging begin!

❑ 240. Go Navy! Go Army! Visit a Surplus Store

The best thing about an army-navy surplus store is the huge selection of unique and cool stuff. What's in it for you and your kids? Plenty. Patches, army hats, sailor caps, lanterns, flashlights so powerful you can shine them up to the moon, red-filtered flashlights that won't ruin your night vision, telescopes, periscopes, T-shirts, uniform jackets, camouflage face paint, temporary tattoos, and camouflage nets that can be strung up in the backyard and used as a fort. What else? Helmets, jungle boots, flack jackets, old military canteens, can openers, old maps, and a popular favorite—dog tags with your kid's name and maybe even a message on the back from Mom and Dad. It's one thing to read about history in a book, but at an army-navy surplus store, history comes to life with real souvenirs.

❑ 241. Turn Lemons into a Lemonade Stand

A sure sign of summer is a lemonade stand on the corner and a bunch of eager kids shouting to passersby, "Lemonade! Lemonade for sale!" What a fun way to make money and supplement the allowance parents give. A kid's first experience in running his or her own business can start with a lemonade stand in the front yard or on a path where bikers and runners may provide ample customers. The lessons learned from something as simple as a lemonade stand include adding up the cost of ingredients and paper cups, then deciding what to charge so a profit can be made. Keeping a cash box and learning how to make change is another handy skill. Help your kids get started by setting up a card table, mixing up the lemonade, and showing how to make change. Then step back and let them take charge!

❑ 242. Make a Shake or Smoothie

Shake it up, baby! You can shake the smoothie industry up by creating your own shakes and smoothies right at home. All you need is an electric blender. Try this recipe or create your own.

BERRY GOOD SMOOTHIE

- 2 cups milk
- ¾ cup fresh strawberries, blueberries, raspberries, or mixed berries
- 2 scoops vanilla ice cream

Pour the milk and berries into the blender and blend until mixed. Add the ice cream, and blend again until thick and smooth. Pour, drink, and say "Ahh! Delicious!"

❑ 243. Visit the Kennedy Space Center

There's more to offer in Orlando, Florida, than Mickey Mouse. The Kennedy Space Center is the only place on Earth where you can tour launch areas, meet a real astronaut, see giant rockets, try out a spaceflight simulator, and even view the launch of a space shuttle. There is an entry fee to the Kennedy Space Center Visitor's Complex and additional fees for guided tours. But the educational value of the visit and tour are well worth the price of admission.

❑ 244. Invent a Sandwich

It may seem pretty ordinary to you, but the sandwich was once a groundbreaking invention. Popular lore has it that 18th-century English aristocrat John Montague, 4th Earl of Sandwich, came up with the idea of putting meat between bread in order to keep his hands clean while playing cards.

FAST FACT

Did John Montague really invent the sandwich? According to some sources, the creator of the sandwich was really an ancient Jewish sage, Hillel the Elder, who wrapped lamb meat and bitter herbs in a matzo.

But just because the sandwich has been around for centuries doesn't mean there isn't room for improvement. The great thing about the sandwich is that it can be made of anything stuffed between two slices of bread. So gather the family together in the kitchen, and brainstorm some sandwiches of your own. Go to the store together to buy the ingredients, and come home to make the bread-encompassed meal of your dreams. Be sure to share! Then, in the true spirit of the great multitasking Earl himself, gather round the table and deal out some cards. The stakes? The winner gets to judge the best sandwich!

❑ 245. Guide Your Kids in Decision-Making

Life is full of hard choices. Arm your kids with the knowledge they'll need to make the important decisions in their lives. Help them by breaking the decision-making process into five simple steps, as outlined below:

1. Identify the problem. State it clearly so you know exactly what it is you are trying to decide.

2. Think about alternatives—what are your choices? It might be as easy as deciding whether or not to do something. Are there any other alternatives?

3. Analyze the alternatives. Do a **SWOT** analysis. **SWOT** is the acronym for **S**trengths, **W**eaknesses, **O**pportunities, and **T**hreats. **Example:** You are deciding whether or not you should try out for a team. The strengths of joining the team might be: fun, good for school record, friends will be there. Weaknesses related to joining the team: extra work, weekend practice. Opportunities if you join the team might include making new friends, getting noticed by the coach, winning awards. Threats or things that make it a bad idea to join the team might include getting injured and the expense of a uniform.

4. Make your decision. Look over your analysis and drop the alternatives that don't make sense.

5. Do what you've decided to do.

▲ ▲ ▲ ▲ ▲

"A tree is known by its fruit."
—Proverb

▼ ▼ ▼ ▼ ▼

❑ 246. Join Your Neighbors in a Block Party

A neighborhood is only as good as the relationships of the people in it. Your kids will feel a sense of community if your family engages with those who live next door, in your circle, on your block, and in the development in which you live. One way to close the gaps that may exist in relationships is to organize a neighborhood block party. Choose a site in a common area where you can set up buffet tables, chairs, and have room for mingling. Invite each family to bring an appetizer, side dish, main course, dessert, or drinks—or have a barbeque grill going with hot dogs, hamburgers, and grilled vegetables. Set a time and date that allows the most people to come—a Saturday afternoon or evening will probably work best—and send the invitations two weeks in advance. Plan games for both the children and adults to get everyone mingling and having fun together. Bingo is a great crowd-pleaser that will appeal to young and adult alike—especially if there's a money prize involved.

❑ 247. Compare a Book to Its Movie

Charlotte's Web, Stuart Little, and a whole host of Grimms' and Hans Christian Andersen's fairy tales started out in print before they made it to the big screen. Oftentimes, when a book is turned into a movie, important material can be lost in translation. Sharpen your child's powers of observation by making a game out of comparing the book you just read together to the movie you're watching together.

Questions you might ask could include:

- Did the characters in the movie look like you imagined when you read the book?
- What scenes did the movie have that were not in the book?
- What scenes did the book have that were not in the movie?
- Why do you think they made these changes? Were they for the worse or for the better?
- Which did you like better—the book or the movie? Why?

❑ 248. Take a Ringside Seat

The souvenirs at ice hockey games are probably the coolest of any sport—miniature hockey sticks and genuine official game pucks if you walk down to the players' box at the end of the game. The game official often pleases the crowd by handing out NHL pucks as a way to build the audience. Ice hockey is a fast and rough sport to watch, but it's definitely exciting as players zoom back and forth on the ice toward their goals. If your child plays on an ice hockey team, seeing the professionals play will be a real treat.

❑ 249. Learn How to Eat a Lobster

Chances are if you live in Maine you know all the ins and outs of eating a lobster. But for the rest of us, these lobster-eating tips may make the difference between fun and frustration. It's a little tricky at first, but the sense of accomplishment at tackling the task is worth the energy expended.

YOU WILL NEED:
A lobster
A lobster- or nutcracker
A fork
Melted butter

INSTRUCTIONS:

1. Hold the lobster by the back and carefully twist to pull off the five pairs of legs. Save them to eat later.

2. Next, twist off the two claws.

3. Remove the "thumb" of the claw. Check inside for a small bit of meat. Dip it in melted butter and eat.

4. Use your cracker to crack the tip of the large section of the claw. Here you'll find a good chunk of meat to

FAST FACT

Why bother with a lobster? Nutrition experts say that 3 ½ ounces of lobster meat is only 90 calories (without the butter, of course!). Lobster meat also contains omega-3 fatty acids—the good cholesterol that decreases the risk of heart attacks.

eat. Use your pointer finger to push the meat from the tip of the claw out the large open end.

5. Holding the tail portion with one hand and the back with the other hand, twist the tail off the body.

6. Shove your fork into the tail meat, twist, and pull. When you become more expert in this delicate task, the whole tail will come out in one piece.

7. Use your fork to scrape away the green stuff, also called *tomalley*. The red stuff, or roe, is edible, but you don't have to eat it if you don't like it.

8. Cut up the tail meat, dip it in the butter, and eat it. Enjoy!

▲　▲　▲　▲　▲

"In dwelling, live close to the ground. In thinking, keep to the simple. In conflict, be fair and generous. In governing, don't try to control. In work, do what you enjoy. In family life, be completely present."

—Lao Tzu

▼　▼　▼　▼　▼

❏ 250. Take in a Soccer Game

Someone once said that the best part about going to a soccer game in the United States is having the stadium seats all to yourself. While soccer is one of the most popular sports for young kids, professional soccer teams have yet to build a huge audience in the United States. Meanwhile, in Europe and South America, the sport draws crowds like U.S. football teams do. Taking your kids to a professional soccer game will give them a feel for a sport that's enjoyed internationally by many enthusiastic fans. Kids who play soccer will have a special appreciation for the skill and speed with which professionals make a goal. The game may just inspire your young soccer player to try some fancier moves on the field, too!

❏ 251. Tour a Ship

From ancient times to our modern era, ships have played a vital role in the advancement of civilization. The idea of life at sea has also sparked many an imagination. How many people have looked out over a harbor and dreamed of all the fantastic places to visit, all the adventures to be had? Join the long line of oceanfront dreamers by taking your family to the waterfront for a tour of a ship. Preserved ships and replicas can be found in harbors on both coasts of North America. If your kids are interested in history, tour a historic vessel, where you'll learn all about shipboard life from firing cannons to trimming sails to eating salted beef. If modern naval technology strikes your fancy, take a tour of a battleship or an aircraft carrier. These behemoths of the ocean are truly impressive to behold, and they require a lot of coordination and commitment on the part of the crew. Whether old or new, a ship is like a building, a city, an ecosystem, and a society all in one. It's tightly designed and tightly run. But there's always room for a little dreaming, and there's always a new horizon up ahead.

❏ 252. Visit a Hot Spring

A visit to a hot spring can be the hottest ticket in town. There are hot springs all over North America, most of which are clustered in mountain areas and in the western regions. The hot springs found in Yellowstone National Park are among the most famous, though with temperatures reaching 400 degrees Fahrenheit, you certainly won't want to bathe in them! Another popular spot is Hot Springs, Arkansas. You can tour historic Fordyce Bathhouse—one of the grandest bathhouses of its time—then head to Bathhouse Row to enjoy an indoor soak at one of the bathhouses operated by park concessioners.

In the end, when you visit a hot spring, it's worth remembering that you are at a point where the inside of the earth meets the outside. That alone is worth marveling over.

❑ 253. See the Sparks Fly

Is there anything more magical than watching your child experience fireworks for the first time? And what better time to take in a fireworks display than the Fourth of July? Check your local paper for listings of fireworks near you. Plan to arrive early to get a good spot (and decent parking). Pack the fixings for a picnic dinner and eat as you wait for darkness to fall. Keep kids entertained with games of catch or tag. As the fireworks finally begin, snuggle up together and take in the beautiful sights. It will be a night your family won't soon forget!

FAST FACT

Fireworks originated in China some 2,000 years ago, and legend has it that they were accidentally invented by a cook who mixed together charcoal, sulfur, and saltpeter—all items commonly found in kitchens in those days. The mixture burned and when compressed in a bamboo tube, it exploded. There's no record of whether it was the cook's last day on the job.

❑ 254. Visit a Construction Site and Watch a Building Grow

There is an unexpected beauty to a construction site—the cranes rising up into the air, the scurry of activity around the site, the off days in winter when snow falls on naked girders. It's a poetry that is both organic and magical. The construction of a building is like the growth of a flower on a slower and more massive scale. It is a beauty beheld both instantaneously, as the welders weld and the riveters rivet, and over a long period of time, as significant changes can only really be witnessed from day to day or week to week. It is an exercise in the seemingly simultaneous suspension and passage of time. Given this, it is no surprise that the construction of skyscrapers captivated the imagination of so many throughout the 20th century. Now, in the 21st century, large-scale construction projects may have lost some of their cachet to those outside the fields of architecture and engineering, but they are an important testament to the growth of civilization and to the culture in which we live. Consider taking your family to watch a building go up. Spend some time at the site to take in all the details. Then revisit the site a few more times as the building grows. Maybe you will be inspired to learn more about building construction or maybe you will need nothing more than to quietly witness the ascent of a skyscraper. However you experience it, watching a building grow will leave a lasting impression on you and your children.

▲ ▲ ▲ ▲ ▲

"Tell me who admires and loves you, And I will tell you who you are."
—Charles Augustin Sainte-Beuve

▼ ▼ ▼ ▼ ▼

❑ 255. Take a Walk

You don't need to go far or spend a lot of money to experience cool things. The world outside your front door is ripe with possibility. Take your family on a five-senses walk to see what's in store for you in your own neighborhood. Smell the freshly cut grass or the newly bloomed roses. See the light shine through tree branches and play off leaves rustling in the breeze. Taste the nectar of a honeysuckle growing along a fence. Hear the buzzing lawnmowers and chirping birds battle for sonic supremacy. Feel the wind on your faces and the ground under your feet. Try to experience each sense to the fullest, and let yourself get lost in the beauty of the world around you. It's the perfect immersive vacation—and it's free!

❑ 256. Finger Paint

The fun of finger painting is obvious for little kids—messy, squishy, gooey, and colorful—and it's no wonder that it's a popular activity in school. But when's the last time *you* purposely made a mess with your kids? Take some giant paper and make a family painting, or paint some smaller individual works. Finger painting is fun no matter how old you are, and it's a worthy activity to bring out of the closet even when your kids are older. You'll all enjoy the simple nostalgia that comes from doing something you did when you were younger, and you'll get a kick out of the creative liberation experienced from using a material that is completely lacking in seriousness or pretension. Just let loose and paint or smear whatever comes to mind. When you're done, hang the paintings on the wall and have a mock critique. There may be a great artist among you!

❑ 257. Try Your Hand at Soap Carving

What hobby is so clean that even when you make a mess you're dirt-free? Soap carving! Soap carving is a fun and relatively easy way to tap into your family's creative potential and work with your hands. Just decide what you want to carve, and then follow the instructions below to learn the basics. There are plenty of Web sites devoted to this popular little hobby, so look it up online to find out more, or visit your local library for a detailed book or two. Just make sure your hands are dry when you start. Soap carving may be clean, but it can also be slippery.

1. Start with a simple white bar of soap. Ivory soap is said to be ideal for soap carving.

2. Have your child use a pencil to draw the outline of the shape they want carved into the bar of soap.

3. Using a sharp knife, gradually carve away from the soap until you have reached your outline and have the basic shape. (We recommend that only adults handle knives!)

4. Gently slice away from the soap with the knife to round harsh edges and refine your miniature sculpture.

5. Your soap carving is done. Use it as a decorative soap in the guest bathroom, or give it as a gift. But if you want to save it, be sure to keep it away from water!

❑ 258. Ride on a Carousel

There's a potent mix of fantasy and nostalgia in a carousel. The spinning platform, the whirling music, and the galloping horses all combine to transport you to a delightful dream world of imagination and joyful abandon. Share the magic with your kids by taking them for a spin. Ride with them for a shared experience but also give them the opportunity to ride alone as you watch from the sidelines. It's a chance to give them a small sense of independence as they rotate away from you, and it's a reminder that you will always be there for them as they rotate back around. As strange and fantastic as a carousel is, the defining characteristic of the ride is that it always reminds you of where you began.

❑ 259. Make Your Own Sundaes

There's nothing quite like an ice-cream sundae. It's the most personal and customizable of all desserts. Chocolate ice cream with peanut butter sauce, almonds, and gummy bears? That's a sundae. Vanilla ice cream topped with chocolate-covered raisins in caramel sauce with whipped cream and a cherry on top? That's a sundae, too. Sundaes give you and your family the perfect opportunity to tantalize your taste buds in new and creative ways. Set up a sundae station in your kitchen so that every family member can create his or her own, then pass sundaes around to share. You'll have fun on a hot summer evening, and you'll learn a little bit about each other's tastes, too!

❑ 260. Play Frisbee Golf

The object of Frisbee golf is to work your way through a pre-designed "course" from start to finish in as few throws as possible. As in the real game of golf, each consecutive throw is made from the spot where the last throw landed. Your score will be based on the number of throws made on each "hole." Add penalty throws, and the winner of the game is the one who goes through the entire course with the lowest score.

While there are more than 1,000 disc courses in the United States and about 200 abroad with professional-quality tee pads and hole posts, you can make your own and have just as much fun. Set up the course using paper plates numbered 1 through 18 (or 9, or any other number divisible by 3). Tape or tack the "hole" numbers on trees, on the ground, or on poles. Take turns throwing the disc from the teeing area to hole #1, and keep track of how many throws it takes to reach the hole area. Continue until all holes have been played by all players. This game works for all ages from five and up.

❑ 261. Travel to Foreign Lands

A child's world is as big as your house, your town, their school, and maybe the homes of some relatives. But if you have the oppor-tunity to show them the bigger world by traveling to other coun-tries—experiencing the sights, sounds, smells, tastes, and textures of other lands—you and your children will broaden your scope of knowledge and gain a feeling of worldliness. Traveling to Europe one country at a time is an extravagance, but the return is priceless as you and your children have more to contribute in conversations, new interests to pursue, new views of other nations and the people in them, and an expanded base of knowledge regarding those with whom you share the planet. The great big world becomes smaller as other parts become familiar, and experiencing travel together is something you'll always have to talk about, remember, and treasure. If a family trip is out of the question, consider taking one child at a time for graduation presents or to celebrate milestone birthdays. The time shared between parent and child on a one-on-one basis is a wonderful gift.

If the expense of real travel is a barrier, venture out virtually with travel DVDs that have narration describing what's unique and interesting about the place featured. Make a monthly trip to a foreign country from the comfort of your own home. Serve the food of the country about which you are learning. Make native costumes or handicrafts that represent the culture. Keep a scrapbook of your "trips" and have real discussions about what each person likes or doesn't like on each virtual journey. There is no limit to the amount of information and knowledge you can provide and share.

▲　▲　▲　▲　▲

> "A man travels the world over
> in search of what he needs,
> and returns home to find it."
>
> —George Moore

▼　▼　▼　▼　▼

❑ 262. Be a Scout— Work on Badges

Whether or not your kids are officially in the Scouts, the books for scouting at all levels are a treasure trove of fun and educational things to do. Available directly through the Boy Scouts or Girl Scouts of America or—better yet—at a garage sale, these books are filled with activities that must be accomplished to earn a variety of badges in many different categories including cooking, woodworking, knot tying, canoeing, outdoor survival, building a fire, swimming, water skiing, and much more. Joining an existing troop introduces your kids to structured fun, new friends, and character-building activities. When you volunteer to be a leader, you'll add to your kids' experience and you may learn a few things too. Find a Boy Scout troop near you at www.scouting.org. Find a Girl Scout Troop near you at www.girlscouts.org.

❏ 263. Be Instrumental

Before television, computers, and video games, music was a great source of family entertainment. Families who played together stayed together, and it wasn't unusual for every member of a family to play a different instrument, making for many a memorable musical evening.

If your child has expressed interest in playing a musical instrument, consider checking with instrument stores to see whether they offer a try-before-you-buy program. That way, your child can try the expensive violin, clarinet, or drums they're so sure they want to play before you shell out the money for them. Music lessons cost money, the instruments cost money, and perhaps the biggest investment is the time dedicated to practice. It is not unusual for children to express genuine excitement and make sincere promises at the very beginning of the music lesson experience, and then discover that practice is time-consuming and not always their first choice of things to do. A serious discussion about the reality of such a commitment and a trial period after which your child can reconsider his or her choice without consequence is a good way to determine whether or not the interest is sustainable.

Music is a wonderful element of a well-rounded education. Playing an instrument instills a greater appreciation for music in general, and for those students who stick with it, the rewards are immeasurable.

❑ 264. Rent a Houseboat

Why go for the same-old, same-old when planning your next vacation? Where there are lakes, there are often houseboats for rent, and if you're thinking that spending a week on a raft with your whole family is not your idea of a vacation, think again. Houseboats are fully equipped floating houses that usually sleep six to eight people. Furnished with private staterooms, air-conditioning, entertainment centers, fully appointed galley kitchens, gas barbecues, and more, houseboats easily offer all the amenities you're used to. And you and your kids will have a blast living on the water, swimming off the boat, using the water slide, and paddling around in a rowboat, canoe, or whatever other extras you choose to add to your package. Plan a vacation that will provide a lifetime of memories for everyone. It will really float your boat!

❑ 265. Organize a Neighborhood Cookie Swap

Hosting a cookie swap is a great way to get to know your neighbors, cut down on your holiday baking, and involve your kids in an event with very sweet rewards. Invite each guest to bake a few dozen of their favorite cookies and bring them to the swap house. Display all the cookies on a table. Each guest goes around the table and take two of each cookie (or however many you decide). Guests should provide copies of the recipe for their cookies to share with everyone. Be sure to let the kids make their favorite cookies as well and include them in the fun of collecting all the different kinds of cookies. Sing holiday songs and send everyone on their merry way with a tin full of the best cookies in the neighborhood!

❑ 266. Walk in the Snow

"It's snowing!" No matter how young or old members of your family are, that first snowfall elicits the same squeals of excitement year after year. Covered in a blanket of white, the world around you looks, smells, sounds, and feels different. Before the plows and shovels break the silence, bundle everyone up and go for a walk. Catch a snowflake on your tongue. Listen to the silence. Look for birds and animals to see how they are responding to the snow. Look for animal footprints and try to figure out what animals were out before you. Look up and get lost in the sky and the falling snow. Catch snowflakes on the top of your mitten or glove and see if there really are no two alike. Wear snowshoes, cross-country skis, or snow boots, and when everyone's legs are tired, toes are getting cold, and cheeks are rosy-red, go home, have hot chocolate, and draw pictures of your snowy-day walk.

❑ 267. Go to an Opera

The word *opera* means "work" in Italian, and attending an opera might seem a lot like work to your kids. But opera doesn't have to be intimidating. It is, after all, simply a drama set to music. Prepare your family for the performance ahead of time by familiarizing yourselves with the story before you go. You can look up the libretto of any opera

FAST FACT

The most performed opera is *Tosca*. The longest opera, clocking in at 18 hours, is Wagner's *The Ring Cycle* (probably not a good choice for the little ones in your household!). The shortest opera is Darius Milhaud's *The Deliverance of Theseus,* which is only seven minutes long.

on the Internet and get a word-by-word translation, or you can simply search for the summary. Puccini's *Madame Butterfly* and *La Bohème* and Mozart's *The Magic Flute* are a few operas that preteens and teens might like. They'll never forget the experience of sitting in the theater, hearing the live orchestra, seeing elaborate costumes, and listening to professional voices singing out their tales of love, death, and hope. Try it!

❏ 268. Find Your House on Google Maps

Get a bird's-eye view of your house without leaving your chair! Satellite views of Earth are so detailed that you and your kids can sit down at the computer and search for the very house you're in! Simply type in the address of Google.com. Then click on Maps. Type your address into the search box and click. Once you're in your neighborhood, you can zoom in and see your house. Since the satellite is not always photographing, you might be surprised to see a car in the driveway that you haven't owned for years. For more fun, find the house where you lived when your kids were born, the house where you were born, the house where grandparents were born, and any other buildings about which you're curious.

❏ 269. Get Fishy!

Fish can be great pets for young kids. Plus, you have the added bonus of not having to deal with taking them for walks or changing a litter box. Aquarium fish come in all shapes, colors, and sizes, and they're so much fun to watch as they swim in and out of sunken treasure chests, old castle ruins, coral fans, and caves. The more you involve your children in the decisions of what kind of fish to buy and how to decorate the tank, the more interest they will show in the aquarium once it's set up. Here are some tips to get you started:

- Learn about the kinds of fish you'd like to keep. Learn what type of care they need and if the variety of species you're considering are compatible with one another and the space you're planning on creating. Although goldfish are often chosen as starter fish for children, they're not really suited to small bowls. Goldfish can grow to be quite large and actually need fairly big tanks to be happy and healthy.

- Once you determine what types of fish you want to keep, you'll know how large or small your aquarium should be. For instance, if you have your heart set on angelfish, you'll need a much bigger tank than you'd need if you were interested in neon tetras or guppies. Your budget may be a determining factor in the kinds of fish you'll keep and the size tank you'll need.

- Be sure your tank fits the space you have for it in your home. Clean it, fill it with water, and give it a few days to operate without fish in it just to make sure everything is working properly.

- When you shop for fish, keep in mind that you want to allow one gallon of water for one inch of fish. Select fish that are small, hearty, and inexpensive. Start with only one or two at a time until your aquarium is properly cycled.

- Do not overfeed your fish. Follow aquarium maintenance and fish care instructions offered by the store from which you've purchased your equipment and fish.

For more detailed information, talk with the staff at your local pet store and do some research on the Internet.

❑ 270. Take a Botanical Walk

Walking with the specific intent of finding rare species of wildflowers, native flora, trees, shrubs, grasses, and waterfalls is a discovery activity that increases awareness of one's surroundings and sparks an interest in nature's most beautiful masterpieces. Tour guides are botanical experts who will point out fascinating sights. Did you know that some of our most common wildflowers are also some of our most ancient? Ever wonder how forget-me-nots got their name? What plant will make you beautiful if you eat it? Did you know that flowering plants provide almost 25 percent of the basic ingredients for modern drugs? There are thousands of facts, folk tales, and love stories with botanical roots. Take a walk on the wildflower side and grow plant wise!

❑ 271. Go Greek

You've probably seen or heard of a Greek festival near you, but have you ever actually attended one? If not, now's the time to seize the opportunity to experience Greek food, Greek music, and Greek culture, including artifacts from Greece and Greek dancing performed in traditional dress. The opportunity to join in the festivities of another country right in your hometown is one that exposes you and your kids to other members of the community who celebrate in different ways. You'll also find good shopping for pastries and jewelry. The festivals are often run by volunteers who are eager to keep their traditions alive and willing to put in many hours cooking,

YOU'RE SPEAKING GREEK!

Just for fun, learn a few phrases and practice them at the festival!

Good morning: Kalime'ra
Good evening: Kalispe'ra
Good night: Kalini'chta
Hello/goodbye: Yia'sou
Cheers: Yia'sou
Please: Parakalo'
I'm hungry: Pina'o
The bill: To'n Logariasmo'
How are you: Ti' Ka'nis
Fantastic: Fantastiko'
Excellent meal: Poli' oreo' fagito'
Thank you: Efharisto'
See you again: Tha' se do' ksana'
Let's go: Pa'me
Do you speak English: Mila'te Angklika'
Let's go dance: E'la na' Hore'psoume
Let's go eat: Pa'me na' fa'me
Let's go have fun: Pa'me na' Glenti'soume
I am leaving: Fe'vgo
We are leaving: Fe'vgoume
We had a lot of fun: Diaskeda'same Poli'

planning, and preparing for the three-day events that bring out crowds of all cultures. Fun for all is guaranteed.

❏ 272. Do the Dude Ranch Vacation, Dude!

Today's world moves at a pretty fast pace, so if you can find a vacation that offers your family the chance to slow *way* down, why not take it? The experience of being on a ranch is exciting in and of itself and is most likely quite different from your family's typical lifestyle. Dude ranches vary in activities and accommodations. You'll find working dude ranches on which you can actually join in the daily tasks of caring for cattle and sheep, and you'll find ranches that are more like resorts. Accommodations vary depending on the ranch you choose. Often you'll find individual log cabins, gourmet ranch dining, fishing, cattle drives with real cowboys and cowgirls, cookouts, biking, mountain hiking, horseback riding, and pretty much everything else the great outdoors has to offer.

❏ 273. Make Your House a Green House

Wait—are you going to throw that away? Before you toss something, think twice: You might have a hidden treasure in your hands! All you need are a fresh pair of eyes and an attitude set on reusing items instead of throwing them away. Here are some cool ideas for turning trash into treasure.

Egg cartons: Use them to store golf balls. Or cut off the tops of the cartons and use them to store jewelry in a drawer. Egg cartons also make great packing material.

CDs: Decorate them and use them as coasters; make holiday ornaments and tape a photo in the middle hole.

Tissue boxes: Use an empty one to store plastic shopping bags.

Glass jars: Fill them with colored sand and use them as bookends, or clean them thoroughly and fill with homemade candy or cookies for holiday gifts.

Shower curtains: Use as a drop cloth for a painting project.

Paper towel tubes and toilet paper tubes: Store extension cords inside them or tape one end and store batteries in them.

Wine corks: Use them as pin cushions, corn holders, or bobbers for fishing.

FAST FACT

The average person throws out one ton of trash per year!

☐ 274. Watch a Caterpillar Turn into a Butterfly

Lepidoptera (lep-eh-dop-tera) is the scientific family to which butterflies belong. Teach your kids this ten-dollar word for *butterfly*, and they'll easily impress their friends and teachers with their vocabulary. But don't stop there. When it comes to butterflies, the real fun is in watching their metamorphosis. There are four stages to a butterfly's life cycle: In stage 1, the egg is laid on the underside of a leaf. Stage 2 takes place about six days later when the egg develops into the *larva*, or caterpillar. During stage 3, the *pupa* or *chrysalis* stage, the caterpillar forms a cocoon. While in that cocoon amazing changes take place. At the end of stage 4, the butterfly comes out of the cocoon.

You and your kids can watch this process in action with a live butterfly garden. These kits, which are similar in concept to ant farms, provide the habitat for butterflies as well as a certificate for a few live caterpillars. Your kids will be transfixed as they watch the caterpillars spin their cocoons and ultimately emerge as butterflies. Once all the butterflies have hatched, bid your new friends good-bye as you release them into the wild.

❑ 275. Start a Pen Pal Relationship

Back in the day—before e-mail rendered "snail mail" almost extinct—people looked forward to the arrival of the postal carrier. Before the art of letter-writing is totally lost, help your kids start a pen pal friendship with someone. It could be a cousin, a friend from summer camp, a friend of a friend, or anyone else who meets with your approval. Buy special stationery just for the pen pal letters and help your child write a letter that is newsy, asks questions about the other person, and talks about interests they have in common. The real fun begins when the first letter arrives from the new pen pal. Send pictures, cartoons, jokes, drawings, and other surprises. No matter how high-tech computers are, the joy of receiving a real letter to open, read, and save is irreplaceable.

▲ ▲ ▲ ▲ ▲

"That is happiness; to be dissolved into something completely great."
—Willa Cather

▼ ▼ ▼ ▼ ▼

❑ 276. Head to Spring Training

If there's a tried-and-true baseball fan in your household, nothing could be more exciting than experiencing spring training. Kids and adults alike will get a special thrill from watching their favorite players practice. Even the nonbaseball fans in your family will catch the fever. One of the best parts is being able to meet the players and get autographs after a practice. It's easy to find your favorite team's spring training schedule and location. Simply go to www.spring trainingonline.com/. Everything you need to know is right there. Meanwhile, brush up on your baseball trivia by learning the names of all the teams in the Cactus League (teams who practice in Arizona) and the Grapefruit League (teams who practice in Florida). Here's a list!

CACTUS LEAGUE

Arizona Diamondbacks

Chicago Cubs

Chicago White Sox

Cincinnati Reds

Cleveland Indians

Colorado Rockies

Kansas City Royals

Los Angeles Angels of Anaheim

Los Angeles Dodgers

Milwaukee Brewers

Oakland Athletics

San Diego Padres

San Francisco Giants

Seattle Mariners

Texas Rangers

GRAPEFRUIT LEAGUE

Atlanta Braves

Baltimore Orioles

Boston Red Sox

Detroit Tigers

Florida Marlins

Houston Astros

Minnesota Twins

New York Mets

New York Yankees

Philadelphia Phillies

Pittsburgh Pirates

St. Louis Cardinals

Tampa Bay Rays

Toronto Blue Jays

Washington Nationals

❏ 277. Play "Art Smart"

The museum or gallery experience is what *you* make it. Airplanes, trains, dollhouses, and dinosaurs hold attention on their own. But art and all the subtleties that come with it are not always quite as captivating to kids. Give the new viewers things to look for as they stroll through the museum. How many paintings with apples can you find? How many paintings with clocks? Dogs? Cats? Mothers and children? Men with beards?—gives a stroll through an art museum a purpose. Planning ahead with specific knowledge of the exhibits or paintings you are about to see enables you to prepare questions or lists of scavenger hunt items to be found in the exhibit. For added fun, provide children with notebooks for sketching a favorite item found in a painting. Museum and gallery visits needn't be filled with lectures and shared information about the artists. It can be more fun and more memorable if it is turned into an inter-active experience. Art appreciation starts with being able to stay awake through a tour of the gallery. Give it a try and your kids will look forward to it the next time you go to the art museum.

❑ 278. Emphasize Independence

We do our children no favor by making them too dependent on us. Just as mother birds must eventually push their babies out of the nest, so too must we give our children the guidance, the confidence, and the encouragement to venture out on their own in little ways every day. Having the patience to allow your child the time to slowly tie their shoes even if you're in a hurry, feed themselves even if it's a little messy, dress themselves even if the buttons don't always line up right—these small steps are what lead to their eventual capabil-ity to solve problems and make intelligent decisions. Problem-solving involves step-by-step thought processes, and your willing-ness to guide a child through that process rather than step in and take the problem into your own hands is a gift for successful living.

❑ 279. Accept Your Children for Who They Are

This is a lesson from which many parents could learn and benefit. Perhaps Mom is very social and outgoing. Maybe Dad is a rough-and-tumble type of guy. And maybe the little girl or boy born into this family is quiet, does things in his or her own time, or prefers to figure things out alone rather than engage in big group activities. Children are not clones of their parents. They are individuals who develop at their own pace. Accepting your children, respecting them, encourag-ing their interests even if they don't mirror yours, and letting them express their views and individuality is a gift you can give to them. Encourage curiosity and help them make new discoveries. Provide what they need to express their creativity and give honest praise for a job well done, a great idea, and questions asked. Your acceptance of your children is the most important acceptance of all. When they leave their house with the knowledge that the people who love them the most value them for who they are, they will proceed with confidence and will show the same respect for others.

❏ 280. Shoot Hoops Together

There's something pretty satisfying about watching a basketball rise up into the air and curve downward in just the right arch and "whoosh!"—the ball falls through the hoop and net. It's good! This is the joy of a basketball game played in a driveway or schoolyard court. It's just you and your kids out on the court, dribbling the ball, dashing in and out of each other's way. You're shooting hoops, and it's one of the sure-to-be-remembered times that you'll all hold dear. When the kids are young, remember not to always be the super champ yourself. Some of the fun is in beating the parent. And later, when your competition grows taller, stronger, and more able-bodied, you can hope they'll show you the same consideration you showed years ago. Maybe they'll let you win sometimes, too.

Here's a fun game that holds up through the years. It's called HORSE, but you can really use any word. The rules are as follows:

- Players take turns shooting baskets from anywhere on the court.

- If a player makes their shot, the other players shoot from that same spot.

- If the next players miss the shot, they each get the first letter in the word HORSE.

- Shooting continues in this manner until someone spells out the whole word. Then that player is out.

- The last one standing wins!

❑ 281. Watch the Sunrise

In the wee hours of the morning, when the dew is fresh and the birds are just beginning to sing, the sun makes its magical appearance. Watching the day break is a thrilling experience worth sharing with your kids. Plan a sunrise breakfast to be enjoyed out on the deck, yard, or rooftop, and learn to appreciate the beauty and glory of a new day.

❑ 282. Visit Colonial Williamsburg

There's no better way to learn history than to experience it first-hand. Colonial Williamsburg, located in Virginia, is the nation's largest restored colonial village. In the years from 1699 to 1776, this capital of Virginia was England's oldest, largest, most populous, and richest American colony. In 1926, Reverend Dr. W.A.R. Goodwin and John D. Rockefeller Jr. took on the task of restoring and preserving the 18th-century capital and the ideals of the courageous patriots who helped create the American democratic system that still lives on today. The town is set up for families to visit and enjoy, with hotels outside and inside the Colonial Village, reenactments day and night, shops, and tours of a variety of buildings and businesses—all hosted by

SOMETHING FOR EVERYONE!

Activities for children abound at Colonial Williamsburg. Kids can help with seasonal farm chores, play colonial games such as ninepins and blind man's bluff, make soap, dip candles, and draw water from a well. Once they've demonstrated how handy they can be, your kids won't have any excuse for neglecting their chores at home!

costumed colonists who are happy to tell you all about their daily lives in colonial times. The souvenirs, the foods, and all the fun of seeing history come to life are great reasons to travel to Virginia.

❑ 283. Read Classics Out Loud

Research has shown that children who have been read to in their very early years grow up to be voracious readers. While television requires less concentration, good books still hold the attention of children whose parents, siblings, and grandparents take the time to sit down with them and read aloud. Sometimes even children who can read on their own enjoy the luxury of just listening. Many modern-day books are written for the reader who has little patience for long sentences and elaborate descriptions. But the classics are rich with detail, character development, and plots that keep a reader and listener glued to the chair, sofa, or bed. Find a great reading spot and share your favorite books as well as some of these classics:

Ages 1 to 3:

Goodnight Moon by Margaret Wise Brown

Pat the Bunny by Dorothy Kundhardt

The Real Mother Goose by Blanche Fisher Wright

The Runaway Bunny by Margaret Wise Brown

Ages 3 to 8:

Caps for Sale by Esphyr Slobodkina

Curious George by H. A. Rey

Make Way for Ducklings by Robert McCloskey

The Tale of Peter Rabbit by Beatrix Potter

Ages 5 to 8:

Frog and Toad Together by Arnold Lobel

The Cat in the Hat by Dr. Seuss

A Bear Called Paddington by Michael Bond

The Shrinking of Treehorn by Florence Parry Heide

Now We Are Six by A. A. Milne

Ages 8 to 10:

Harry Potter and the Sorcerer's Stone by J. K. Rowling
Stuart Little by E. B. White
Charlotte's Web by E. B. White
Winnie the Pooh by A. A. Milne
Charlie and the Chocolate Factory by Roald Dahl
Pippi Longstocking by Astrid Lindgren

Ages 10 to 13:

Blubber by Judy Blume
Little Women by Louisa May Alcott
A Wrinkle in Time by Madeline L'Engle
Harriet the Spy by Louise Fitzhugh
The Secret Garden by Frances Hodgson Burnett

❑ 284. Teach the Value of Hard Work

"All play and no work makes Jack a very dependent boy." While that's not exactly how the original saying goes, it can be very true. Chores that contribute to the whole family's lifestyle are a good way to teach children to be responsible. Age-appropriate jobs assigned with a positive attitude and praise for being a valuable member of the household will be engaged in by happy and willing workers. When you set definite expectations, children want to please and will strive to meet them.

Here are some jobs that help foster a strong sense of responsibility and community within the household.

- Picking up toys and returning them to their proper place
- Setting the table
- Clearing the table
- Loading the dishwasher
- Feeding pets

- Making one's bed
- Keeping one's room neat
- Watering houseplants
- Mowing the lawn, raking leaves
- Helping to take out the trash
- Folding laundry and helping to put it away

▲ ▲ ▲ ▲ ▲

"What greater thing is there for human souls than to feel that they are joined for life—to be with each other in silent unspeakable memories."

—George Eliot

▼ ▼ ▼ ▼ ▼

❑ 285. Visit an Ancient Architectural Ruin

Before building codes, which are ever-changing as technology and materials improve, buildings were built to last and last and last. The extraordinary condition of architectural ruins is a testament to the idea that even without modern technology, ancient peoples built houses, tombs, government buildings, and public forums that continue to draw tourists who are interested in learning more about past civilizations. Throughout the world there are hundreds of famous ruins worth visiting either virtually or in person. Here are some to consider:

- **Pompeii** near Naples, Italy
- **Giza Pyramids** in Egypt
- **Machu Picchu** in Peru
- **The Acropolis** in Athens, Greece
- **Chichén Itzá** on the Yucatán Peninsula

- **Ayutthaya** in Thailand
- **Great Wall** of China
- **Petra** in Jordan
- **Mesa Verde** near Cortez, Colorado, United States
- **Pueblo Bonito** in Chaco Canyon, New Mexico, United States
- **Moai** on Easter Island, Chile
- **The Coliseum** in Rome, Italy
- **Stonehenge** near Salisbury, England
- **Fort Mountain,** Georgia, United States

❏ 286. Visit a Mystery Spot

The United States is dotted with spots where gravity is defied, optical illusions abound, and tennis balls roll uphill. It may be true that these mystery spots are simply tourist traps that have wallets opening and cash strangely flowing from your hands to another's hands, but if you're not too much of a skeptic and just go with the flow, you and your kids will have some interesting stories to tell afterward.

Here's a list of some mystery spots across the United States and Canada:

- **Gravity Hill,** Sylacauga, Alabama
- **Spook Light,** Gurdon, Arkansas
- **Gravity Hill,** Helena, Arkansas
- **Gravity Hill,** La Jolla, California
- **Mystery Spot,** Santa Cruz, California
- **Confusion Hill,** Piercy, California
- **Spook Hill,** Lake Wales, Florida
- **Gravity Hill,** Cumming, Georgia
- **Gravity Hill,** Mooresville, Indiana

- **Big Mike's Mystery House,** Cave City, Kentucky
- **Gravity Hill,** Greenfield, Massachusetts
- **Gravity Hill,** Burkittsville, Maryland
- **Mystery Hill,** Irish Hills, Michigan
- **Mystery Spot,** St. Ignace, Michigan
- **Paulding Lights,** Watersmeet, Michigan
- **Spook Light,** Hornersville, Missouri
- **Tri-State Spooklight,** Neosho, Missouri
- **House of Mystery,** Hungry Horse, Montana
- **Gravity Hill,** Franklin Lakes, New Jersey
- **Mystery Hill,** Blowing Rock, North Carolina
- **Mystery Hill,** Marblehead, Ohio
- **Oregon Vortex,** Gold Hill, Oregon
- **Gravity Hill,** New Paris, Pennsylvania
- **Cosmos Mystery Area,** Rapid City, South Dakota
- **Mystery Lights,** Marfa, Texas
- **Ghostly Gravity Hill,** San Antonio, Texas
- **Wonder World,** San Marcos, Texas
- **Gravity Hill,** Salt Lake City, Utah
- **Mystery Hole,** Ansted, West Virginia
- **Magnetic Hill,** Chartierville, Quebec

▲ ▲ ▲ ▲ ▲

"In every child who is born, under no matter what circumstances, and of no matter what parents, the potentiality of the human race is born again."

—James Agee

▼ ▼ ▼ ▼ ▼

❏ 287. Make a "Cozy Hotel" out of Sofa Cushions

The world's most comfortable, most affordable, and most family-friendly hotel is closer than you think. At least it will be when you make your very own "Cozy Hotel" out of blankets and sofa cushions. This is the perfect rainy-day activity. Rearrange the furniture in your living room and set up walls with the cushions and chairs. Use a blanket for the roof, and don't forget to leave a door wide enough for Mom and Dad to crawl through! Bring some flashlights inside with you, and you'll have a cozy hotel of your own that's perfect for play time. Encourage your kids to decide where in the world your hotel is located and what tourist sites are located nearby. Have them act as tour guides as they lead you around the house to different locations. Is that a sleeping cat or is it the Sphinx? Is that a mess of building blocks or is it Stonehenge? Pretty soon you've gone from building a "Cozy Hotel" to creating a whole cozy world for yourselves right in your own home. Who knew rainy days could be so much fun?

❏ 288. Try Public Transportation

Outside of big cities, North America is designed around cars. It was the automobile that enabled the suburb, and the highway that enabled the exurb. In most towns, however, there still exists public transportation in some form or another. Spending some time riding public transportation is a great way to instill in your children a greater understanding of the community in which they live. If your town has train service, ride the train, and feel the rhythm of the tracks. Take the bus and listen to the sounds of morning conversations as people get on and off. Take the experiment a step further and commit to using only public transportation for your errands and trips for an entire day. How does this experience differ from the regular automotive lifestyle? Maybe it's a little hard for errands, but commuting might be a whole lot more pleasant as riders lack the illusion of control that defines the psyche of the driver. Talk it over with your kids, and discuss what different modes of transportation mean for different people. You can learn a lot about yourselves by changing something small in your lives—even if only temporarily. The road may be the same, but how you travel it can open new insights and possibilities.

▲ ▲ ▲ ▲ ▲

"Insanity is hereditary;
you get it from your children."
—Sam Levenson

▼ ▼ ▼ ▼ ▼

❏ 289. Enter a Wacky Contest

There are many prizes that deserve respect and honor: the Nobel Prize, the Pulitzer Prize, an Academy Award, a Grammy. And then there are other awards, like those for taffy sculpting, putrid pun-making, or artistic pie-eating. These prizes may not be on the same scale as the Nobel Prize—but they'll still merit lasting fame and admiration among the members of your family! Cast off your inhibitions and do something silly together. After all, collective silliness is a great equalizer and will bring your family together faster than any serious activity ever could.

❏ 290. Meditate Together

Togetherness doesn't have to mean activity, hustle and bustle, or constant entertainment. Sometimes it's important to relax, to shut everything out and breathe deeply, to reflect calmly on nothing at all and let the world fade away. Life can be stressful no matter how old you are, and learning stress-relieving breathing and meditation techniques is a soothing way to be together as a family and refresh your minds for all the activities and responsibilities that come your way. You can learn more about meditation by visiting a yoga studio in your area and taking some classes. In addition to breathing and meditation, you'll also learn some gentle exercises to rejuvenate your entire body, and that's something everyone in a family needs once in a while.

▲ ▲ ▲ ▲ ▲

*"Families are like fudge—
mostly sweet with a few nuts."*
—Author Unknown

▼ ▼ ▼ ▼ ▼

❏ 291. Visit Museums Online

The Internet can play a big role in expanding one's horizons without spending a nickel on gas, hotels, or entry fees. Virtual tours enable you to see art exhibits, science exhibits, history exhibits, and a whole lot more. A fantastic traveling exhibit that may be coming to a location nowhere near you is just a click away if you know where to look. Here are some quality museums that make their exhibits available online. Sit down with the kids and explore…virtually!

1. **The Metropolitan Museum of Art,** New York City
   www.metmuseum.org/home.asp

2. **The Louvre**, Paris, France
   www.louvre.fr/llv/musee/visite_virtuelle.jsp?bmLocale=en

3. **Smithsonian National Air and Space Museum,** Washington, D.C.
   www.nasm.si.edu/exhibitions/online.cfm

4. **The Field Museum,** Chicago, Illinois
   www.fieldmuseum.org/exhibits/online_exhib.htm

5. **University of California Museum of Paleontology,** Berkley, California
   www.ucmp.berkeley.edu/exhibits/index.php

In fact, most major museums and many smaller ones, too, have online exhibits complete with audio support. All that's missing are the tired feet and sensory overload that sometimes come with an actual tour of a museum.

❏ 292. Practice Argument Enders

Even members of the closest of families sometimes get into arguments or spats. Being fair and showing respect for one another is the best way for family members and friends to get along. Ending an argument is the only good thing about an argument. Here are some easy ways to turn frowns into smiles:

1. Saying "I'm sorry" is the fastest way to end an argument. In fact, it stops one dead in its tracks, because once you say it, there's nothing else to be said.

2. Sometimes arguments happen when two people can't decide who should do something (a chore perhaps). Instead of standing there arguing, flip a coin. Let the coin decide. The one who wins the flip wins the decision. And the one who loses the flip gets to keep the coin.

3. Can't bring yourself to apologize out loud? Write a note instead. Keep the message simple and wrap the note around a piece of candy. Sweetness is hard to resist and the argument is sure to be over.

4. Take a time-out from each other. Sometimes it doesn't matter who is right or wrong—you've just gotten so mad you can't back out of the argument. Take a break in different rooms. Pretty soon you'll both decide it's more fun to do things together than separately.

❏ 293. Play at the Park

Take advantage of the time when your children are young and still think playing with Mom and Dad is the coolest. Slide down the slide, swing on the swings, walk across the rope bridges. The park is the perfect place for children to test their courage, try new things, and accomplish great physical feats. Be there to catch them at the end of the slide. Be there to push them on the swings. Be there with your full attention for every new and wondrous thing they do. You'll never regret taking the time to play!

❑ 294. Create a Trunk Full of Costume Fun

Little kids love to play dress up. Having a costume trunk filled with costumes, accessories, and props provides the basis for creative and imaginative playtime. Let the kids choose their costumes, and you'll be amazed at the stories they make up to fit the attire. This is when your camera will be the best accessory of all. For fun and wacky memories, leave a disposable camera in the costume trunk for the kids to use. Keep adding new things to the trunk so that it's always a source of surprise. This will be a very handy thing to have at Halloween time, too.

❑ 295. Learn Self-Defense as a Family

Keep your friends close, your enemies closer...and your family closest of all. That's exactly what you'll be doing when you learn self-defense as a family. Self-defense training is about a lot more than fighting. You'll learn discipline, confidence, and respect— important qualities. Plus, learning a martial art is lots of fun and great exercise! You'll all start at the same level, and you'll learn from each other as much as you'll learn from the instructor. The confidence you build will be enhanced by the knowledge that you worked together in your training. You will also share in humility as you make mistakes and learn from them in the presence of others. From this humility, you'll reinforce the strongest notion of family—that you support each other in success or in failure.

❑ 296. Make a Wacky Wallet

Got a problem? Duct tape is almost certainly the answer! In fact, the fashion world has started putting duct tape to good use in the form of wallets, belts, pocketbooks, vests, and anything else designers can think up. And believe it or not, duct tape fashions sell for big bucks. Save your money. Make a duct tape wallet with the kids and then fill it with funny phony cards that will get a laugh whenever they're presented. You can find step-by-step instructions for making a duct tape wallet online. Once you've got your wallet all ready, make some funny accessories out of poster board. Here are some ideas:

Elephant Charge Card: "Only a herd of elephants can stop me from charging!"

Social Insecurity Card (with photo of crying person): "Do not disturb the bearer of this card; they're disturbed enough already!"

EXXCESS GAS Card: "Bearer of card has unlimited gas!"

Driver's License: "Permission to drive friends and family crazy!"

❑ 297. Play Name That Tune

Do your family members have good ears for music? Now's the time to find out!

Name That Tune was a television game show that premiered in 1953, ran until 1959, and showed up again several times in the years following. It was popular because it was a game everyone could play, and the better an individual was at identifying songs with one, two, or three notes, the better their chances of winning. It's a perfect car game. To start, play some songs all the way through from beginning to end. Then select a song and play only a few notes. Players compete to see who can name that tune in as few notes as possible. Everyone's a winner because it's fun to listen to music and race to name the song before the other person does.

❑ 298. Visit a Fish Ladder

One of the most fascinating rituals in nature is the voyage of certain fish from salt-water to freshwater in order to spawn. Fish such as salmon regularly participate in this natural cycle, but with all the construction on riverfront areas and the industrialization of North American water-ways, the fish sometimes need help getting to their spawning grounds because their regular route has been interrupted by dams or other artificial struc-tures in the water. Fish ladders are our answer to the problems human development has cre-

NOTABLE FISH LADDERS IN NORTH AMERICA

- Ballard Fish Ladder, Seattle, Washington
- Whitehorse Rapids Dam and Fish Ladder, Whitehorse, Yukon, Canada
- Bonneville Dam Fish Ladder, Portland, Oregon
- Amoskeag Fish Ladder, Manchester, New Hampshire

ated for the fish. They make a great sight during mating season, with scores of fish jumping up each watery step. A visit to a fish ladder gives your family the opportunity to witness nature in action. Take the opportunity to reflect upon the relationship we have with our surroundings and the things we can do to make the world work bet-ter both for us and for the creatures with which we share it.

❑ 299. Hit the Rails

The railroad was an integral part of North American expansion and development. Although the railroad isn't as important for transpor-tation today as it may have been in the 19th century, you can still experience romance and imagination on the tracks. Today, families can reserve a compartment on any number of historic trains for short or long rides around the country and spend some quality time together while living it up the way we used to in days gone by. Have a meal in the dining car or step out onto the caboose and see the horizon retreat behind you. Go sightseeing at various stops along the way, then crawl into your bunks at the end of the day and let the swaying and clacking of the train gently rock you to sleep.

HISTORIC TRAIN RIDES IN NORTH AMERICA

- Santa Fe Southern Railway
- Durango and Silverton Narrow Gauge Railway
- The 1880 Train on the Black Hills Central Railway
- Delaware and Ulster Railroad
- Royal Gorge Route Railway

❑ 300. Swim with Dolphins

The ocean is full of life, but it's a lot harder to identify with its marine inhabitants because they're not as personable or as available as the landlubber animals we know so well. Also, for the most part, fish just aren't that cute, especially when compared to puppies and pandas. Enter the dolphin. The dolphin is the ocean's most lovable, most personable, and most communicable denizen, which may not be surprising considering it is a mammal, just like the land's most lovable creatures. Next time you're by the ocean, get to know dolphins a little better by swimming with them. Many dolphin research and education centers in tropical climates have swim-with-the-dolphins programs available for the whole family, and you'll build a relationship your kids will never forget. For more information, look online to find a dolphin swim near your next vacation spot.

▲ ▲ ▲ ▲ ▲

> "Treat your family like friends and your friends like family."
>
> —Proverb

▼ ▼ ▼ ▼ ▼

❑ 301. Climb a Tree

Remember how you used to climb trees when you were a kid? Do you remember your parents ever joining in the fun? Probably not. Tree-climbing tends to be a kids-only activity, but it doesn't have to be. You may not be as nimble as you used to be, but you can still scale the heights with your children and relive a bit of your own childhood in the process. The main thing is to get off the ground for a while and get into the mind-set of your children. You'll learn that they see the world as a place of both reality and fantasy, and they'll learn that you still have a little kid in you. Save the tree as the place where your minds meet, and climb it often. There's a little family magic in the branches.

❑ 302. Attempt to Break a World Record

How many times have you heard your kids or their friends claim that they can do something better than anyone else—that they're the best in the world? Well, give them a chance to prove it. There are world records for almost anything you can imagine, and you can find them in *Guinness World Records*. Pick out some wacky records and see if your family can break them together. Care to challenge the record for most cockroaches eaten (36) or the most books typed backward (67)? Whatever record you choose to challenge, you'll also

FAST FACT

Guinness World Records got its start as a result of an argument in 1951 at a shooting party. The debate was whether the golden plover was the fastest game bird in Europe. Now there's probably a record for who can eat golden plover the fastest! Care to break it?

be challenging yourselves. And even if you don't break a record, you'll have some good, silly fun speculating who can do what amazing feat.

❑ 303. Visit at Least One of the Seven Wonders

THE SEVEN NATURAL WONDERS

1. Mount Everest
2. Ayers Rock
3. The Matterhorn
4. The Grand Canyon
5. The Meteor Crater
6. The Great Barrier Reef
7. Victoria Falls

Most people are familiar with the Seven Wonders of the Ancient World: the Great Pyramid of Giza, the Hanging Gardens of Babylon, the Statue of Zeus at Olympia, the Temple of Artemis at Ephesus, the Mausoleum of Maussollos at Halicarnassus, the Colossus of Rhodes, and the Lighthouse of Alexandria. Unfortunately, of these, only the Great Pyramid remains today.

As luck would have it, though, oodles of other Seven Wonders lists have cropped up in recent centuries. You'll find lists of the seven engineering wonders or the seven natural wonders or the seven modern wonders. The beauty of the Seven Wonders list is that it can't be pinned down. So find your favorite list of seven wonders, and try to visit one (or all) of them. Then discuss what you and your family find to be wonderful and come up with your own lists. Choose the top Seven Wonders of your country, your state, your town. For added fun, find pictures of the places on your list and make your very own Seven Wonders book!

❑ 304. Stomp Grapes at a Winery

Wine: the nectar of the gods, the refined drink of connoisseurs. Sure, wine has a highbrow reputation, but did you know that historically, one of the key steps in the winemaking process was grape stomping? That's right, mashing grapes with bare feet! You may be familiar with the famous scene from *I Love Lucy* when Lucy and Ethel get into a hilarious stomping mess. Didn't that look like fun? Lucky for you, many wineries across North America are now giving visitors the chance to leave their footprints on a barrel of grapes. Grape stomping—with all its inherent fun and silliness—can be the perfect activity to bring a family together and ease any tensions. The drinking age may be 21, but the stomping age is whatever you want it to be!

❑ 305. Create a Secret Hideout

A secret hideout has timeless appeal. After all, don't *you* have times when you'd like to lock yourself in some hidden fortress? Enlist your children in finding the perfect spot, whether it's inside or outside. Consider the attic, closets, or that spot underneath the basement stairs. Decorate your hideout and stock it with some games, snacks, and books. Come up with a secret password or special knock. Cramming yourselves into a small space and playing a little make-believe will bring you closer in more ways than one!

❑ 306. See an Endangered Species in Its Natural Habitat

It can be quite sobering to realize just how many species are on the endangered list. Many of these animals, including the lynx, the panther, and the grizzly bear, live in North America. Take the opportunity to experience one of these endangered species in its natural habitat—while you still can. Visit a national park or wildlife preserve where some endangered species live and are protected by conservation programs. While there, talk with park rangers, guides, or scientists to find out what you can do to help these species survive. No doubt you will be encouraged to consider your own place in the world and wonder at the fragility and beauty of life. For more information on endangered species, visit the U.S. Fish and Wildlife Service at www.fws.gov.

❏ 307. Participate in an Organized Nonviolent Protest

We all have different beliefs—some more different than others. Sometimes these beliefs are at odds with the prevailing society or government. There are many ways to deal with this, whether through letter writing, voting, or petitioning. But sometimes the discrepancy is so egregious that we may feel more drastic measures are needed. When your family feels this strongly, perhaps you can consider participating in an organized nonviolent protest or gathering to unite your voices with those of other like-minded individuals. When you voice your opinion, you take your place in a long history of organized dissent, and you show your children that they are part of a larger community and can make a difference in the world.

❏ 308. Volunteer at School

Parenting is as much about understanding your kids as it is about raising them, and every parent knows that a good understanding doesn't always come easily. Once your kids start school, they start living independent lives—at least during the day. As kids get older, you have to rely on their limited information about the school day or wait for teacher comments and conferences to get an insight into their time away from you. Volunteering at school is the perfect opportunity to experience a day in the life of your children. Attend a class field trip or offer to help in the classroom a few days a month. Volunteering will give you a chance not only to experience your children's day-to-day routines, but also to participate in their activities and therefore gain a better understanding of how their minds work and how they interact with their friends and other classmates. You are sure to come away from the experience feeling a little bit closer to your child—even if he gives you a funny look when you try to wipe the jelly from his cheek.

❏ 309. Share Your Favorite Music with Your Child

Every meaningful song has a story, not just to the singer, but to you, too. Recall some favorite memories and share them with your kids by going through some of your old records, cassettes, or CDs and playing your favorite songs for the whole family. Tell the stories behind the songs, what they meant to you, what you were doing when you first heard them, and what feelings they evoke. The past lives on in every note. Don't be afraid to delve into it once more. Your kids will appreciate the opportunity to know you a little better and to understand the different periods of your life. In turn, encourage your kids to tell stories about *their* favorite songs. Why not take everyone's favorites and create a CD or playlist to listen to in the car? Every movie has a soundtrack. Every family can have one, too.

▲ ▲ ▲ ▲ ▲

"We do not remember days; we remember moments."

—Cesare Pavese

▼ ▼ ▼ ▼ ▼

❏ 310. Make Paper

Where would we be without paper? There would be no Gutenberg Bible, no Shakespeare plays, and no *500 Things to Do with Your Children Before They Grow Up*! Paper is definitely an essential part of daily life. So what could be more fun than learning how to make it?

Get your family together and gather all sorts of paper products— printer paper, newspaper, magazines, egg cartons, paper bags, toilet paper, tissue paper, construction paper, or any other fiber that you think would be good. Experiment with different textures and colors.

Papermaking is a great way to let your family's creativity shine through, and it's also a fantastic way to reuse and recycle unwanted paper to make new and beautiful paper.

YOU WILL NEED:
Sponge
Window screening
Wood frame
Plastic basin/tub
Blender or food processor (for making paper pulp)
White felt or flannel fabric
Staples (for tacking screen on frame)
Cookie sheets
Liquid starch (optional)

1. Select the paper or paper mix that you want to use.

2. Rip the paper into small pieces and put them into the blender until it is about half full.

3. Fill the blender with warm water and turn it on until the paper looks smooth and well blended.

4. Make a mold by stretching and stapling screen material to a frame. You can be as creative as you want with your paper shape. Who says paper has to be rectangular?

5. Fill a basin halfway with water and add three blender loads of pulp. The more pulp you use, the thicker your paper will be. Optional: You can add 2 teaspoons of liquid starch for sizing. If you plan to write on the paper, this is a good idea, as the starch helps prevent inks from soaking into the paper fibers.

6. Place the mold into the basin and level it out while it is still submerged. Then slowly lift the mold to the surface. At this point you can add or remove paper pulp depending on how thick you want your paper to be.

7. Lift the mold above the basin and allow the water to drip through the mold.

8. When the mold stops dripping, gently place one edge on a fabric square. Ease the mold down flat with the paper directly on the fabric. Use a sponge to press out as much water as possible.

9. Slowly remove the mold from the paper (be careful—this is tricky). Gently press out any bubbles and loose edges at this point.

10. Repeat these steps until you run out of paper pulp or until you have the desired amount of paper.

11. Stack the paper/fabric squares on a cookie sheet and use another cookie sheet on top to squeeze out the excess water. This will make a mess so it is easiest to do this outside or in the bathtub.

12. Gently separate the sheets and allow them to dry by hanging them on a clothesline or laying them out on a table.

13. When the sheets have dried, peel the paper off the fabric. Voilà! You have homemade paper that your family can use any way you want!

❑ 311. Ride a Ferris Wheel

FAST FACT

Did you know that the first Ferris wheel was built in 1893 by George Washington Gale Ferris Jr. for the World's Columbian Exhibition in Chicago? It was a marvel of engineering designed to give visitors a vista they would never forget.

Ferris wheels are not the hot item they once were. Today's roller coasters and interactive rides can promise more immediate thrills. But a Ferris wheel has something the newer rides don't: charm. Bring a camera to capture the view from the top. Your children will be thrilled at the heights a Ferris wheel ascends, the views it affords, and the time you spend together—isolated for a moment in the sky.

❑ 312. Pick Up a Hula Hoop

Hula hoops are an integral part of childhood. You probably played with one as a kid, and your kids probably play with them now. Who would have guessed that such a simple idea—a hoop—could create such a craze? This just goes to show that real fun comes from the creativity of the participant, not the fanciness of the toy. Test your whole family's skills in a hula hoop contest, and break out some of the tricks you knew as a kid: the Knee Knocker, the Stork, Wrap the Mummy, or the Hula Hop.

The hula hoop is the perfect equalizer: Everyone has a few clumsy moments. In fact, you may not be able to keep up with your kids. That's part of the fun—it's their turn to teach you. No matter what ages your children are, the hula hoop is a timeless, simple pleasure anyone can get wrapped up in.

FAST FACT

Did you know the hula hoop was used in ancient Greece as a form of exercise? Maybe the real reason Odysseus took so long to get home was because he got sidetracked hula hooping with Poseidon!

❑ 313. Visit a Sculpture Park

We normally think of art's habitat as a museum or a gallery—a serious place with plain walls and directed lighting where we must behave quietly and reverently. But art can exist in many locales and take many forms, whether it be in the architecture of a building or even graffiti on the side of a bridge.

When you visit a sculpture garden, you'll experience the marriage of art, horticulture, and landscape design all in one spot. A sculpture garden is about creating a prevailing mood and letting that mood sink into you. Each of you can experience and appreciate the art in your own way, whether that means quietly strolling the paths or running in and around the sculptures for a more hands-on appreciation of the pieces. You can find sculpture gardens all across North America, but five that are worthy of a road trip are:

1. **Storm King Art Center,** Mountainville, New York

2. **Dr. Seuss National Memorial Sculpture Garden,** Springfield, Massachusetts

3. **Minneapolis Sculpture Garden,** Minneapolis, Minnesota

4. **Hirshhorn Museum and Sculpture Garden,** Washington, D.C.

5. **di Rosa Preserve: Art & Nature,** Napa, California

▲　▲　▲　▲　▲

> *"Pleasure is the flower that passes;*
> *remembrance, the lasting perfume."*
> —Jean de Boufflers

▼　▼　▼　▼　▼

❏ 314. Visit a Flea Market

Your kids may laugh when you tell them you're taking them to a flea market, but when you explain that they won't actually be shopping for fleas, they're sure to change their tunes. Flea markets may be held in the parking lot of the local high school, on the side of a rural road, or in an out-of-the-way plaza in a big city. Finding one just depends on where you live and how far you want to drive. When you get there, stroll through the tables and booths looking for treasures in plain sight—old wooden toys, first-edition books, valuable artwork, or antiques—you never know what you might find, and that's half the fun. Consider giving each of your children $5 (or some other amount you deem reasonable) so they can do some shopping. A flea market is the perfect place to encourage your children's imaginations to run wild, and that may be the best treasure of all.

❑ 315. Institute a "Choose-Your-Own-Adventure" Day

It may sometimes seem like your kids rule the roost. Their activities—soccer games, swim team, school, music lessons—dictate your schedule. But being a kid is harder than it appears. They can't drive, and they don't really have much say over their lives (no matter how much they may whine). It's easy for a family to get out of balance with everyone feeling like someone else is making all the decisions. Get yourselves back on track by planning a choose-your-own-adventure day for your kids. Let them plan everything for the entire day from breakfast to activities to dinner (even if they choose double chocolate chip ice cream for every meal, they'll learn it's not quite so good when they eat it all the time). Of course, the flip side of this is that you're secretly making a deal with them. By giving them a designated day to be in control, you're reinforcing that you are in charge. And you'll have the opportunity to teach them about decision-making. Kids like order, and they like the opportunity to make decisions once in a while. Combine these two desires, and you'll all understand each other a little better, and you'll have a happier, more balanced family life.

❑ 316. Paint Pottery

The things most special to us are often the things we have had a hand in making. Visiting a paint-your-own pottery place is an ideal opportunity to flex your creative muscles while spending quality time together as a family. The pieces are already made, but it's up to you to paint them. When you're done, the pottery place will glaze your artwork for you. Pick your pieces up later, and you'll be ready to eat from, drink from, or simply admire your work. Consider making this a family tradition. Go every year at the same time and paint a new mug, jug, or bowl. Don't forget to sign and date the bottom. That way, you will not only be able to trace the growth of your collection, you'll also be able to see how much your family's artistic abilities improve over time!

❏ 317. Tour a Submarine

Ever since Captain Nemo took his accidental passengers (or captives!) on the *Nautilus* in Jules Verne's classic *20,000 Leagues Under the Sea*, submarines have captured the imagination of children and adults alike. Submarines played important roles in WWII, through the Cold War, and even in today's conflicts. But there's more to a submarine than war. Several submarines are out of commission now and are available for tours, so consider giving your family a taste of life in the deep. It's a simply fascinating experience, and it will take you out of your everyday lives and into the cramped and musty quarters of your imagination.

"WE ALL LIVE IN A YELLOW SUBMARINE . . ."

Here are three submarines worth checking out in person:

USS *Pampanito*, a U.S. sub from WWII, is located at San Francisco's Fisherman's Warf.

U-505, a German submarine from WWII, is located at the Museum of Science and Industry in Chicago.

USS *Nautilus*, the world's first nuclear-powered sub, is located at the U.S. Navy Submarine Force Library Museum in Groton, Connecticut.

❏ 318. Eat Cotton Candy on a Stick

Among the carnival barkers, the human statues, and the giant stuffed animals at the county fair or amusement park, there is a magical place—a place where candy comes in brightly colored airy wisps of sugar that have to be caught on sticks and eaten before they blow away again, a place where this silky, sticky web of candy

captures the imagination
as well as the tongue. It's
the fresh cotton candy
maker's booth, and every
family should visit it at
least once. The fun isn't
just in eating the candy,
it's in watching it being
made, in seeing the spin-
ning centrifuge full of
fluffy candy, and looking

on in anticipation as the candy seller inserts the
stick to capture the flitting, finely woven strands of sugar that are
about to become your dessert. With all of the prepackaged candy
available today, it's a pleasant throwback experience to get something so fresh.

❑ 319. Tour a Big City

There's no denying the lure and magic of a big city—even if you're
from one! With so many people crammed into such a small space,
diverse cultures and food, iconic architecture, theaters, museums,
and parks, you can find pretty much anything in a big city—except
free parking. Take your family on a trip and see what all the noise is
about. It's almost like visiting a different world on every block. There
are organized bus tours, Duck tours, or even walking tours, as well
as stadium tours, theater tours, and restaurant tours. Splurge on a
fancy hotel and pamper yourselves. Even consider renting a limo.
Big cities can be a lot of fun, but they can also be a great learning
and bonding experience for your family. Navigation, for example,
can be a fun challenge in an unfamiliar city. Let the older kids have a
turn with the map and see how well they can find their way! Let the
whole experience sink in, then discuss it later over dinner. What was
the family's favorite place? Is the lure of the big city real or is it just a
myth? Was the whole experience incredible, or was it just a trip to a

really loud and crowded land of Oz? Whatever you decide, when it's over and your car pulls up in front of your house, you're all sure to remember that "there's no place like home."

❏ 320. Decorate T-Shirts

T-shirts are one of the primary modes of personal expression. Just think about all of the snarky message T-shirts you see around town on everyone from teens to college students to young, urban hipsters. Ironically, the majority of those personal expression T-shirts are designed and produced in multiples, so instead of showing individuality, they show similarity. If your family wants to show true expression, try designing your own T-shirts—items that are one-of-a-kind and just for you. For younger kids, puffy paint, glitter, and markers will do the trick. If you have older kids, consider branching out into tie-dye designs. Gather around the table, and turn them loose on their own designs, or help them by creating templates out of cardboard and painting on the fabric with fabric-safe paint. Continue the trend when your kids get older, and encourage them to design their own shirts rather than buy something that already exists. You'll be fostering self-reliance, creativity, and individuality—all of which are more important than consumer selectivity— and you'll be getting to know them a little better by witnessing their sartorial choices firsthand.

❏ 321. Share Your Hobbies

Your hobbies can be an important way to escape from daily concerns, to relax or blow off steam. You may think of them as the only way to get some alone time. But they can also be an important way to have some relaxing, pressure-free bonding time with your kids. If you're a runner, take your children with you for a jog. They may not be able to keep up, but that's okay. Run back inside with them when they're too tired, and go out again for yourself later. If you like to build things in the garage, show them how to use the tools. Or if you're into spectator sports, teach them about your favorite team. They may not be interested in your hobbies, but just as you learn about them from playing their games, they'll learn about you from playing yours, and your whole family will be closer because of it.

❑ 322. Host a Silly Family Tournament

If you have young kids, you've seen them do this already: stare cross-eyed at each other, challenge each other to thumb wars, play rock-paper-scissors. Turn these activities into a family competition to determine who can be the winner of your family's Crazy Zany Games! Buy or make a silly trophy, and give it a wacky name. Then engage in the craziest, zaniest competitions you can think of: who can make the funniest face, who can flex in the strangest way, who can blow the biggest chewing gum bubble, who can burp the loudest. Stage the games every year, and add a new event each time. Keep a running tally of the winners at each tournament so you can remind your kids later when they're all grown up and dating. Being ridiculous together breaks down barriers between family members and brings you closer together. So remember as you cross your eyes so far your pupils become invisible: The sillier you feel, the stronger a family you'll become.

❑ 323. Compliment Your Children

No matter how old your children are, they will always want to impress you and make you proud. Every family has its own way of showing pride and its own measures for success, but whatever these are, it is important that you recognize your children for their achievements and contributions. At the very least, positive reinforcement encourages continued good behavior and success, and it can even set your children on a path to a bright and promising future. A little pride can go a long way. You can show your pride through big rewards or through small words of encouragement, through a look in your eye or a hand on the shoulder after your child has done something positive. If you make recognition and pride a part of your family's life, you will all benefit from a lasting feeling of love and support—the true strength of a family.

❑ 324. Hook a Rug Together

You could spend hours searching for the perfect rug for your home, and once you find it, you might flip over the price tag and wonder how that many nines and zeros can fit on such a tiny piece of paper. Instead of spending all day shopping, why not spend all that time with your family making a rug that will weave you a bit closer together? You can buy a wide variety of rug-hooking kits online or at craft stores, or you can make your rug one-of-a-kind by designing your own pattern. Measure your space to determine what size rug you want and let the kids help pick out the color scheme and shape—this is a good opportunity to teach them about taste in decor—and keep everyone involved all the way through. The rug may get threadbare and old over time, but the bond you share will never wear out.

❑ 325. Set Up an Obstacle Course

Sometimes you may look around your house or your yard and wonder whether you have children or Tasmanian devils as offspring. Make the most of that mess by using it as an obstacle course for some fun family competition. Set up cones (in the driveway or on the sidewalk) in patterns to weave through on bikes. Lay trash cans on their sides and use them as hurdles for a footrace. Or simply use the trees and mailboxes in your neighborhood as markers for a cross-country race. Not only will you all get some valuable exercise, but you'll also be encouraging ingenuity and resourcefulness in your children. Best of all, you'll be creating some healthy competition for bragging rights in the family!

❑ 326. Be an Angel

Being a good neighbor means more than taking out the trash or bringing someone else's paper to their door. It also means looking out for those in need. Whether you work through a religious organization or a secular charity or simply visit a local senior center, homeless shelter, or a sick or elderly neighbor, you'll teach your children the value of lending a hand in your community on an individual level. Cook someone a homemade meal and bring it over to them, or take your children to read a book to a blind person or to an elderly neighbor whose vision may be failing. These small gestures bring immense joy to the lives of others and can really change the nature of their day or even their whole outlook on the world. Your blood family may be small, but the love you share between you can be a wonderful benefit when shared with the larger family of your community.

❑ 327. Dig for Buried Treasure

X MARKS THE TIP

If you've ever wondered how to get your kids to help in your garden, try making it a pirate game: Draw your garden layout as if it were a treasure map, and place an X anywhere you want to plant something new. Then get the kids out there to dig for treasure!

Treasure isn't just for pirates, it's for families, too. You may not have a treasure map, but that doesn't mean you can't dig. You never know what you might find—even in your own backyard. You might discover an arrowhead, a dinosaur bone, or even the TV remote the dog buried years ago. Dig at the beach, and you may find jewelry or fascinating shells. It doesn't matter what you dig up, it's the search and the anticipation, the stories you tell to each other about what might be found in the next shovelful of earth that are the real treasure. Ask any pirate when he's alone, and he'll say the same thing.

▲ ▲ ▲ ▲ ▲

"Making the decision to have a child—it's momentous. It is to decide forever to have your heart go walking outside your body."
—Elizabeth Stone

▼ ▼ ▼ ▼ ▼

❑ 328. Tell the Story of How They Were Born

The days your kids were born were the best in their lives—after all, no matter how good the rest of their days have been or will be, they couldn't happen without the first. And chances are, their birthdays were some of the best days of *your* life, too. Recall these precious moments together by sharing with your children the stories of their births.

Start with the moment you found out you were expecting and tell them about the excitement you felt knowing that your lives would change. It's okay if you were nervous at first. Every good story has some drama. Tell them about how Mom's belly grew, how you started to prepare the house for them, how you got to the hospital, and how you fell in love the moment you first held them in your arms. The story of their birth isn't just a story for them, it's part of the story of your whole family, a part of your own legend, so tell it often, and always remember the joy you felt on that day.

If your children are adopted, tell the story of your decision to adopt and the process you took to find them. Include the details of that phone call when you found out your child was waiting for you and the lovely first moments of meeting him or her for the first time, how you knew in your heart they were meant for you, and how you fell in love that lucky day.

❑ 329. Get Hands-On at the Petting Zoo

You probably wouldn't want to stroke the fur of a Bengal tiger, but what about stroking the mane of a horse or giving a treat to a rambunctious billy goat or riding on an elephant? You and your family can do all these things and more when you visit the petting zoo. You'll find a wide variety of animals to get close to, whether your child's favorite is a monkey, a sheep, or even a funny-looking emu. Your family will learn that many animals are friendly and have great personalities. Animals are an important part of the world, and a visit to the petting zoo will help your children understand that.

▲　▲　▲　▲　▲

"In time of test, family is best."
—Burmese Proverb

▼　▼　▼　▼　▼

❑ 330. Create an Artist's Studio

Easels, paints, drawing paper and canvases, felt-tipped markers, chalk, and a space devoted to creating art send a message that creativity and art are valued in your family. Make art a choice for something to do, and make it an easy choice by having the studio area ready at all times for artistic self-expression. Cover the floor with newspaper and set up easels or tape plain brown paper to the wall with art paper over it. Keep drawing and painting materials in clear plastic containers on shelves low enough for the youngest artist to reach. Set up the studio area together so everyone knows where things are and where they need to be returned to at cleanup time. Add a table complete with supplies needed for collage. Work on your own art projects while your children work on theirs. Make a point of critiquing and offering positive reinforcement. Display the finished masterpieces as a way of showing your appreciation for their wonderful talents and attempts.

❑ 331. Make Invisible Ink

Got a secret? Keep it! Mum's the word when you and your kids learn the secret formula for invisible ink! Write an important note in this disappearing ink, and the paper will appear blank unless you know how to read it. All you need for this top-secret mission is a lemon wedge, toothpicks, plain white paper, and a lamp with a 100-watt bulb. Lemon juice will be your ink, and a toothpick will be your pen. Squeeze the juice into a bowl and dip the tip of the toothpick into the juice. Plan on dipping the toothpick in the "ink" often. Write the note on the paper. Let the juice dry for a few minutes. Then, to read the secret note, hold it over the lamp. Be careful not to touch the lightbulb because it will be very hot. The secret message will appear in a few seconds. The heat from the lamp turns the lemon juice brown, revealing your secret message!

▲ ▲ ▲ ▲ ▲

"Call it a clan, call it a network, call it a tribe, call it a family. Whatever you call it, whoever you are, you need one."
—Jane Howard

▼ ▼ ▼ ▼ ▼

❑ 332. Write a Haiku

Can you Haiku? Sure you can! You just need to learn the basic formula for creating this short poem format. Haiku is a Japanese style of poem that has three lines. The object of haiku is to say something important using just a few words. The first line has five syllables.

The second line has seven syllables. The last line has five syllables. The lines do not rhyme. They simply tell a very short story. Often the last line has some significance or reflects thoughtfully on the first two lines.

Here's an example of a Haiku poem:

The sun is hot now.

1　2　3　4　5

Crops are turning brown and dry.

1　2　3　4　5　6　7

He hopes rain will come.

1　2　3　4　5

Have every member of the family try their hand at writing a Haiku. Then take turns reading the poems aloud. Maybe you'll discover that one of you has a secret talent for poetry!

❑ 333. What's in a Name?

"That which we call a rose by any other name would smell as sweet...." Juliet said it in Shakespeare's *Romeo and Juliet*. In other words, our names don't define who we are. But it's still fun to explore the hidden meaning behind our names. Look up the meaning of your child's name and the names of their siblings and swell with pride when you find out that Audrey is English and means "noble strength," Richard comes from French and means "strong power," and Danny comes from Hebrew and means "God is my judge." The next time someone says "What's in a name?" you'll have the answer!

❑ 334. Everybody into the Pool...Hall, That Is!

Billiards and pool have a history dating back to the 15th century. Despite the image some may have of a dark hall filled with bikers and slackers, billiards is actually a game of kings, noblemen, ladies, gentlemen, and commoners alike. In fact, the game of pool requires mental, physical, and emotional control, three skills that—when mastered—come in handy throughout life.

Many pool parlors offer special "kids' corners" made available for families and birthday parties. Check your local phonebook for a place near you. Make an afternoon of it and find a new family sport when you do!

❑ 335. Float Paper Boats

Start with a few sheets of plain 8½″×11″ paper and some colored pencils, and your fleet of boats is at your fingertips.

Follow the simple step-by-step directions on any of these Web sites:

- www.wikihow.com/Make-a-Paper-Boat
- www.mathematische-basteleien.de/paper_ship.htm
- www.laits.utexas.edu/hebrew/personal/toolbox/acm/boat/boat.html

When you've finished your folding and decorating and have named the fleet, take your boats to a pond, lake, puddle, or stream and launch them. Add to the interest level with discussions of famous ships and their roles in maritime history, or keep it simple and just have a race to see whose boat floats the farthest, longest, and fastest.

❑ 336. Jump Rope

Jump ropes—they're easy to pack, easy to carry, and there are hundreds of rhymes and reasons to learn how to jump rope, both alone and in a group. If you're nimble enough to demonstrate, well then, cheers to you, but if you'd rather play the role of coach, here's what you need to know to get the jump rope games going.

1. Regulation jump ropes are sold in toy stores, or you can make your own by knotting both ends of a rope for easy handling. Choose a rope that fits the jumper. To do that, hold one end of

the rope in each hand and stand on the middle of the rope. The ends should reach the armpits of the jumper.

2. To start the jumping, the jumper should hold one end of the rope in each hand. Elbows should be next to the body with arms bent. If the rope has handles, the thumbs should be on top.

3. The jumper should start with the rope behind her heels and swing it over her head. When the rope meets her feet, she should jump just high enough to clear it.

4. Jumpers should jump on the balls of their feet, keeping their feet together with knees slightly bent.

5. Elbows should always be kept close to the body, even when the rope is swinging overhead.

6. Practice!

JUMPING RHYMES

There are many well-known jump rope rhymes. Here are two to get you started:

"Down in the Valley"

Down in the valley where the green grass grows,
There sat <jumper> pretty as a rose.
Up came <a boy in the class, particularly one the jumper likes> and kissed her on the cheek,
How many kisses did she get this week?

Count until the jumper misses a step.

"Cinderella"

Cinderella, dressed in yella
Went downtown to meet a fella
On the way her girdle busted,
How many people were disgusted?
10, 20, 30, 40, 50 . . .
Count until the jumper misses a step.

❑ 337. Track an Animal

Animals have paws (or hooves). Paws leave tracks. Hunting for those tracks with the help of a field guide, a magnifying glass, a notebook and pencil, or a digital camera, provides an opportunity for a day of detective work and possibly a hobby that lasts a lifetime. Whether you track birds, beetles, bear, deer, squirrels, groundhogs, foxes, or just the neighbor's dog, identifying the different tracks and following them is exciting and educational. There may be surprises in store when your kids discover they've got a family of rabbits living under the porch or a herd of deer just passing through the backyard. Start close to home to get the idea, then take the new tracking skills to the woods or on a walk along a canal, river, beach, or lake. Footprints are everywhere. Matching them up with the critters that left them is fun!

▲ ▲ ▲ ▲ ▲

"We've had bad luck with our kids—they've all grown up."
—Christopher Morley

▼ ▼ ▼ ▼ ▼

❑ 338. Hide-and-Seek

It was good enough for you when you were a kid, and it's just as much fun for the next generation. The rules are simple, and the game lasts as long as everyone wants it to. Play inside or outside— just be sure to set boundaries if you're playing outdoors. You'll be surprised how much fun you have, and your kids will enjoy the game that much more if Mom and Dad are playing. The more games you play, the more laughs you'll share, and the closer your family will be.

❑ 339. Practice the Art of Leaving

When the leaves start falling, you can rake them, bag them, and take them to the recycling dump, or you can give some of them another chance at life by collecting the most colorful ones to use in craft projects. Autumn delivers these lovely souvenirs just in time for the gift-giving season. Give the kids some ideas for things to make for family and friends using leaves as the basis for their artistic creations. Here are a few ideas for projects where leaves leave a good impression!

1. Create leaf art suitable for framing. Lay leaves down on plain construction paper. Paint or color around and over them. Remove the leaves, and you'll see a stencillike design.

2. Do leaf rubbings. Place a leaf under a piece of plain paper. Using a piece of chalk, crayon, or artist's charcoal held on its side, rub over the paper covering the leaf. You'll see the "skeleton" of the leaf when you're done.

3. Make leaf placemats. Place your colorful collection between two sheets of clear contact paper and press firmly.

❑ 340. Color Your Giving Green

Going green? Continue the trend when it comes to wrapping paper. Don't buy it—make it! What you and your kids can create using recyclable paper is more clever, more interesting, and more beautiful than anything you can buy. In fact, this could be a new holiday tradition in the making! As the holiday season approaches, set aside a weekend for designing and creating wrapping paper. Break out your supplies, including white shelf paper, brown grocery bags, newspapers, cereal boxes, oatmeal canisters, and any other containers that will serves as gift boxes or wrap. Use sponges dipped in poster paints, potatoes sliced in half and dipped in paint, markers, crayons, and other decorative items such as sequins, feathers, googly eyes, and buttons. Let your imaginations run free as you play holiday music in the background and applaud each other's efforts when you're done. When the papers are dry and ready for use, set aside another time for wrapping the gifts! Holidays take on a new significance when handiwork is part of the celebration.

❑ 341. Visit a Movie Studio

Lights! Camera! Action! It's all about a behind-the-scenes tour of movie magic! Hollywood, California, is the heart of the television and movie industry, and that's where the biggest studios are. In the early days of film, movie sets were created and entire movies could be filmed without ever leaving the grounds of the studio. As technology advanced, on-location filming became more popular and studios were used less and less as the backdrop for films. However, a handful of major motion picture studios still offer tours to the public, as do television studios on both coasts and in major cities. Getting a look behind the scenes gives you and your family a better understanding of how movies and television shows are made. It's a thrill to see a familiar "living room" set from a favorite show or movie. Often tours offer the opportunity to see yourself on camera, try out a blue-screen special effects experience, and even talk to some of the stars.

Here are some studios to visit if you just happen to be in Hollywood:

Warner Bros. Studios
VIP Studio Tour
4000 Warner Blvd.
Burbank, CA
(818) 977-TOUR

Universal Studios
Studio Tour and Theme Park
100 Universal City Plaza
Universal City, CA
(818) 508–9600

Paramount Studio Tour
5555 Melrose Avenue
Hollywood, CA
Advance reservations: (323) 956–1777

Sony Pictures
Studio Tour
10202 W. Washington Blvd.
Culver City, CA
(310) 244–8687

❑ 342. Extra! Extra! Read All About Us!

Some people wait for the end of the year to send out a family news-letter that tries to catch everyone up on every detail of every family member. Why wait for a pileup of news when you could be creating a family newspaper with a more frequent publication date? Parents may be the best editors, depending on the ages of the kids, but if you've got budding reporters, photographers, and graphic design-ers on your "staff" you can share the assignments and the credit for every issue! If you've got a computer, you've got unlimited space for "Kid's Sports Reports," "Birthday News," "Out and About with the ___ Family," "News, Notes, and Nuttiness," and any other features you want to include. Each child can write a story; Dad and Mom can write a column; and an older child can type, proofread, add photo-graphs, and create funny fake ads. Send copies to the grandparents and anyone else who wants to keep up with your family. Each issue becomes a souvenir journal of what you've all been doing. Reading them again years later will be even more fun than creating them in the first place.

❑ 343. Skip Stones Across the Water

It takes just the right kind of stone—a little flat, rounded on the edges, big enough to fit snugly between the thumb and the index finger while resting comfortably on the curled middle finger. And then it takes the right current on the lake or ocean—smooth, slightly rolling, but not too much. And then it takes a challenge: Think you can skip your stone more times than mine? Take the dare. Stand at the edge of the water with your pile of perfect stones at your feet. Pick one up, aim, and flick your wrist so the stone goes gliding across the surface of the water, skipping once … twice … again … and again! Practice makes perfect. And this is one family challenge you definitely don't want to skip.

❏ 344. Spit Watermelon Seeds

Every year in June, the town of Luling, Texas, holds an event called the Watermelon Thump. It started in 1954 and today attracts more than 35,000 people. And could this crowd really be gathering just to spit watermelon seeds? You bet! In 1989, Luling local Lee Wheells set a Guinness World Record by spitting a watermelon seed a distance of 68 feet and 9 ⅛ inches. At the time of this writing the record had not yet been broken. Think you can beat it? Why not take advantage of the next family summer picnic to try? Let the kids who aren't at risk of choking join in the fun, and set your own records to break. You demonstrate first, then see who's your spitting image!

▲　▲　▲　▲　▲

"The habits we form from childhood make all the difference."

—Aristotle

▼　▼　▼　▼　▼

❏ 345. Invite the Teacher Over for Dinner

Back in the days of one-room schoolhouses, teachers lived with students' families to save the town money. Families invited the teacher for dinner and in doing so fostered close and respectful relationships with their educators. It's a tradition worth reviving. In an era when school populations grow, budgets shrink, and time to get to know teachers and school administrators is eaten up by so many other commitments, inviting the teacher for dinner brings back a personal touch that could be valuable to your child. Every child needs an advocate at school. Your role as that advocate is made much easier when you are known to the teacher and have a personal relationship. Your child will feel special, and the teacher will feel valued. Make it an informal and fun occasion ending with an apple for teacher—baked into an apple pie!

❑ 346. Spend a Day at the Farmers' Market

Nutritionists recommend that we eat five servings of fresh fruits and vegetables every day. What better way to do it than to go straight to the source—the farm where the fruits and vegetables are grown? Many towns have farmers' market stands on a weekly or monthly basis. Make visiting one near you a regular family excursion, giving the kids the opportunity to pick out the freshest of the fresh and even talk to the farmers who grew them. Plan a dinner around the available fresh produce. Check out the selections of fresh breads, pastries, and cheeses. And don't forget to stop and smell the flowers (literally). Farmers' markets often have a beautiful selection of blooms from which to choose. You'll all enjoy getting some fresh air and taking in the hustle and bustle of the farmers' market experience.

❑ 347. Preserve Beach-Day Memories

Does your family take a beach vacation every summer? Why not start a new tradition this year? Choose a spot and write your child's name and date in the wet sand. Then snap a photo of him or her standing next to their name. Use this beach photo as your holiday card, or frame each one for a yearly record of how much your child has grown.

❏ 348. Come Fly with Me

They glide with precision toward their target, delivering the secret message: I made this paper airplane myself! Paper airplanes come in many designs and levels of difficulty, but mastering the production of the simple arrow plane is a great way to start.

1. Fold a plain piece of paper in half the long way. Crease it along the fold and open it again.

2. At one end of the paper, fold each corner toward the center crease so they are even. Crease the folds. You should have a point.

3. Starting at the very tip of the point, fold the paper down on each side so the inside edges line up with the center crease.

4. Turn the paper plane over and fold it in half along the center line.

5. Fold the first wing with the line of the fold running nearly parallel to the centerline of the plane. Make this fold ½ to 1 inch from the center.

6. Fold the second wing exactly as you did the first wing.

7. Write a message on the wing or inside. Hold the plane by the body and throw. Not bad for a first try. Practice the toss and fill the skies with your friendly airplanes!

❏ 349. Have Fun While Waiting in Line

Yep, you read that right! Turn waiting into a fun time filled with built-in laughs. Keep this list of things to do handy the next time you take the kids to a movie, doctor's appointment, amusement park, or anywhere else where lines keep you waiting.

1. Count the number of blondes, brunettes, and redheads standing in the line.

2. Look up and keep looking up. See how many people look up, too, to see what you're looking at.

3. Yawn. See how many people yawn, too.

4. March in place. Count how many marching steps you make until you get to the front of the line.

5. Draw pictures on each other's backs and try to guess what they are.

6. Listen to see how many people are complaining about waiting. How many are talking about work? Friends? Boyfriends? Girlfriends? School?

7. Play "I Spy."

8. Count how many things you can see that begin with the letter *D* (or any letter).

9. Play Simon Says.

10. Look at signs around you and try to make new words out of their letters. For example, the letters in "STOP" on the stop sign can become *pots, spot, tops,* or *post.*

▲ ▲ ▲ ▲ ▲

> "Every child is an artist. The problem is how
> to remain an artist once he grows up."
> —Pablo Picasso

▼ ▼ ▼ ▼ ▼

❑ 350. Go to a Dress Rehearsal

The night before a play or show opens, the actors usually participate in a dress rehearsal. Community theaters often welcome an audience for this final run-through before opening night. It's the last chance for the director, the lighting engineer, and the actors to make adjustments before the paying audience arrives. If you don't demand perfection and you want to see a show for free, ask the box office of your local theater if they allow preview audiences. If dress rehearsals aren't open to viewers, ask about other rehearsals. This is another opportunity to let your kids in on some behind-the-scenes action. The more experiences your children have, the more everyday knowledge they'll bring to their school writing assignments, drama club activities, or even just their conversations with others. Dare to do something different!

❑ 351. Get Fancy for Dinner at a Nice Restaurant

Fast-food restaurants may be fast, but the manners required to eat in them are minimal. Starting your children young in the proper behavior for finer dining establishments allows you to enjoy better experiences as well. Everything doesn't have to change the minute children become part of your lives. You're the ones who set the standards and the tone for every situation. Make dinner at a fancy restaurant a monthly treat. Dress up for it and require that proper table manners be used. Good manners. Good food. Good job, parents!

❑ 352. Go to an IMAX Movie

See more! Feel more! Hear more! IMAX! If you haven't experienced the gigantic screen images and surround sound of an IMAX movie, you're in for an eye-opening, earsplitting cinematic surprise! With more than 320 IMAX theaters in 42 countries and 65 percent of them in North America, there's a good chance you'll find an IMAX theater near you. It may be in a museum, science center, or regular theater complex. Wherever it is, GO! Subject matter varies and can include 3-D. Be ready to be amazed!

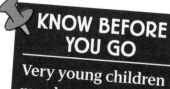

KNOW BEFORE YOU GO

Very young children may be overwhelmed by the IMAX experience. It can get pretty loud.

❑ 353. Go to the Dogs

Dog shows are a serious business in which dog owners and their purebred animals compete for hefty prizes and recognition by the American Kennel Club (AKC). They also make a fun outing. The AKC Web site

FAST FACT

The American Kennel Club recognizes more than 160 breeds of dogs.

(www.akc.org) lists events, clubs, and a whole lot more. In addition to finding an event to attend as a family, you'll find 101 useful tips on being a responsible dog owner and information on how to choose the dog that's right for your family. There's even a special section for kids. It's doggone good entertainment!

❑ 354. Pull Taffy

Long before candy was something that came from a factory, pots of sugar, butter, molasses, and flavorings were brought to a boil and poured out for greased hands to pull until they could pull no more. That was taffy-making at its finest, and it used to be an activity shared by families, kids, and anyone else who was up for it. Taffy is a fun thing to tackle from the mixing to the pulling to the eating. Here's a basic recipe to try. Keep little hands away until the taffy is cool enough to handle, then let everyone dig in and pull!

YOU WILL NEED:

- 2 cups sugar
- 4 tablespoons butter
- ⅔ cup water
- 2 teaspoons cream of tartar
- 1 teaspoon vanilla extract

INSTRUCTIONS:

1. Mix sugar, butter, water, and cream of tartar in a saucepan. Place it over low heat. Stir until the sugar is dissolved.

2. Increase the heat; don't stir the mixture until a firm ball can be made by dropping a bit of the mixture into cold water.

3. Remove the mixture from heat and add vanilla extract.

4. Pour into a greased pan and let cool.

5. When the taffy is cool to the touch, let the kids and company start to pull it. Stretch it into long pieces about 1 inch thick and lay it out on waxed paper.

6. When the taffy strips are hard, cut them into bite-size pieces.

7. Wrap the pieces in waxed paper and store in an air-tight container.

❏ 355. Surprise Them with a Note

Even a bad day becomes a great one when a happy note shows up unexpectedly. Keep a notepad handy when you're making lunches, putting laundry away in drawers, and filling the medicine chests with toothpaste and supplies. Lunch bag notes from home saying: "Hope your day is going well!," "Milk and cookies when you get home!," or "Good luck on your test!" will bring a smile to your child's face. Stock the sock drawer with a joke or a note saying: "Guess who loves you?" Make the morning routine a happy one with a sticky-note on the mirror saying: "Wake up, sleepyhead, and come eat breakfast!"

Your thoughtfulness will make a big difference in your child's day. Don't be surprised if your child starts writing notes back!

❏ 356. Track Santa with NORAD

The North American Aerospace Defense Command (NORAD) is a binational U.S. and Canadian organization charged with the missions of aerospace warning and aerospace control for North America. That's the serious side of NORAD. But NORAD also has a fun side. The organization tracks Santa beginning on December 1 of every year. Who knew, right? If your kids want to follow Santa's progress, go to the NORAD Santa Web site at www.noradsanta.org. It's their official Santa tracker site. For more fun, check out the North Pole Web site at www.northpole.com to find out everything you want to know about Santa's home village. Ho Ho Ho!

▲　▲　▲　▲　▲

The definition of a family is
the love, sweat, and tears shared
over a lifetime together.

▼　▼　▼　▼　▼

❏ 357. Write a Love Letter to Your Child

Baby books are the natural storage place for all the memories of the very early days, months, and years. But don't stop recording memories just because your children are growing beyond the age limits of the baby book's records. As your children grow and their schedules fill up, you can continue to tell the stories of their lives in the form of love letters written to them and saved for the times they'll ask, "What was I like when I was little?" Love letters are a means for expressing your feelings toward them during the triumphs and the disappointments of their young lives. They are the written proof that you were always there for them, listening, watching, sharing, and loving them. Write a letter once a week or however often you feel like doing so. Save them in a special box and when your children are older, perhaps on a special birthday, bring out the letters and share what you were thinking when they were younger. Love means never having to say "I don't remember."

❏ 358. Tell Them a Love Story

The two most important people in the world to your children are their parents. While *Goodnight Moon* and *Runaway Bunny* may be favorite books, the best story—the one they'll want to hear over and over again—is the story of how Mommy and Daddy met, got married, and made the wonderful decision to have children. Your children's history began the day their parents met. Sharing that story will give them a sense of their place in your lives, in the lives of the extended family, and in the world. Talk about the first date, when you knew you were falling in love, what you liked most about each other, how one or the other of you "popped the question," the wedding, the honeymoon, and the most important part of all—the decision to have the little ones who are listening to the story you're telling.

❑ 359. Go to a Gymnastics Exhibition

From the first time your baby turns over, tumbling is a part of his or her life. Gymnastics is a great sport for children of all ages because it helps build muscle strength, improve balance, and even increase social confidence. The Olympics have made gymnastics a popular exhibition sport, and the accomplishments of even very young athletes are encouraging to many. Not every child who takes a gymnastics class will go on to the Olympics, but the exercise, the improvement in flexibility, and the lessons in posture, correct move-ment, and safety will be valuable to your kids forever.

An easy way to try before you buy is to attend a gymnastics exhibi-tion at a local high school, college, or gymnastics studio. Gymnastics is fun to watch, and your budding athletes will be inspired by what's possible with a bit of hard work!

❑ 360. Catch (and Release) Frogs

Catching frogs gives your kids a chance to get an up-close look at what is making that croaking, peeping, ribbit sound that seems to come from the pond, the garden, or anywhere else there is fresh water. If you take your kids to a pond where frogs can be found, you may see them at their early tadpole stage swimming in the shallow water close to the shoreline. Talk about the fact that frogs lay their eggs in the water, and as they hatch into tadpoles, they breathe with gills and swim using their tails. As frogs mature, they lose their tails and develop lungs for breathing air. While catching frogs and studying them is fun, releasing them again is imperative. Many frogs are endangered species. They're valuable to the balanced natural cycle because they eat insects. Get hopping!

❏ 361. Institute an Allowance

Money isn't really the root of all evil, but not knowing how to manage money can be. Handing your kids money without a lesson in how to save it and spend it does them a disservice. Instead, help them lay the groundwork for a positive money experience. Here are some things to think about when deciding whether or not to give an allowance, how much to give, and whether or not allowance should be connected to a chore chart.

1. A fixed amount each week lets kids know exactly how much they have to work with—for example, how much they have to spend and how many weeks they have to save up for something they want to buy.

2. A fixed amount makes your kids think about how much things cost and helps them make choices about what's worth buying or saving up to buy. Kids will appreciate what they buy more when they use their "own" money.

3. One way to determine how much to give for an allowance is to figure out how much you are already giving them. Give them that much, and instead of being the manager of their money, let them make their own choices and figure out the best way to spend or save what they get. If what you are giving them already seems like way too much, an allowance of a lower amount—an amount you really can afford and wish to give—may actually save you money!

4. Allowance should be given once a week and may start when children begin to take an interest in picking out things to buy.

❏ 362. Be a Rock Star

Rocks rock. Especially when you make a concerted effort to collect rocks of a certain shape and size. Collect rocks with the idea of painting them, and be sure to select just the right "rock canvas" for your needs. While there are craft books devoted to the art of rock painting, you can use your own imaginations to create colorful additions to your gardens, windowsills, front step, or display cases.

You'll need smooth rocks, a few paint brushes, acrylic paint colors, and a cup or container of water to rinse your brushes and thin the paint. Spread newspaper on your work surface. Let the rock's shape help dictate the design. For example, an oval rock might make a perfect bumblebee or rabbit. Paint the rock with a white base first so that colors will be brighter. Then paint faces on the rocks or turn your rock into a flower, frog, or the background for a scene. Rock painting is so much fun it can be habit-forming. Keep some of your finished designs for yourselves and give others as gifts. Those on the receiving end are sure to say, "You rock!"

▲ ▲ ▲ ▲ ▲

A family's love is as sure as the taste of an orange,
as certain as the flow of rivers toward the sea,
as familiar as the fragrance of a rose,
and as steadfast as the warmth of the sun.

▼ ▼ ▼ ▼ ▼

❏ 363. Hunt for "Rare Things"

The thrill of a treasure hunt comes, in part, from the hunt itself. And there's definitely excitement at finding something rare and precious! Decide on some "rare" things to be on the lookout for wherever you and your family go. Four-leaf clovers, Indian arrowheads, falling stars, rare wildflowers, crystal-clear moonstones, and fossils are some examples of the rare items you might seek out. And then, of course, there's always Big Foot, the Loch Ness monster, and the Abominable Snowman. But we think four-leaf clovers would be much more fun to find!

❏ 364. Make a Daisy Chain

Daisy chains are pretty simple to make. All you need are bunches of daisies, a plastic knife, and a comfortable setting. Start with a daisy-picking party. Let the kids do the picking, but make sure they take care to keep the stems as long as possible. Each chain will require about 25 daisies.

When the flowers have been gathered, follow these easy steps:

1. Use the plastic knife to slit the stem of the first daisy about 2 inches down from the flower.

2. Thread the stem of a second daisy through the slit of the first.

3. Slit the stem of the second daisy and thread a third daisy through it.

4. Continue slitting and threading until your chain is long enough for a bracelet, a crown, or a wreath.

5. When you're ready to bring the ends together to make the circle of daisies, make a slit in the last stem and thread the head of the first daisy through it. Voilà! Your crowning achievement is complete!

❏ 365. Say "Yes" to a YaYa Box

As the caterpillar in *Alice in Wonderland* asked, "Who are you?" A Ya Ya box may help your kids answer that question. It's a box decorated inside and out with objects and mementos that represent the owner's outermost and innermost self. What is painted, glued, or sewn to the outside of the box represents the *you* that other people see and know. What is inside the box represents the private you—the you only *you* know best. Work together to create a Ya Ya box that represents the whole family, or have each individual family member create a box of his or her own. The idea is to gather photographs, ticket stubs, charms, fabric scraps from important T-shirts, poems, books, collectibles, song lyrics—anything that helps create the explanation of who you really are. Select a box with a lid and use acrylic paints, collage materials, and white craft glue to decorate the outside of the box. Line the inside with fabric, photographs, baseball cards, or anything else meaningful. Add to the box as the years go by. Use it for special keepsakes and keep it up to date as the personalities of the owners change and grow.

▲ ▲ ▲ ▲ ▲

"Govern a family as you would cook a small fish—very gently."

—Chinese proverb

▼ ▼ ▼ ▼ ▼

❑ 366. Make Magic

Good magicians are never supposed to reveal the secrets of their tricks. But lucky for you, they don't always follow that rule! Why not learn a magic trick or two as a family? Learn new tricks each week and practice until everyone knows how to perform at least one. There's a wealth of information online, and your local library almost certainly has books on magic tricks that you and your children can study. Take in a magic show together so you can see the pros in action. Then perform a magic show of your own for friends and family. Abracadabra—instant fun for all of you!

❑ 367. Pan for Gold

Is there gold in "them thar" hills? Maybe. You might be surprised to learn that it's not uncommon for streams to contain gold that has sunk to the bottom and gotten stuck in the bends and curves. Gold is about 19 times heavier than water and 7 times heavier than most other minerals, so if it does exist in a stream, lake, or river, it gets trapped in the sandy bottom and slower-moving sections. Before you set out on a gold rush, investigate the particular body of water you're planning to "mine" to see if other people have had any success. While you might only come up with flakes, the thrill of discovery is the same as if you'd found boulder-size nuggets. Beginner gold panners should bring a milk crate to sit on and a shovel for lifting rocks from the bottom of the stream bed. You'll also need a good gold pan, a suction pipette to suck the flakes and tiny nuggets from the sand in your pan, and an old film case in which to store your treasures. The Internet is a great source of information on how and where to pan for gold. Don't miss this golden opportunity to spend time with your kids!

❏ 368. Moon Over the Moon

Lullabies, nursery rhymes, and love songs often center around the moon and its phases. From the Old Moon of January to the Milk Moon of May to the Harvest Moon of October to the Moon Before Yule of December, the moon holds

THE TOAD IN THE MOON?

People in different parts of the world have different ideas about just who, or what, is "in the moon." In the United States, we look at the shadows on the full moon and say it is the man in the moon. In Germany, people say that man was sent to the moon for something he did wrong. In Africa, the Masai people say it's the "woman in the moon." And in China, they say it's a rabbit or a toad.

a fascination for everyone who beholds it. Choose a clear evening to set up some chairs outside and gaze at the moon. Spend time together looking up at the moon and talking about the phases—

new moon, first quarter, full moon, last quarter—and take comfort in knowing that no matter where you all are in the future, you'll always be watching the same moon.

❑ 369. Build a Terrarium

Terrariums allow you and your kids to plant and tend an indoor garden. It's fascinating to watch as everything grows right before your eyes. For an open-air terrarium, a dish at least 2 inches deep and 8 to 12 inches wide will work. Place a layer of coarse sand or pebbles in the bottom of the dish. A layer of sphagnum moss or a very fine screen on top of the pebbles allows the water to filter down and prohibits the soil from settling into the pebbles. Add regular potting soil. Then create your terrarium "landscape" design by placing plants and/or seeds in the soil. Let your eye for design guide you. Keep your indoor garden watered and enjoy the changes as it grows.

❑ 370. Plan a Family Reunion

The more crazy relatives you put together in a room, the more fun everyone has. Plan a family reunion, and see for yourselves! When families get together around a feast of food, the stories come out and history is told, revised, and made. Let your kids in on the family secrets, and more importantly, let them discover their wonderful background. Encourage the kids to help with the planning. Should there be reunion T-shirts? What color should they be, and what should they say? Plan the location, the games, the food, and the invitations. Your kids will get a real sense of belonging from being included in such an important event.

❑ 371. Coach the Team

It's the bottom of the ninth, and bases are loaded. Your kid is up at bat. He hits it out of the park, everyone comes home, and your kid saves the game! But wait, it's not just your kid, it's *your* team because you're the coach! What better way to share, to bond, to celebrate wins and commiserate over losses? Coaching your son's or daughter's team is a commitment with big paybacks in pleasure, appreciation, and fond memories. No matter what the sport, parents who volunteer to coach are valuable to the community—not to mention to their immediate family and their child in particular. Check out the sidebar for some important tips on being the best coach you can be!

TIPS FOR COACHING YOUR KID'S TEAM

- Lay the ground rules with your own child first. Explain that as the coach for the whole team, you will be fair, and fair means treating everyone equally.
- Know the game and the rules; rules limit the need to make calls and decisions based on opinion.
- Teach the game.
- Involve everyone.
- Make the practices fun and enjoyable.
- Don't baby them. Explain that a certain amount of exercise and drills are necessary to be physically ready to play the game. Provide plenty of water and rest between drills.
- Act your age—don't argue with referees; don't yell. Exhibit good sportsmanship.
- Care, but not too much. It's not about winning or losing but how you play the game. Positive reinforcement is what gives kids the courage to play the next game.

❏ 372. Celebrate Father's Day

Father's Day is a great opportunity for your whole family to learn what makes Dad tick. Once you've served him breakfast on the veranda (or in bed) with the sports section spread out for easy reading, ask Dad to tell some stories about his happiest moments as a father or to tell some tales about his own upbringing. Have the kids figure out Dad's favorite things, and then plan a day around those activities. When you celebrate Father's Day this year, make it a point to get to know Dad better!

▲ ▲ ▲ ▲ ▲

"Whatever they grow up to be, they are still
our children, and the one most important of all
the things we can give to them is unconditional love.
Not a love that depends on anything at
all except that they are our children."
—Rosaleen Dickson

▼ ▼ ▼ ▼ ▼

❏ 373. Celebrate Earth Day

Until citizens of this world figure out how to sustain life on another planet, planet Earth is going to be the place where our civilization stays, grows, and thrives … or doesn't. That is why it's important to recognize the value of protecting and preserving our environment and the earth that is the very foundation of our existence. Back in 1970, Senator Gaylord Nelson was instrumental in declaring April 22 the official Earth Day. Now recognized in most countries, Earth Day is celebrated by conscious efforts to clean up streams, plant trees, support and maintain wildlife habitats, and educate people on the value of using less energy, creating less waste, and thinking "green" when consuming and disposing of material things. You and your family can join an Earth Day celebration sponsored by your school or town, or celebrate Earth Day right at home with an inspection of all that you're doing (or would like to start doing) to protect the planet. If we all teach our children to preserve our natural resources, we can help safeguard the planet for future generations.

❑ 374. Go to a Track-and-Field Meet

As soon as kids learn to walk, they want to learn to run. The more they run, the more you run. Maybe your little runner is going to grow up to be a big runner—a track star! High schools are a great source of entertainment and inspiration for budding athletes. Watching professional sports is exciting and fun, but watching high school sports gives young athletes attainable goals. Track-and-field events include running, throwing, and jumping—things most kids do from an early age. Find out your local school's schedule for home track meets and exhibition events and take the kids to see the local stars do their stuff. Don't be surprised if your kids want you to measure their long jumps and time their 100-yard dashes at home!

❑ 375. Visit Madame Tussauds Wax Museum

Want to rub shoulders with the rich and famous? For more than 200 years, Madame Tussauds Wax Museums have been introducing the public to historical figures, political figures, musicians, sports stars, world leaders, cultural figures, and Hollywood stars—all made of wax with measurements and features so exact one would think the real people were actually posing for the audience's enjoyment. Madame Tussauds has museums in major cities all over the world, including Amsterdam, Berlin, Hollywood, Hong Kong, Las Vegas, London, New York, Shanghai, and Washington, D.C. In addition to the astonishingly real celebrity likenesses, the museum features historical facts about each person portrayed. Photo opportunities abound. To find out more about Madame Marie Tussaud and the history of her wax figures, visit her on the Web at www.madametussauds.com.

❑ 376. Make New Year's Resolutions

New Year's Eve is a time to celebrate. The old year has passed, and new opportunities await us. When the party's over, take some time to reflect upon the past year and what you would like to do in the coming year to bring your family closer together. Making a family resolution is the perfect place to start. Anything is possible when your whole family is committed to a resolution, and you'll all grow closer together just talking about your goals. That's an achievement in and of itself.

❑ 377. Play with Your Food

You've told them over and over again, "Don't play with your food!" Well, now it's time to tell them, "Play with your food." It's okay. It's a parent's prerogative to change his or her mind. Playing with food isn't so bad after all. In fact, it can be a whole mess of fun, no matter how old your kids are. Finger paint with pudding or make mountains of mashed potatoes complete with parsley trees and skiing peas. How about an onion igloo or a pretzel and cracker lean-to? The best thing about this mess is the cleanup. All you have to do is dig in. Yum.

❑ 378. Visit a Ghost Town

These tumbleweed-inhabited towns were once homes and outposts on the trails of expansion and opportunism. They're the standing remnants of another time, another way of life that has passed. A visit to a ghost town can be both fun and educational—fun because these are places that ignite imaginations, and educational because they provide the impetus to consider the difficulties endured on the march of history. Be sure to learn about some of the inhabitants of the ghost towns, and notice that in nearly all cases, when times got tough, individuals pulled together as families to make it through. It's that sense of family that can bring a little life back into a ghost town.

❑ 379. Plan a Mystery Date

Dates aren't just for spouses and teenagers—they can be for the whole family. In fact, dates are a great way to bring some of the spirit and excitement of your early courtship to your kids' lives. Plan an outing with your spouse, then surprise the kids. There are plenty of great ideas in this book, from hot-air ballooning to bungee jumping to going out for a retro dinner. Whatever the date, make it surprising, make it fun, and make it for everyone.

GREAT FAMILY DATE IDEAS

- Have brunch at a pancake house
- Rent a canoe or rowboat and picnic "out at sea"
- Go for a bike ride in a park with trails
- Go to a drive-in movie
- Attend story hour at a bookstore or the library
- Throw an indoor pool party
- Head to an indoor ice rink
- Take a day trip to a historic site or town

❑ 380. Eat at a Restaurant with Carhops

Ah, the halcyon days of carhops and drive-ins, soda fountains and bubblegum. Crank up the jukebox, and put on your blue suede shoes to dine to the rocking sounds of Elvis Presley, Chuck Berry, Gene Vincent, and Eddie Cochran. Go ahead and let loose as a family. Good tunes and good food? Can't beat that!

❏ 381. Visit an Offbeat Museum

Most people are familiar with the world's major museums—the Louvre, The Guggenheim Museums, the Museum of Modern Art, and the Smithsonian Institution Museums. These storied places offer the best in art and culture. But there are other museums that offer the *worst* in art or the *weirdest* in culture. Whether in the interest of fairness, balance, or just plain wackiness, plan to visit some of these

WEIRD AND WILD MUSEUMS

At the **Woodman Institute Museum** in Dover, New Hampshire, you can check out a two-headed snake and a four-legged chicken!

If you like bugs, then the **Cockroach Hall of Fame** in Plano, Texas, is the place for you! You'll find preserved roaches that have been dressed in costumes and placed in themed dioramas. Have a laugh with David "Letterroach" or enjoy a piano concert with "Liberroachi." This offbeat museum is crawling with weird and wild stuff!

If you're feeling particularly hungry, you might want to give the **Idaho Potato Museum** in Blackfoot, Idaho, a shot. They've got the world's largest potato chip on display!

nutty museums. If you're outside of Boston, Massachusetts, pay a visit to the Museum of Bad Art (MOBA) and see works ranging from the simply bad to the mistakenly ambitious. If you happen to be in Minneapolis, Minnesota, check out the Museum of Questionable Medical Devices. This is a definite must for the side of your family with an interest in the oddly gruesome! Or consider visiting the

Kansas Barbed Wire Museum in LaCrosse, Kansas. Your whole family will get caught up in the 2,100 samples of 700 different varieties of barbed wire. Weird museums may at first seem more than a little useless, but it's important to remember that every failure is just one step on the road to success. This is an important lesson for every family—especially when you're all acting a little weird.

❑ 382. Start a Cousins' Camp

You all get together every summer anyway. Why not formalize the visit with a well-organized plan for a day camp? No need to spend money on summer fun when you and your siblings or in-laws can work together to create a day camp experience that builds memories as well as muscles, skills, relationships, and character. Plan a daily schedule that includes games and sports, swimming or running through the sprinkler, crafts, acting, field trips to the zoo, museums, or parks. Eat lunch together on a picnic blanket. Take lots of photos for the family album. This will become a tradition that all the cousins will look forward to each summer.

THINGS TO DO AT COUSINS' CAMP

- Morning exercise
- Hike
- Bike
- Relay races
- Carnival games (ring toss, baseball throw, tug-o-war)
- Pool or sprinkler games
- Crafts
- Camp songs
- Field trips

❑ 383. Plan a Surprise Party for Dad or Mom

Being in on a surprise creates an instant bonding between parents and children. In addition to teaching your kids how to plan a great party, you're also teaching them how to keep a secret. Pick a time, place, and theme for the party, and allow everyone except the person being surprised to contribute ideas for foods, games, and gifts. Have one person distract the party guy or gal—perhaps with a trip to the grocery store for milk, a call from a neighbor who "needs a helping hand," or a walk to the park while the other party planners and guests assemble at the party location. Plan favorite foods, make appetizers, make and bake a cake together, and then pop out and yell "Surprise!" at the magic moment. Don't forget to take pictures!

▲　▲　▲　▲　▲

"If there is love,
there is hope to have real families,
real brotherhood, real equanimity, real peace."

— Dalai Lama

▼　▼　▼　▼　▼

❑ 384. Plan a Treasure Hunt Complete with Clues and a Treasure

Why save all the games for birthday parties? While you may not want to make a daily practice of pinning a tail on a donkey, a treasure hunt is quite a different animal and is one that can involve the entire family, both in the treasure hiding and in the hunting. First decide on the treasure. Possibilities include a special treat, movie tickets for the whole family, or coupons for ice-cream cones. Each player is given the first clue, which leads to a place where the next clue can be found. Clues can be as simple or as difficult as you see fit. To make the hunt last longer, add some misleading clues and plant some silly "treasures" with notes saying, "Ha ha! Fooled you!" Make the clues funny, write them in verse, or just be clever with your directions to the next place. You'll treasure the time spent on the hunt!

❏ 385. Collect Pinecones and Get Crafty!

Are you pining for something fun to do? Get outside and collect some pinecones! Pinecones are perfect for craft projects such as Christmas tree ornaments, door decorations, centerpieces, mantle pieces, pine-cone bird feeders, pinecone people, and a whole lot more.

To get started, prepare your pinecones by following the steps below:

1. Preheat the oven to 200 degrees Fahrenheit.

2. Line a cookie sheet with foil, and spread your pinecones out.

3. Heat in the oven for 45 minutes until all the sap is melted and any bugs or other dirt have been baked off.

4. Allow to cool before handling.

If you want to make pinecone people, decorate using glue and glitter, acrylic paints, pipe cleaners for arms and legs, and cotton balls or acorns for heads. To make a fun decoration, use craft wire to wire bunches of pinecones together, add a ribbon, and hang on the front door or place in a bowl as a table centerpiece. Use your imagination, and let the kids use theirs as well. Pinecone crafts make great gifts for grandparents, neighbors, and teachers. Best of all, they make great keepsakes for family time well spent.

▲ ▲ ▲ ▲ ▲

"That man is richest whose pleasures are cheapest."
—Henry David Thoreau

▼ ▼ ▼ ▼ ▼

❏ 386. Make Up a Lullaby Just for Your Child

You don't have to be a great singer or songwriter to please your children at bedtime. The lullaby you make up especially for them is the best song they'll ever hear and one that will bring back happy memories all their lives. Sing a simple tune, include your child's name, and fill the lyrics with words of your love. A lullaby signals to your child that it's time to close their eyes and dream sweet dreams. The soothing, soft sound of your voice is relaxing and comforting. Good night, my little baby, good night.

❑ 387. Create a Cheerful Good Morning, Wake-Up Ritual

Start the day the cheerful way, with a wake-up routine that makes kids happy to see the morning come—even on school days. Although the ever-cheerful sing-song voice of Mom or Dad may grow old fast, quieter tickles on the neck or back and a soft-spoken assurance that great things lay ahead in this new day start the day with positive, comforting feelings that will stay with your children all day long. The time that you have to spend just between the two, three, four, or more of you are few and far between. Finding these intimate moments to give full attention and enjoy a little silent time together is just as valuable in the morning as it is at bedtime. Add a little morning song or help your child think of what he or she has to look forward to at school, after school, and that evening when the whole family is together again. Your time is the greatest gift, and morning time is the perfect time for giving.

❑ 388. Eat at an Outdoor Café

When you say you're eating out, you mean you're eating *out!* Europe is famous for outdoor cafés where people can sit for hours just people-watching, reading the newspaper or a book, and enjoying a cool drink or a coffee. Let your kids in on this experience. Try it first at a less crowded time—late breakfast, early lunch, or early din-ner. Teach your children the fun of watching the pedestrian traffic go by. Keep them interested with observation games: How many people are talking on a cell phone? How many people are walking a dog? How many are wearing red? An awareness of the world around them gives children a broader world view and helps them learn to be respectful of neighbors and fellow diners.

❑ 389. Go Spelunking

Spelunking is a fancy word for cave exploration. Spelunkers have equipment that helps them navigate through small crevices, crawling on their stomachs through cold water and climbing down rocky cave walls while ducking bats and other cave creatures. If this sounds a little too adventurous for you, there are plenty of caves and caverns that can be explored via well-lit tunnels with walkways leading to spectacular sights of stalagmites and stalactites, clear pools, and gnarly rock formations. Surf the Web to find a cave near you!

❑ 390. Visit an Old Car Museum

Honk if you love old cars! Exploring the history of the automobile is fascinating for children and adults alike. Whether you visit a museum devoted specifically to old cars or attend an exhibit within a science and technology museum or history museum, you and your kids will find lots to look at, talk about, and explore.

❑ 391. Walk (or Ride) to the Top of a Historic Building

Good shoes, a good attitude, and a good historic building have all the makings of a great day with a great view. The thrill of the hike to the tippy-top of a historic building such as the Washington Monument in Washington, D.C., or the Statue of Liberty in New York City is an "I knew I could do it" experience that kids of a certain age—8 and up—will like. But whether or not walking up is an option, there are many historic towers, lighthouses, monuments, and buildings that offer skyboxes, protected balconies, and walkways featuring 360-degree views of a city, island, or town. Seeing the "world" from a bird's-eye view brings a greater understanding of the topography, landscape, and layout of the grounds and towns we walk on and in every day. Start with the tallest building in your own town, then make it a vacation mission to always take time to climb to the top of a place that offers a view.

FAST FACT

In 2009, Chicago's Willis Tower (formerly known as the Sears Tower) opened The Ledge, a glass-box viewing platform 1,353 feet in the sky. Not for the faint of heart, The Ledge offers unparalleled views of Chicago from one of its most historic buildings.

❑ 392. Visit a Waterfall

How do you describe the sound of icy mountain waters crashing down upon the ground? The short answer? You don't. To fully appreciate the wonders of a waterfall, you need to experience it in person. There are nine million known waterfalls in the world, and the United States has its fair share, with Niagara Falls, located in New York on the border between the United States and Canada, being one of the most famous. Niagara Falls is actually made up of three separate waterfalls: Horseshoe Falls, American Falls, and Bridal Veil Falls.

But even if you have no plans for a trip to upstate New York, there are plenty of other waterfalls to see. Here's a list of some of the biggest and best waterfalls in the United States:

- **Havasupai Waterfall** in the Grand Canyon
- **Yosemite Falls** in California
- **Multnomah Falls** in Oregon
- Yellowstone's **Lower Falls** in Wyoming

- **Malchite Falls** in Washington
- **Amicalola Falls** in Georgia
- **Honokohau Falls** in Hawaii
- **North Clear Creek Falls** in Colorado
- **Shoshone Falls** in Idaho
- **Punch Bowl Falls** in Oregon

▲ ▲ ▲ ▲ ▲

"Those who bring sunshine into the lives of others,
cannot keep it from themselves."
—James M. Barrie

▼ ▼ ▼ ▼ ▼

❑ 393. Get Scientific

When it comes right down to it, science is at the heart of everything. Whether you're talking about global warming, drinking water, DNA, infectious diseases, animals, bugs, amphibians, the sky, the sea, shadows, photography, makeup, or movie making, there's a scientific element to almost everything. And that's exactly why science museums are so interesting—and so relevant—to so many people. Chances are, you have a science museum (or a museum with a science section) near you. Most have fun, interactive exhibits that will appeal to even the youngest members of your family. You'll all have such a great time, you won't even realize how much you're learning!

❑ 394. Visit the Mariners' Museum

If you find yourself in the neighborhood of Newport News, Virginia, a stop at the Mariners' Museum is a must. Founded in 1930, this museum is one of the largest of its kind in the world. With more than 60,000 square feet of gallery space exhibiting rare artifacts; ship models; and exhibits showcasing the history of shipbuilding, ocean navigation, and cartography, you and your family will be swept up in a wave of enthusiasm for all things nautical. Explore a full-scale replica of the USS *Monitor*, then take some time to roam the 550-acre grounds overlooking the James River. It's a full day's worth of exploring. If you can't make it to Newport News, check out the museum's Web site instead. There are plenty of virtual tours available there. It may not be quite as hands-on as the real deal, but there's plenty to see and learn right from the comfort of your own home!

▲ ▲ ▲ ▲ ▲

"To fill the hour—that is happiness."
—Ralph Waldo Emerson

▼ ▼ ▼ ▼ ▼

❑ 395. Make a Memory Mobile

Vacations are great opportunities for picking up free souvenirs. Shells on the beach, postcards from the hotel, and leaves or pinecones from a walk in the woods are some examples of things your family might bring home. Add family photographs to the collection and you've got the ingredients for a Memory Mobile. Albums and scrapbooks are great, but mobiles put your memories on display for all to see. The next time your family takes a day trip or a holiday vacation, collect things that will remind you of a special moment. Take a corresponding photo of your kids in action. When you get home, gather your photos and souvenirs together. To make the mobile, start with something as simple as a wire hanger with strings of different lengths hanging from it. Attach your souvenirs and photos to the ends of the strings, or glue them to a shaped piece of construction paper and punch a hole in the paper for hanging. Don't forget to add a card with the date, place, and occasion. Hang your Memory Mobile in a doorway, by a window, or any place your kids can see it on a daily basis. It will serve as a reminder that it's fun to "hang around" with the family!

❑ 396. Make Rice Krispy Bars

These crispy, marshamallow-y treats are easy and fun to make. Let your kids help with both the making and the eating!

YOU WILL NEED:

- 3 tablespoons margarine
  A large saucepan
- 4 cups fresh mini marshmallows
- 6 cups crispy rice cereal
  9″×13″ pan
  Cooking spray
  Wooden spoon

INSTRUCTIONS:

1. Over a medium heat, melt the margarine in the saucepan.

2. Add 4 cups mini marshmallows.

3. Stir the mixture until all the marshmallows are completely melted.

4. Remove the pan from the heat and add six cups rice cereal.

5. Stir the mixture until the cereal is coated with the melted marshmallows.

6. Spray a light coating of cooking spray onto the bottom and sides of the 9″×13″ pan and press the mixture into the pan. Use the back of the spoon to press until the mixture is spread evenly.

7. Allow the mixture to cool and then cut into squares.

❑ 397. Write a Résumé with Your Child and Update It Each Year

Everything you do is a brick in the building of who you become. In the beginning, your child's activities will be for fun and development.

But at a certain point, what your child is doing becomes an important entry on a résumé for an application to a private school, a summer camp, an exchange student program, college, or employment.

Starting a résumé at a young age saves a lot of endless searching through memories, papers, and files when the need for one arises. Plus, it gives your child a fun way to list and celebrate his or her accomplishments. A résumé also gives you, the parents, a look at the bigger picture of who your child is becoming. Maybe you'll notice trends, particular interests, specific skills, and noteworthy recognition in certain areas. These observations will help you be a better guidance counselor when it comes to choosing what's important and worth the time and money that might be spent on extracurricular activities. Update your child's résumé at the same time each year, and keep it with other important papers relating to your child. When the time comes to look back, you'll be glad you did!

❑ 398. Give Thanks

What makes your family's Thanksgiving different from every other family's Thanksgiving? Maybe it's your secret ingredient for stuffing or your famous corn pudding, or maybe it's the fact that every member of the family pitches in to help make the feast. Getting the kids involved in meal preparation gives them an opportunity to shine at the table. Let little hands get involved in the mashing of the potatoes, the stirring of the gravy, the shaping of the crescent rolls, or the shelling of the peas. Once the meal is on the table, make sure to give thanks for your family!

❑ 399. Walk in the Rain and Look for Rainbows

Splish! Splosh! Stomp! Splash! What could be more fun than walking in the rain together and splashing around in some puddles? Looking for rainbows while you're doing it! Seeing a rainbow—in the sky, in the fine misty spray from a hose or fountain, or in a droplet of dew catching the sun at just the right angle—is a thrill. You're more apt to find a rainbow in the morning or the evening when the sun isn't too high in the sky. Set out just after the rain has stopped, and keep your eyes to the skies for the beautiful arc of colors. Bring a camera and try to capture the extraordinary

RAINBOW OF INFORMATION

Rainbows are really very interesting, and your child is sure to want to know more about them. Arm yourself with information by checking out one of these Web sites:

- www.earthboundlight.com/phototips/finding-rainbows.html
- www.photocentric.net/rainbow_physics.htm

sight, or even better, snap a shot of your child smiling at the end of the rainbow.

☐ 400. Have a Picnic in a Rowboat

Row, row, row your boat,
gently down the stream.
Merrily, merrily, merrily, merrily,
life is but a dream.

You know the little ditty, but something was left out of the song: lunch. Without it, life might be a pretty bad dream because all that rowing can work up quite an appetite. You wouldn't want to be caught downstream without a good meal, would you? In the great chaos of modernity, a simple family activity like a picnic on a rowboat can bring out the most basic appreciations in all of you. Take turns on the oars as you paddle through the water—your kids will learn about responsibility and delegation with each stroke—and be sure to keep your eyes out for wildlife and a place to idle in the shade. Then pull in your oars and listen to the hum of dragonfly wings as you nibble on some sandwiches and cool off with a refreshing glass of lemonade. If you want to have a little fun with this, take along a few lace parasols, a wicker basket, tea, and some cucumber sandwiches and make an English afternoon of it. However you choose to picnic, the whole activity can be a great metaphor for life: Sometimes you struggle against the current, and sometimes you cruise with it, but as long as you're together with a basket of food, you'll all float along just fine.

❏ 401. Go to Summer Camp as a Family

Summer camp—the perfect place to stash the kids for a couple of months while you parents have a little time to yourselves. It's a tempting thought, but time away from the kids is not all it's cracked up to be, especially with kids as wonderful as yours, right? Deep inside, despite the responsibilities of adulthood and the drudgery of the workaday world, you're still a kid at heart. So why not join your children at summer camp? There are family camps all over North America. The first that come to mind are likely to be classic outdoors camps with rustic cabin lodging and dining halls just like you may remember from your own childhood. You'll play flashlight tag at night, go for moonlit hikes, canoe on the lake, or soar through the forest on a zip line. Then, when each day is over, you can get to know some of the other families at camp. You can even reminisce about your own childhood camp experiences and give your kids a little insight into your upbringing. If this kind of general camp experience isn't for you, there are also all sorts of specialized family camps ranging from folk music gatherings to art camps, where you'll hone your existing talents or maybe even find some new ones. Whatever camp you choose, the experience is sure to bring you all together like a macaroni necklace.

❏ 402. Build a Fire

Fire is one of the great communal gathering points of all time. Since its discovery, people have clamored around its dancing flames to cook meat, stay warm, engage in conversation, sing songs, and roast marshmallows. When the snow falls outside your window and great gusts of wind blow it into drifts against your doors, start a fire in the fireplace. There's nothing cozier than gathering around a fire on a cold winter evening and reading stories to each other— except possibly gathering around a bonfire on the beach, roasting marshmallows and singing campfire songs and telling ghost stories. No matter when you build a fire, make sure to teach your kids about fire safety. Fire is beautiful, captivating, and fun, but it can also be dangerous. Managing a fire is a great responsibility that should not be taken lightly.

❏ 403. Ride in a Cable Car or Gondola

You don't have to be a daredevil to see the world from high above, to gaze down upon the ground and gain a new perspective on Earth-bound life. You can witness it in comfort from a cable car, also known as a gondola (not to be confused with the Venetian canal boat), or an aerial tram. Cable cars might first come to mind as transportation at ski resorts, where you ride them from the base of the hill up the high mountains. The views from these gondolas can be spectacular. The only catch is you have to ski back down! For those without alpine abilities, cable cars are also used for commuting. Two noteworthy examples in the United States are the Roosevelt Island Tramway in New York, which connects Roosevelt Island to Manhattan over the East River, and the Portland Aerial Tram in Portland, Oregon, which connects the South Waterfront District with the Oregon Health and Science University. And if you're anywhere near any sort of mountain, a quick look in the phone book or a call to the local chamber of commerce or tourism board will tell you where the nearest tram ride can be found. So if you're looking for a good view and an unusual mode of transportation, keep an eye out, and up, for a cable car to ride.

❑ 404. Listen to Audio Books in the Car

Let's face it: We spend too much time in the car. For kids, time in the car can be boring, and boredom can turn into backseat fights (which means headaches for you!). Books on tape or CD are a lifesaver on long trips or even short ones if the stories are compelling. Listening to a book can raise your children's interest in reading and help to develop a sense of story construction, while also introducing new characters and new experiences. Plus, an audio book allows kids with high interest levels but lower reading skills to enjoy books they might not choose to read on their own. Libraries and book stores have a large selection of recorded books from which to choose. Or you can make the experience more personal by taping yourself reading a favorite story.

▲ ▲ ▲ ▲ ▲

"Parents can only give good advice or put them on the right paths, but the final forming of a person's character lies in their own hands."

—Anne Frank

▼ ▼ ▼ ▼ ▼

❑ 405. Teach Some Cool Tricks

Remember when your dad scared you by taking off the tip of his thumb and putting it back again? Or how about the time you caught your older sister hugging someone in the corner? And don't forget the hand that reached out and pulled your brother out of a doorway by the neck! These are all eye-fooling tricks that look like one thing but are really another thing entirely. Try them out on your kids, then pass the traditions along by teaching them how to do the tricks themselves. Here are some quick tips on how to fool the eye and get the giggles going!

Thumb-Thing Strange:

1. Close the fingers of your right hand and flatten them against your palm.

2. Put your closed hand in front of you with your palm facing your chest.

3. Bend the tip of your thumb down so the base of your thumb is even with the base of your index finger.

4. Hold your left hand out and bend your thumb in half just as you did on the right thumb. Rest the knuckle of your left thumb on top of your right thumb's knuckle so the two thumb knuckles meet.

5. Wrap the index finger of your left hand over the spot where your two thumbs meet.

6. Curl the rest of your fingers on your left hand into a fist.

7. Slowly slide your left index finger and thumb tip along the side of your right index finger. It should look as if the tip of your left thumb is separating from the right one. Practice in front of a mirror and then show Thumb-Thing Strange to your family.

Corner Warmer:

1. Stand in a corner facing the wall.

2. Wrap your arms around yourself. Put one hand over each of your shoulders, resting on top of your back.

3. Tip your head to one side and begin moving your hands on your neck and back.

4. Say "Oh, I never loved anyone as much as I love *you*!"

5. Turn around and reveal that the one you love is really *you*!

Grabbed by the Neck:

1. Stand in a doorway with your body half covered by the wall. Face into the room where people are.

2. Grab your neck with the hand that is hidden by the wall. Only let your hand and wrist show.

3. Lean your head toward the open doorway so it looks as if a hand is trying to pull you away.

4. Say, "Help! Save me!"

5. When everyone jumps up to run to your rescue, smile and say, "Gotcha!"

▲ ▲ ▲ ▲ ▲

"To nourish children and raise
them against odds is in any time,
any place, more valuable
than to fix bolts in cars
or design nuclear weapons."
—Marilyn French

▼ ▼ ▼ ▼ ▼

❑ 406. Joke Around

A sense of humor is a wonderful thing to share with your kids. Teaching them how to tell a joke does more than give your kids the good feeling they'll get when they can make others laugh. It also gives them an idea of how to set up a story and a punch line. Start with some easy jokes, such as these knock knock jokes, then encourage your kids to tell a few of their own!

Knock Knock!
Who's there?
Boo.
Boo who?
Don't cry little boy. Your Mommy is right here!

Knock Knock!
Who's there?
Ach!
Ach who?
Gesundheit! Want a tissue?

Knock Knock!
Who's there?
Olive.
Olive who?
Olive You (I love you).

Knock Knock!
Who's there?
Peekab.
Peekab who?
Peek-a-boo! I see you!

❑ 407. Learn a New Dance Move Together

When they're very little, children swing, sway, bounce, and bobble to the rhythm of any music they hear. But self-awareness brings with it inhibitions, and the freedom to dance like no one is watching disappears. Knowledge of "how to do it right" helps break down such inhibitions. Dancing is a physical skill that requires flexibility. It's also a means for getting in shape while learning a social skill. There are basically two types of dancing: fast dancing and slow dancing. Both require certain steps—moving to the beat of the music, leading or being led in pair dancing, knowing a box step or side-to-side step, knowing when to move your arms or keep them in place. Consider signing up for a dance class at a local community center or college. Or rent an instructional video so you can learn and teach in the privacy of your own home. Helping your kids master some dance basics will give them confidence when that first school dance rolls around. So go on—dance!

❑ 408. Teach the Golden Rule

"Do unto others as you would have them do unto you." This golden rule of behavior is also known as the "Ethic of Reciprocity," or the moral practice of mutual respect. Teaching your children the importance of treating other people the way they themselves would want to be treated is a lesson in sensitivity, tolerance, and understanding. The practice encourages good manners, kindness, and confidence in the knowledge that goodness is reflected in goodness. We share, and others share with us. We say "please" and "thank you," and others respond with the same respect and gratitude. A social environment governed by the Golden Rule is peaceful, safe, secure, and pleasant. This one simple life lesson introduces a positive quality of life. Do unto your children as you would have them do unto you. Do unto your parents, your spouse, your friends as you would have them do unto you. Set the example of mutual respect, and you will see your goodness reflected in the goodness of your children.

▲ ▲ ▲ ▲ ▲

"Youth is when you blame all
your troubles on your parents;
maturity is when you learn that everything
is the fault of the younger generation."
—Bertolt Brecht

▼ ▼ ▼ ▼ ▼

❑ 409. "Hunt" for Animals in Your Local Woods

As construction projects proliferate, eliminating natural habitats, animals become more daring in their hunt for food. Deer frequent residents' gardens; foxes come out during the day; and woodland animals of all types show up where least expected. Before they're all out of the woods, pull on your boots, pack a snack, and head out for a walk on the wildlife side in search of animals in their natural environs. The hike alone is worth the time spent, but the thrill of treading lightly on slightly beaten paths with eyes darting to the left, right, front, and rear and suddenly seeing a doe and her fawn is the purpose of it all. Showing your kids where the animals live and telling them a little bit about when and where they sleep, when they venture out, what they like to eat, and what purpose they serve in the ecosystem gives your young audience another source of information about the world in which they live. Bring along a field guide and learn to recognize animal prints, wildflowers, and animal habitats. There will be lots to report around the dinner table after a day spent "hunting!"

CAMOUFLAGE

Having trouble spotting animals no matter how hard you hunt? Try a few of these tips:

Blend in: Birds see colors, so colorful clothes will give you away. Wear gray, tan, or brown. Mammals don't see color but can tell if your clothing is light or dark compared to the background. Choose clothing that won't contrast with your background.

Change shape: Wild animals recognize predators and prey by their shape. Many animals have patterned coats, which make it harder for predators to spot them. Drape yourself in a dull-colored tarp or blanket and assume an outline that animals won't recognize.

No scents: Wild mammals have an excellent sense of smell. If mammals smell you, they will stay away—even if you hide. When you choose a place to sit, make sure it is upwind of the area you're watching.

Patience: Predators may hide by a water hole for hours waiting for their prey. You must be just as patient. The outdoors isn't a zoo, and animals aren't easy to find. Wild animals follow their own schedules. If you don't see any animals one day, try another day or a different area.

❏ 410. Visit a Police Station

Police officers are responsible for preserving law and order in your town, city, county, and state. They keep traffic running smoothly, patrol neighborhoods to keep them safe, respond to emergencies, and stop crime. They are a resource if someone or something goes missing. Police work to keep you and your family safe. Introducing your children to the police and the work they do adds to their sense of security. Plus, it's a good lesson should your child ever lose you in a crowded place or encounter a police officer during an emergency situation. What better way to teach your children about the police department than to visit it and take a tour? Many police departments have special kid-friendly kits, badges, stickers, and brochures as well as guided tours of the station and the squad cars. Call ahead to find out what your station's policy is regarding visitors. Then take a family field trip and get a heads-up on law and order in your district.

▲ ▲ ▲ ▲ ▲

"Life can only be understood backwards; but it must be lived forwards."

—Søren Kierkegaard

▼ ▼ ▼ ▼ ▼

❏ 411. Bake Bread

Measuring, kneading, and watching the dough rise—there's fun in store for kids who join in the process of making and baking bread. The very act of baking bread can be therapeutic; kneading and punching the dough is a great way to shed some of the day's stress. It's also a lesson in history, in self-sufficiency, and in how to make your kitchen smell delicious! The basic recipe for bread includes four ingredients—flour, yeast, water, and salt. But it's what's added to the basics—nuts, fruits, olives, dates, chocolate, or any number of extra ingredients—that really counts. Kids of most ages can help with bread-making. There are many books and Internet sites offering easy instructions. Any way you slice it, baking and breaking bread together is a recipe for good times!

❏ 412. Teach Ten Tips for Making New Friends

Being the new kid is not always fun. Before you launch your child into a new social situation, arm her with a set of guidelines that will ease the discomfort. Making new friends can be as easy as 1, 2, 3!

1. Don't sit at home, get out!

2. Smile. Looking friendly is the first step toward making a friend.

3. Don't be shy, just say "Hi!" Being the first one to greet another person shows that you're open to new friendships.

4. Say nice things about other people.

5. Join a team, club, or group.

6. Be yourself. Don't try to copy anyone else. Like what you like and share your interests with other people.

7. Ask questions. Show an interest in others.

8. Be a good listener.

9. Be honest.

10. Be a good friend to have a good friend.

❏ 413. Stage a Taste Test

Don't let the advertisers tell you what tastes best, find out for yourselves with an official taste test! Chocolate drink mixes, peanut butters, and chocolate chip cookies are great products to start with. Buy multiple brands of each product, cover the labels, and number each entry in the taste test.

Give each taster a numbered note card and a pencil for scoring. Allow time for tasting and note taking about each entry. At the end of the test, add up the scores for each numbered product. Divide the score by the number of tasters to find the average score. Then do the big reveal! Uncover the labels and let everyone see which one was the winner. Expect the unexpected and don't be surprised to find out that a favorite brand isn't really a favorite at all. For extra fun, send an e-mail and photo to the customer service department of the winning brand telling them the results of your taste test. You may just get a few coupons for your real favorite!

❑ 414. Have Movie Night in the Backyard

Drive-in movies used to dot the American landscape. It was a thrill to drive along a highway at night and see a huge movie screen off to the side. Cars filled with families (and dates) paid one admission fee, found a parking spot with a speaker that worked, hung it in the car window, and watched a movie from the comfort of the front or back seat. Such theaters are now a rare sight, but you can create the feeling right in your own backyard with a DVD projector, a queen-size white sheet, and a wall on which to hang it. If you don't have a DVD projector, look into renting one along with the required cables and speakers. Set up chairs or sleeping bags in the yard, provide bug spray and movie goodies, and get ready to roll. It's show time!

❑ 415. Practice the Six Components of Wellness

Wellness is about more than exercise and good nutrition. Total wellness involves engagement in the six dimensions that experts recognize as necessary for living a long and healthy life. As you and your family plan daily activities, keeping in mind the six components of wellness will help you live a balanced life. Remember: The best way to teach is to lead by example. Here's a sample of how the six components might affect your daily schedule:

Physical: Do a family stretching exercise first thing in the morning to get the blood circulating; go for a bike ride, play a game outdoors, or have a race.

Spiritual: Express gratitude for all that is good in your life and for the family you have; meditate, say a prayer, or take a walk and listen to the birds.

Intellectual: Read the newspaper together, visit a museum, watch a nature program on television and talk about what you've learned.

Vocational: Learn something new together, help with homework, take your child to work with you, take a class together.

Social: Invite friends over, go to a party, visit a grandparent, have a family movie night.

Emotional: Share your feelings, give a hug, find out the other side of the story to explain why someone might have done something disappointing.

Consciously setting goals to lead a balanced life teaches your children a set of values that will keep them strong in mind and body all the days of their lives. Start now!

❑ 416. Start a Book Club

The pleasure of being read to morphs into an even greater joy when your children learn how to read on their own. The next step in reading fun is sharing the experience with others. You may have your own book club that you participate in with friends. Why not let your kids start one of their own? Invite parents and kids from the neighborhood to come to the kickoff meeting at your home. Let your child choose the book that everyone will read for next time. Explain that at the next meeting, everyone should have read the book and be prepared to say what they liked, didn't like, which characters were their favorites, how the ending could have been different or better, and whether or not they would recommend the book to a friend. Serve refreshments that reflect the era or theme of the chosen book. Let the next host select the next book to read. Give everyone a turn at hosting and choosing a book. This could be an ideal way to make summer reading fun rather than a chore. Start a club and get reading!

❑ 417. Get Personal!

How well do you know your family? And how well does your family know you? It's time to find out! Create a trivia game starring the members of your family and the things you've all done together and separately. Give each family member a few index cards. Instruct everyone to write trivia questions on one side of each card and to write the answers to the questions on the reverse side. Here are some sample questions to help you get started:

a. Who has a birthday in the month of May?

b. Where did Mom go to college?

c. What was Dad's nickname in high school?

d. What was baby sister's first word?

e. What did Grandma do for a living?

f. Whose favorite color is yellow?

g. What vacation destination did the whole family vow never to visit again?

Shuffle the cards and place them in the middle of the table, question side up. The first player draws a card and tries to answer the question. To keep score, give 1 point for every correct answer. The player with the most points wins. The winner gets a day off from feeding the dog, taking out the trash, or making the bed. But really, there are no losers, because you'll all have fun!

❑ 418. Ride in an Airplane

When you stop to think about it, the ability to fly in a heavier-than-air craft is pretty amazing. Humans dreamed of flying thousands of

THE WRIGHT STUFF

Brothers Orville and Wilbur worked together as a team, striving to become the first to fly a heavier-than-air machine. On December 17, 1903, Orville Wright made a 120-foot flight into history in the brothers' Wright Flyer while Wilbur watched from the sidelines. Who knows—maybe this story will inspire your kids to get along with one another?

years before any individual ever believed it would be possible. Now that flight is relatively commonplace, it's easy to overlook the excitement your kids will feel when they fly in an airplane for the first time. It's a true adventure all the way from the drive to the airport to the ascent into the sky and back down again. The experience of flying over the patchwork fields, neighborhoods, and city grids and peering out over the wing at the sun shining down on top of the clouds is thrilling. There's such a sense of possibility in flight that it's no wonder kids are so fascinated by it. Let that fascination rub off on you, too, and you'll all feel a little *lighter* for it!

❑ 419. Share Wishes, Hopes, and Dreams

You might know all of your children's hopes and dreams, but do they know yours? Sharing your wishes, hopes, and dreams with your children shows them that even *you* don't have everything. And it gives them a different perspective on you as an individual. Sometimes we have to work and save to make a wish come true. Other times we have to accomplish a number of things on the way to making a wish come true. When your children learn this, they are learning the value of education, training, working toward a goal, and having the power to make their own wishes come true. So wish on that shooting star, on that dandelion going to seed, or on those birthday candles. Let your kids know there's power in wishing and dreaming—just as there is power in working to make those wishes and dreams come true!

☐ 420. Learn to Sign the Alphabet

It can be quite fascinating to see people converse in American Sign Language (ASL). And it can be a whole lot of fun to learn the alphabet in sign language so you can converse as a family! While there are many signs for whole words and phrases, learning the alphabet is the first step to becoming fluent in ASL. You can find charts and videos online to get you started. Before you know it, you'll be spelling out entire words and sentences!

BABY SIGN LANGUAGE

Sign language is catching on with parents of babies and toddlers in a big way. Parents are using simple ASL signs for such words as *milk, eat,* and *sleep* to communicate with children who aren't yet verbal. If you have a little one at home, try saying and signing the words for a few key items in your day-to-day life. If you are consistent, you may be surprised to find your baby signing back one day!

☐ 421. Tour a Prison

At first blush, touring a prison may not seem like the perfect family activity. But it can definitely be an interesting experience—especially if you tour a prison that no longer houses prisoners. In that case, a prison tour can be an adventure. There are many myths and legends in prison lore, and there is

FAST FACT

Alcatraz was used as a military prison as early as 1861 to house Civil War prisoners. From 1934 to 1963, it operated as a federal prison.

perhaps no better place
to get acquainted with
them than in one of the
most famous prisons of all:
Alcatraz, that terrifying
island in the middle of San
Francisco Bay, California.
It is said that no one ever
successfully escaped from
Alcatraz when it was in
use. However, there were
some pretty memorable escape

attempts. One involved spoons, raincoats, and papier-mâché
dummies! Alcatraz is now operated by the National Park Service
and is open for tours. Care to try an escape of your own?

❑ 422. Participate in a Walk, Run, or Hike for Charity

Finding the cure for cancer may be out of your reach right now,
but that doesn't mean you can't contribute with your own two feet.
Many charities, both medical and otherwise, host walks, runs, or
hikes for their causes. If their cause is your cause, too, walking for
charity is a great way for your family to work together to help the
world—and yourselves, too—with some healthy exercise. When you
join in one of these charitable activities, you'll also go out into your
community to raise awareness of the cause and what can be done to
help as you look for sponsors and donors. It can be difficult to ask
people for money, no matter how noble the cause, but this is also an
opportunity for you to teach your kids about communication and
being a good citizen. The whole endeavor may be challenging, but it
will also be fun. Ultimately, it's about the rewards you bring to others through your family's work. A few small steps for your family can
lead to great strides for those in need.

❏ 423. Attend a Wacky Festival

A frozen Norwegian stored since 1994 in his grandson's backyard shed? There's a festival for that. It's called Frozen Dead Guy Days and takes place in Nederland, Colorado. The festival features coffin races, historic hearses, and visitors dressed up as frozen or dead people. What about 200 people competing in the Great International World Championship Bathtub Race? There's a festival for that: the Nanaimo Marine Festival in Nanaimo, British Columbia. There's even a festival featuring cockroach races and flea circuses. Not surprisingly, that's called BugFest, and it's in Raleigh, North Carolina. There are festivals across North America for pretty much anything imaginable. Take your family to participate in one of them, because you'll never know what normal is until you've seen the truly bizarre.

WACKY FESTIVITIES

Want to find a wacky festival near you? Here's a list of some of our favorites:

- **Frozen Dead Guy Days,** Nederland, Colorado
- **Secret City Festival,** Oak Ridge, Tennessee
- **Nanaimo Marine Festival,** Nanaimo, British Columbia
- **BugFest,** Raleigh, North Carolina
- **Rattlesnake Roundup,** Freer, Texas
- **Barnesville Potato Days,** Barnesville, Minnesota
- **Faux Film Festival,** Portland, Oregon
- **Contraband Days Pirate Festival,** Lake Carles, Louisiana
- **Whole Enchilada Festival,** Las Cruces, New Mexico
- **Roswell UFO Festival,** Roswell, New Mexico

❑ 424. Experience the Supernatural

Bigfoot lives! The truth is out there! You know the catchphrases, and you've seen the videos and photographs of purported sightings. Whether you're a believer or not, tales of the supernatural can be fascinating. Give yourselves a little scare and experience the mystery firsthand by visiting the homes of some legendary creatures or by exploring the locations of some UFO sightings. Learn the stories, and try to figure out if they're hoaxes or fantastical truths. You may be surprised by how engrossing the endeavor can become. After all, we all like to make believe sometimes!

A MYSTERY NEAR YOU...

Legend has it that between 1966 and 1967, the town of Point Pleasant, West Virginia, was terrorized by a mysterious, shrieking winged creature described as the **Mothman**. Today the town pays homage to this tall, dark stranger with a 12-foot-tall sculpture and the world's only Mothman Museum.

Bigfoot can probably be "found" in any wooded area, but he is particularly fond of the Pacific Northwest. His cousin, the **Skunk Ape,** tends to roam the hinterlands of South Florida and is studied at the very scientific-sounding Skunk Ape Research Headquarters in Ochopee, Florida.

UFOs have been sighted all over the world, but perhaps the most famous site is **Area 51** in Roswell, New Mexico. The International UFO Museum and Research Center in Roswell is a good place to start if you want to get to the bottom of all this UFO business. If the truth is out there, Roswell seems like a good place to find it!

❑ 425. Visit a Shakespeare Festival

Though nearly 450 years have passed since his birth, William Shakespeare is still regarded as the foremost man of English letters. Kids read Shakespeare in school, but the language can make it tough to appreciate the humor and depth of his writing. When performed on stage, Shakespeare's works really come alive. All of the energy, the depth and breadth of human emotion, the subtlety and brilliance of the acting move the audience and reveal the true art of the Bard's plays. There is no better place to see one of Shakespeare's plays than at a Shakespeare festival performance. Contrary to the name, a Shakespeare festival is not like a carnival or a Renaissance fair. Rather, it is a regular theater company of professionally trained Shakespearean actors that puts on plays throughout the year. It is their studied interpretation of these works that will inspire and enrich your family's life. Get thee to a festival near you!

▲ ▲ ▲ ▲ ▲

*"Let us be grateful to people
who make us happy;
they are the charming gardeners
who make our souls blossom."*
—Marcel Proust

▼ ▼ ▼ ▼ ▼

❑ 426. Hit the Road

North America is a very diverse continent, full of different climates and landscapes. There's so much to see, from the snowy winters of New England to the warm sun of Florida, from the great plains of the Midwest to the Rocky Mountains, from Alaska to the great Pacific Northwest all the way to the Yucatán Peninsula. Who could resist the allure of a grand road trip across the country? Go to your library and check out an atlas of North America to learn about the different landscapes, then get together as a family to talk about what you'd like to see. Plan your route on a map, and when you're driving, keep the kids involved (and out of each other's hair) by having them navigate or by asking them to take pictures of interesting roadside vistas and sites. Stop whenever you come across something that seems interesting. You'll find there's a lot to see beyond the typical tourist sites. Sure, it may seem like a lot of family time in close quarters, but it's trips like these that ultimately bring you closer together no matter how far you travel.

GET YOUR KICKS...

Before the U.S. interstate system was developed, it wasn't always easy to get from one part of the country to another. One road, however, which wound from Chicago to Los Angeles, became the stuff of legend. Route 66 was established by Congress in 1926 and traversed Illinois, Missouri, the corner of Kansas, Oklahoma, the Texas panhandle, New Mexico, Arizona, and Southern California. In his Depression-era novel *The Grapes of Wrath*, John Steinbeck dubbed it "The Mother Road." Route 66 inspired many to look West for their fortune and was also the subject of a song performed by everyone from Nat King Cole to the Rolling Stones to Depeche Mode. The Federal Highway Act of 1956 led to its demise with the creation of several new interstates, and, by 1985, Route 66 had been formally decommissioned, though most of the winding route through Illinois, Missouri, Kansas, Oklahoma, Texas, New Mexico, Arizona, and California can still be traveled today.

❏ 427. Play Hooky Together

We all live by the rules day in and day out, going to work and going to school, doing our chores and our homework. But we have a little Tom Sawyer in each of us, too. Let the rascal out in a controlled manner by playing hooky together and enjoying some quiet time as a family with nothing in particular to do. Rent some movies and pop some popcorn, read a book together, play a board game, or sing some songs. Sometimes a personal day is the perfect remedy for the high-stress world in which we live. Just make sure there aren't any big tests or meetings that day to ruin the fun and leave you and your kids in the dog house when you go back to the real world. And don't worry too much about starting a trend of bad behavior. Makeup homework is no fun at all, and as long as you keep on top of your kids, they'll walk away from the experience knowing that playing hooky is great once in a blue moon, but it's not worth practicing regularly.

▲ ▲ ▲ ▲ ▲

"Life isn't a matter of milestones, but of moments."
—Rose Fitzgerald Kennedy

▼ ▼ ▼ ▼ ▼

❏ 428. Visit the World's Largest of Something

Ladies and gentlemen, boys and girls, step right up and see it, the finest, the most wonderful, the world's *largest*...ball of twine. Maybe that doesn't sound all that exciting at first (or maybe it does, in which case, you've probably already been there), but there are some fascinatingly bizarre "world's largest" sites around the world. Some are pretty silly, but then that's half the fun, isn't it? Other sites are sublimely beautiful and amazing, such as Victoria Falls—the world's largest waterfall—on the Zambezi River between Zambia and Zimbabwe, or Rainbow Bridge in Utah, the world's largest known natural bridge. Visiting a world's largest site is fun and amazing while you're there, but it will also provide each member of your family with a lasting memory. After all, the best stories often begin with, "When I was visiting the world's largest concrete buffalo in Jamestown, North Dakota…"

A SMALL LIST OF BIG THINGS

- Eartha, the World's Largest Rotating Globe, Yarmouth, Maine
- World's Largest Bug, Providence, Rhode Island
- World's Largest Uncle Sam Statue, Lake George, New York
- World's Largest Baseball Bat, Louisville, Kentucky
- World's Largest Chest of Drawers, High Point, North Carolina
- World's Largest Peanut, Ashburn, Georgia
- World's Largest Chair, Anniston, Alabama
- World's Largest Ball of Twine, Darwin, Minnesota
- World's Largest Cuckoo Clock, Wilmot, Ohio
- World's Largest Basket, Newark, Ohio
- World's Largest Penny, Woodruff, Wisconsin
- World's Largest Killer Bee, Hidalgo, Texas
- World's Largest Rattlesnake, Freer, Texas
- World's Largest Artichoke, Castroville, California

❏ 429. Go for a Horse-Drawn Carriage Ride

Horse-drawn carriage rides aren't just for couples in love. They're a delightful, escapist adventure your whole family will enjoy. Instead of the cacophony of horns and buses, you'll move along at the slow, sonorous pace of clopping hooves. Many cities and towns throughout North America offer these charming jaunts. You can ride through Central Park in New York; go on a tour of historic Charleston, South Carolina; see the scenery of Mackinac Island, Michigan; or take in the lights of Chicago's Magnificent Mile. The ride has its own fun to offer, but you'll also enjoy stepping away from the hustle and bustle of modern life for some quiet time together as a family.

▲　▲　▲　▲　▲

> "Children's games are hardly games.
> Children are never more
> serious than when they play."
> —Michel de Montaigne

▼　▼　▼　▼　▼

❑ 430. Ride a Roller Coaster

The thrill of being launched on tracks speeding toward the unknown with adrenaline running through your body—this is the wonder and delight of a roller coaster. Roller coasters are not only a source of great fun, they are also engineering marvels and have evolved dramatically over the years as technology has grown more and more advanced. Enjoy some high-speed adventure by taking a spin on some of the country's most popular coasters. If you have a taste for nostalgia, visit Coney Island to ride The Cyclone, which was built in 1927, and is one of the best-known historical roller coasters. Or if you've got a daredevil among you, why not visit the tallest roller coaster, Kingda Ka at Six Flags Great Adventure in Jackson, New Jersey? You'll soar to a height of 456 feet! There are even indoor roller coasters you can try, such as the one at the Mall of America in Bloomington, Minnesota. Wherever you go, a ride on a roller coaster brings with it the exciting illusion of danger, but also the very real security of family. So clutch each other's hands in anticipation of the big ride.

LOOKING FOR A GREAT RIDE?
WHY NOT TRY ONE OF THESE:

The Matterhorn Bobsleds

While not necessarily the tallest, fastest, or scariest ride in the world, the Matterhorn deserves a nod as the grandfather of modern coasters. Still thrilling riders at Disneyland, this ride was the world's first major steel coaster when it opened in 1959. Inspired by the Matterhorn, a 14,692-foot mountain in the Swiss Alps, the structure is made up of two linking steel roller coasters with loops and corkscrews. Top speed is 18 miles per hour.

Apollo's Chariot

Opened in 1999, Apollo's Chariot is an award-winning steel coaster at Busch Gardens in Williamsburg, Virginia. Holding the world record for a gulping 825 feet of drops on a coaster, Apollo's Chariot starts with a 170-foot lift hill, then hits a maximum speed of 73 miles per hour. At the peak, riders drop down a few teasing feet before the cars swoop down 210 feet to graze a water-filled gully at a 65-degree angle. Riders then soar up a second hill and back down a 131-foot drop. Then, the coaster screams through a short tunnel and takes off up a third incline before screeching around a curved 144-foot plunge.

Steel Dragon 2000

Steel Dragon 2000, located at Nagashima Spa Land Amusement Park in Japan, represents "The Year of the Dragon." As of 2006, it had the longest track of any coaster in the world, hurtling its riders along at speeds up to 95 miles per hour for 8,133.17 feet. With a peak at 318.25 feet, it is also the world's tallest coaster to use a chain lift: Two chains are utilized, one for the bottom half and one for the top half because a single chain would be too long and heavy. For earthquake protection, more steel was used in this $50-million machine than in any other coaster in the world.

❑ 431. Make Snow Ice Cream

It's getting colder outside, and the downy soft snowflakes are falling from the sky. They are beautiful to watch, but why let the fun end there? If you and your family get a craving for something sweet and there is fresh snow on the ground, try making snow ice cream. It's tasty, and it's easy. All you have to do is mix the ingredients and dig in!

Snow Ice Cream Recipe

- 1 cup half and half
- ½ cup sugar
- 1 teaspoon vanilla extract
  dash of salt
- 5 cups fresh, clean snow

❑ 432. Play in the Mud

How many times have you told your kids not to track dirt into the house and not to play in the mud? Well, now it's time to retract those orders. A little mess can go a long way in terms of bonding with your kids and meeting them on their level. After all, they get messy naturally. It's you who will have to get over your aversion to mud. Once you dig in, you'll find a new world—one without inhibitions and with almost endless possibilities. For your kids, mud is the building block of imagination. Make mud castles and mud pies—even mud sailboats. The main thing is to let your imagination run freely. Don't forget to hose off outside before coming in, though. No matter how much fun you had in the yard, you know you haven't changed enough to actually *want* to track the mud in with you!

❑ 433. Visit a Foreign Country

Our big world is getting smaller every day. With the Internet, information flows freely across borders, and our products, our food, even elements of our language either come directly from overseas or are influenced by cultures around the world. But nothing can take the place of an actual, real-life visit to another country—especially one that none of you have been to before. Visit the main tourist sites, of course, but also go exploring. Be sure to get lost for a little while. Eat at some restaurants off the beaten path, catch an impromptu gathering of musicians, or watch a group of old men play bocce ball in the village square. Whether the pleasures you pursue are simple and tranquil or modern and fast-paced, you'll learn about other cultures around the world, see beautiful sites, and make the world of your family a little broader by sharing these experiences together.

▲ ▲ ▲ ▲ ▲

"Home is the place where boys and girls
first learn how to limit their wishes,
abide by rules, and consider
the rights and needs of others."
—Sidonie Gruenberg

▼ ▼ ▼ ▼ ▼

❑ 434. Pass Down the Games of Your Childhood

"Kids today. All they do is play video games and watch TV. Back when we were young, things were so much simpler." Sound familiar? Your parents probably said it about you, too. All parents have nostalgia about their own childhood games, along with misgivings about the games today's kids play. Admit it: Even your video games were simpler and purer than the wild games of today. So get your whole family outside and play a game from your childhood, whether it's tag, capture the flag, kick the can, or ghost in the graveyard. If it's raining, pull out the video games you played as a kid. Not only will you have fun reliving your childhood, but you'll also show your kids that you were once like them—that you can understand how they feel and what they like. Everybody wins when you play together!

❑ 435. Experiment

Science is all around us, and you don't need a degree and a lab coat to see it. You just need some imagination and a few household products. Have you ever wondered what makes plastic, what makes things glow in the dark, or if a bowling ball can float on water? These are fascinating questions you and your family can explore together when you have a family science day. Pick your experiment and get your gear ready. Make sure everyone has a role. Even the littlest ones can do something to participate, even if it's just observing. After all, observation is just as important to science as participation. No matter what your roles, get ready to experiment together, and discover how important science is to our everyday lives.

Visit www.scifun.org to learn more about experiments you can do at home, or try the one listed below!

EXPLOSIVELY FUN

There's no need to run for cover when you make this safe model of a real, erupting volcano. Better still, an experiment like this will make your kids think that science is pretty cool!

Get a tall, thin jar. The kind that pickles or olives come in works well. In the jar, mix together ¼ cup water, ¼ cup baking soda, 3 tablespoons dishwashing liquid, and a few drops of red or orange food coloring. Put the lid on the jar. Set the jar in the center of a big container. Next, build a mountain of dirt or sand around the jar (this will work best if the dirt or sand is slightly wet). If you'd like, cover the mountain with plaster of Paris, and paint it to look like a real volcano. You can even decorate it with pinecones to look like trees.

Then it's lava time! Take the lid off the jar, quickly pour in ¼ cup vinegar, and stand back to watch your volcano erupt!

❑ 436. Teach Compass Skills

Dads are notorious for refusing to ask for directions. They always claim they know where they're going and that they have an inner compass. But more often than not, that inner compass is wrong. Therefore, it is important for your family to learn how to read a real compass—the kind that's never wrong. Head to your local outfitter to pick out a compass and get a refresher (or starter) course on its use. Then, test it out in preparation for the real adventure: a hike through the woods. Get your bearings, and discuss your plans. Then take turns leading. Try to maintain your course, even if there are obstacles in your way. With a little practice, all of you may eventually get your inner compasses lined up and true.

▲ ▲ ▲ ▲ ▲

"We speak of educating our children.
Do we know that our children also educate us?"
—Lydia Huntley Sigourney

▼ ▼ ▼ ▼ ▼

❑ 437. Go Whale Watching

Thar she blows! Into the boats! Grab the harpoons! There's so much history and legend in whaling that the mere thought of a whale conjures up images of long-bearded seamen or crazy Captain Ahab and his famed white whale Moby Dick. Whaling is not the industry it once was (and the whales are thankful for that!), but whale watching can be just as exciting—and more than a little bit gentler on the whales. You and your family, along with other passengers and a seasoned crew, will brave the high seas in the quest that obsessed Ahab and so many others—the search for whales. You'll marvel as they play in the water and show their tails. You may even catch a glimpse of a happy family of whales. You can find whale-watching tours in seaside ports in Alaska, the Pacific Northwest, or in New England. It's an experience you won't want to miss.

❑ 438. Visit a Famous Replica

What's even better than the real thing? A replica! Okay. Not really. But visiting a replica instead of the real thing is just the sort of bizarre trip that makes for a good story later. Plus, you might find it easier to get to Niles, Illinois, to see a replica of the Leaning Tower than to actually go all the way to Italy!

Here is a list of some replicas you might want to visit:

Statue of Liberty

The real thing: New York, New York

The replica: Birmingham, Alabama

Eiffel Tower

The real thing: Paris, France

The replica: Las Vegas, Nevada (the capital city of artifice)

Stonehenge

The real thing: Wiltshire County, England

The replica: Maryhill, Washington

▲　▲　▲　▲　▲

"Happiness is not so much in having as sharing.
We make a living by what we get,
but we make a life by what we give."
—Norman MacEwan

▼　▼　▼　▼　▼

❑ 439. Experience Wacky Art

Artwork can have a reputation for seriousness and for staid importance, but there are plenty of strange, crazy, and downright wacky works of art around North America to call that reputation into question. Some were conceived as art, such as the oddly decorated cars one might find driving around town with shells, figurines, or pretty much anything else attached to them; others were adopted by artists and architects as models or points of discussion, such as The Big Duck—a duck-shape building on Long Island, New York. Built in 1931, The Big Duck was originally constructed to help its owner's duck farming business, but architect Robert Venturi famously used it as an entry point to discuss the nature of architec-

THAT'S THE WAY WE ROLL!

Want to take your search for wacky art on the road? Consider a trip to the Art Car Parade in Houston, Texas. The parade features wacky cars that make vehicles from *Mad Max* appear almost ordinary. Past parade entries have included a Volkswagen Beetle with another upside-down Beetle welded to its roof, a Sunflower car where driver and friends sit high in an elevated sun pod, and a giant Gold Star car that looks to be uncontrollable. Every year, the entries get more artistic and more intricate.

ture and the spectrum ranging from works of architecture that look like their purpose to works that disguise their purpose. So wherever you are, keep an eye out for some wacky art. Much of the fun comes from happening upon it in unexpected places.

❑ 440. Whistle While You Work

To someone who doesn't know how, whistling can seem like magic. It's a simple skill that can bring pleasure and brighten even the darkest days. Show your kids a little of your whistling magic, then teach them the tricks of the whistling trade so they can do it on their own. This seemingly trivial lesson can pay large dividends beyond the immediate fun of watching your kids' faces as they try to position their lips and tongue properly. It's a challenge that you will have to overcome together. As simple as whistling is, it's not necessarily easy to learn, so guide your kids through their frustration and teach them how to overcome adversity. Watch their little faces light up as they finally figure out how to whistle a happy tune of their own!

❑ 441. Teach the Art of Blowing Bubbles with Gum

CHEW ON THIS!

The first bubble gum was invented in 1906, but it failed miserably. It wasn't until 1928, when Dubble Bubble came out with its famous pink gum, that the stuff started to catch on.

There may be few more useless skills than blowing a bubble gum bubble, but that doesn't mean it isn't fun! It may seem like magic when a skilled bubbler does it, but anyone can learn. Just chew the bubble gum until it's soft, flatten it on the roof of your mouth, position it behind your teeth, and blow from deep in your chest while slowly opening your mouth. It may take a while to figure it out, but keep practicing. For added fun, mix gums of different colors (especially from a gumball machine), and see how big a bubble you can produce. Once you and your family have trained for a while, hold a competition. Or have a bubble gum duel. Set two family members against each other, face to face so that their bubbles will touch once they expand. The winner is the one whose bubble pops first. No poking, though!

❑ 442. Make Shadow Hand Puppets

Like clouds, shadows can accidentally take on many shapes with a little help from the imagination. Put that combination of shadows and imagination to work by creating shadow hand puppets. It's amazing what you can convey with a few fingers and a fist. All you need is an open lightbulb and a wall. Put your hands between the light and the wall, and you have shadows. Learn how to make a rabbit or a camel or a wolf. It may take as much practice as imagination, but you'll be fostering a fun, creative learning environment for the whole family. Once you've mastered some different shapes, put on a little play. Pick your favorite folk tale or bedtime story and act it out in shadows. Get everyone involved, even in the sound effects, and be sure to set up the camcorder, because you won't just be making shadows—you'll be making memories.

▲　▲　▲　▲　▲

"Dad taught me everything I know. Unfortunately he didn't teach me everything he knows."

—Al Unser Jr.

▼　▼　▼　▼　▼

❏ 443. Visit a Hall of Fame

Professional sports are both entertainment and legend in the making. Each sport builds up its own mythology and celebrates its own heroes. These heroes capture the imaginations of children and adults alike. In sports, we see a microcosm of human achievement and frailty. The greatest athletes showcase such admirable qualities as dedication, teamwork, and the ability to overcome adversity. A truly admirable athlete is one who possesses these qualities and is a good citizen in his or her community.

Whatever sport your children love most, be sure to visit its hall of fame. There you'll find the heroes enshrined; you'll have a chance to discuss the values they embody, and you'll be able to guide your own children's goals using the experiences of the athletes as models. What makes these heroes great? What kept others out of the hall of fame? How did they travel their paths? These are worthy questions that can be applied to all of life's challenges.

❏ 444. Celebrate a New Holiday

Holidays are an important time for families to come together to celebrate beliefs and traditions. Holidays also play a key role in our identities as individuals and as families. With increasingly diverse local communities, it is important to get to know your neighbors— to understand them as people and to appreciate the culture of which they are a part. A fun way to do this is to celebrate a holiday you have never celebrated before. Learn the origins and traditions, then practice them at the appropriate times. By learning to value other cultures' holidays and traditions, you will also gain a stronger appreciation of your own, and your family will look forward to your traditional holiday celebrations with even greater anticipation.

▲ ▲ ▲ ▲ ▲

*"What families have in common
the world around is that they are
the place where people learn
who they are and how to be that way."*
—Jean Illsley Clarke

▼ ▼ ▼ ▼ ▼

❏ 445. Have a Backward Dinner— Eat Dessert First!

Every day has its routine. We wake up, have breakfast, go to work or school, come home and have dinner, do homework, maybe take a little time together, and then go to sleep to start it all again. There's comfort in routine, and we feel happy to be together with our family day in and day out. But sometimes it can be fun to break the routine just a little. A family dinner presents the perfect opportunity to do so. It's a simple idea, but try having dinner backward. Start with dessert, move on to the main course, then to the soup, then to the salad, then to the bread. Even place the silverware inside out and in reverse! If your kids are really young, they might even enjoy walking to their seats backward. A little rule breaking is good for everyone now and then. Why not make backward dinner a new family tradition?

❑ 446. Experience a Luge, Skeleton, or Bobsled Ride

Luge, skeleton, and bobsled racing are three of the most exciting Winter Olympics sports, but they are not just for elite Olympic athletes. You can learn to do them, too. Luge, skeleton, and bobsled rides were started in the health-spa town of St. Moritz, Switzerland, in the mid-1800s. At first, wealthy guests entertained themselves with children's toboggans, but they soon discovered that they needed to steer to avoid pedestrians. The development of steering mechanisms and a specific track for the sports followed, and the rest is Olympic history. In Austria, Italy, and Switzerland, these three sports are considered family activities, but they are not as popular in North America, so you will have to search for luge, skeleton, or bobsled clubs online to start. These are dangerous sports, so you won't be allowed to race down from the top of the track on your first try. However, some bobsled tracks in the United States, such as the one in Lake Placid, New York, offer rides with professional drivers. So if your family likes sledding and a little bit of danger, consider learning to ride a luge, skeleton, or bobsled. Who knows, if your kids start soon enough, the Olympics may be in their future.

❑ 447. Splash in a Fountain

You've heard of throwing a penny in a fountain and making a wish. Well, in some town squares and town centers around North America, you can throw your *kids* in, too! Well . . . not exactly. But you *can* splash in the fountains together. Some fountains are being designed to resemble geysers, and they spray at different intervals, right out on to the pavement. It's simple entertainment, but sometimes that's the best kind. And the reward of your child's giggle with each spritz is the answer to every one of your wishes. But don't let your kids have all the fun. You can join in, too!

▲ ▲ ▲ ▲ ▲

"Love is a condition in which the happiness of another person is essential to your own."
—Robert Heinlein

▼ ▼ ▼ ▼ ▼

❑ 448. See an Ice Show

If it made money at the box office and it's for kids, chances are you can find it on ice as well. An ice show is a mix of figure skating, ballet, and popular children's entertainment, and it really does have something for the whole family. Your kids will enjoy the magic and excitement of seeing their favorite characters live, and you'll enjoy their utter delight and captivation. The skating is a lot of fun to watch, too!

❑ 449. Take a Magical Mystery Tour

You probably know your town like the back of your hand. You've memorized the route to school, to the mall, to the grocery store, to the sports fields, to the library, to your friends' houses, to your kids' friends' houses, and so on. But have you ever gotten lost in your own town just for fun? Have you ever wandered off the beaten path? Even small towns are bigger than they appear. Take your whole family on a bus to the end of the line or drive down streets you've never been on before. It can be familiar and strange at the same time— even a little eye-opening. The experience will shift your perspective a little in a new and interesting way. This minor adventure can lay the foundation for curiosity and a broader worldview for your kids and may even embed some interesting small memories that come back in unexpected ways later in life.

❑ 450. Visit a Greenhouse or Conservatory

Throughout history, conservatories housed plants brought back from expeditions. These plants couldn't necessarily survive in the outdoor habitats of the places to which they were imported, so they were preserved indoors. Conservatories still function this way, but they are also fascinating and beautiful places to visit. At a conservatory, you can find tropical plants, desert plants, rare plants, and plants from around the world in themed rooms that not only house the plants, but also give the visitors a sense of what the climate and landscapes are like in those plants' native habitats. A conservatory is also a place ripe for childhood imagination. With so much inspiration and wonder, there's no telling what could blossom in a child's mind!

▲ ▲ ▲ ▲ ▲

"Children are a great comfort in old age—
and they help you reach it much faster, too!"
—Lionel M. Kaufman

▼ ▼ ▼ ▼ ▼

❑ 451. Sponsor a Child in a Foreign Country

You may already help out in your local community, and your kids may understand the importance of their actions when it comes to your community and your neighbors, but have you considered trying to help people across the globe, as well? Talk with your children about the possibility of sponsoring a child their own age in a place where resources are scare and life is far more difficult than in your homeland. Sometimes even small actions such as this can have a profound impact on another person's life. Your kids will grow to understand that no matter where they live, what language they speak, or how old they are, they are part of a global family.

❏ 452. Visit a Haunted Spot

There are places around the world where strange things happen, where people see ghosts, and where the past comes back to haunt the present. Whether the ghosts are real or not doesn't matter. The places still have a certain power over us. Another way to think of them is not necessarily as haunted, but rather as places where history never dies. Is it just coincidence that said history is usually gruesome or bizarre? That's up to you and your family to decide when you visit. You may want to wait to try this until your kids are mentally strong enough or are at least very sound sleepers, because haunted places could leave quite an impression—at least for a night.

Here are three noteworthy haunted places in North America:

The Hotel Chelsea in New York City: Don't worry if you see a ghost here. It's probably writers Dylan Thomas, Eugene O'Neill, or Thomas Wolfe. Their ghosts reportedly haunt this building. Bring a notebook in case they have some beautiful lines to share!

The Lizzie Borden House in Fall River, Massachusetts: Alleged to be the most haunted house in the United States, this was the site of a famous and gruesome double murder and now boasts a charmingly creepy bed-and-breakfast. Who's the guest, you or the ghost?

The Screaming Tunnel in Niagara Falls, Canada: If you light a match in the tunnel, then blow it out, you'll supposedly hear the scream of a little girl who was burned alive there by her deranged father. It is rumored that the ghost of the father still haunts the place as well. The best advice you'll ever receive before going there is this: Don't light a match.

▲ ▲ ▲ ▲ ▲

"There are three ways to get something done: do it yourself, hire someone, or forbid your kids to do it."

—Monta Crane

▼ ▼ ▼ ▼ ▼

❏ 453. Make a Pizza Together

Pizza is the easiest food to order. You just pick up the phone, and 30 minutes later, dinner is at your door. It's like magic. But the real magic in pizza comes when you make it yourselves from scratch. It's a true family affair. Gather together in the kitchen and mix the sauce, then roll out the dough, knead it, and toss it to each other to stretch it. Load it up with sauce and cheese, and get ready for the toppings. When the kids are younger, make one pizza for the whole family and decide on the toppings together. Older kids might enjoy the opportunity to make their own individual pizzas—to let their creativity shine through their dinner. Experiment with recipes and toppings, and when you find the ones you like most, put them in a family recipe book so you can make your favorites again and again. Bon appetit!

NOW THAT'S WHAT I CALL A PIZZA!

The record for the world's largest pizza depends on how you slice it. According to *Guinness World Records*, the record for the world's largest circular pizza was set at Norwood Hypermarket in South Africa in 1990. The gigantic pie measured 122 feet, 8 inches across, weighed 26,883 pounds, and contained 9,920 pounds of flour, 3,968 pounds of cheese, and 1,984 pounds of sauce. In 2005, the record for the world's largest rectangular pizza was set in Iowa Falls, Iowa. Pizza restaurant owner Bill Bahr and a team of 200 helpers created the 129-foot by 98.6-foot pizza from 4,000 pounds of cheese, 700 pounds of sauce, and 9,500 sections of crust. The enormous pie was enough to feed the town's 5,200 residents ten slices of pizza each.

❑ 454. Visit an Island

Whether it's Jules Verne's *The Mysterious Island*, the island from television's *Lost*, or even the real-life islands of Hawaii or Jamaica, islands capture our hearts and imaginations. Perhaps this is a result of the combined and somewhat paradoxical sense of isolation and communion: isolation because an island is geographically cut off from the landed world and communion because everyone on the island shares a small (and beautiful!) space. Visiting an island is a fun way to explore a different way of life and a different part of the globe. Larger islands house many people and offer vacation resorts, sunny beaches, and entertainment such as fishing, boating, and scuba diving. But you might also consider visiting a smaller island or group of islands such as the Thousand Islands in the St. Lawrence River between the United States and Canada. Some of those islands have only a few trees. Others contain a single house and can be rented for a family vacation. No matter what kind of island you visit, an escape to isolation and communion can do any family some good.

❑ 455. Visit a Wetland

Often the forgotten ecosystem—and the first to get drained for real estate or filled in for recreational lakes—a wetland is a valuable resource. Not only are wetlands the most biologically diverse ecosystem, they are also nature's best flood protector and water filter, as well as an important producer of the oxygen and organic matter that support the surrounding ecosystems. The most famous wetland in North America is probably Florida's Everglades. But if you're not near Florida, don't let that stop you: There are wetlands all over for you and your family to visit. Take nature walks to see all of the plant life—mangrove trees, water lilies, cattails, cypress trees, and on and on—and keep your ears open for the little sounds of animals and insects blending together in a natural orchestra. You'll discover that all parts of the world are interrelated—from a smelly bog to a beautiful mountain—and you can learn about what's being done to preserve these valuable ecosystems. You may even be inspired to help in conservation efforts. Visit The U.S. Fish and Wildlife Service Web site for more information on wetlands: www.fws.gov/wetlands/.

❑ 456. Make Butter

Shake, shake, shake. Shake, shake, shake. Shake your butter! Did you know that the main part of making butter is shaking? With a few simple materials and ingredients, you can shake up your own batch of butter right in your own home.

YOU WILL NEED:
Whipping cream (normal or heavy)
1 jar

The whole process takes about 10 to 20 minutes, and one cup of whipping cream usually yields about ½ cup of butter. So put on some music with a good beat, get shaking, and pass the jar around!

A SWEET TIP

Add honey to your butter for some sweetness or add chives for a more savory treat. You can add anything that you like to flavor your butter, so get creative!

❑ 457. Visit a Rain Forest

There are two kinds of rain forests: tropical, like those found in the Amazon, and temperate, like those found in the Pacific Northwest or on the coast of British Columbia. Rain forests are, of course, known for their high rainfall, but you'll find more than just rain when you visit one of these natural wonders. There's adventure waiting around every corner, whether you choose to zip cord through the tree canopy or prefer to stay grounded and hike the forest floors. Keep an eye out for some of the thousands of interesting animals that call the rain forest home. Make sure you bring a raincoat, wear walking shoes with a no-slip sole (the trails can get slippery and muddy), and—of course—a camera.

WHAT MAKES A RAIN FOREST?

Rain forests are typically divided into four main layers:

The Emergent Layer: The tallest trees pop through to find sunlight and provide homes to eagles and bats. In tropical rain forests, the trees are also home to monkeys!

The Canopy: This is the primary layer of the forest, where tree branches lace together to form a roof over the rest. Food is plentiful in the canopy, and in tropical rain forests, animals such as tree frogs and toucans can be found here.

The Understory: Little sunlight reaches this layer thanks to the density of the canopy, so plants have to have giant leaves to grow. Watch out for jaguars and leopards if you're in the tropical rain forest!

The Forest Floor: There's very little light here, so this is where everything in the forest goes to decay. A leaf that would take a year to decay in a normal climate only takes six weeks to decay on a rain forest floor.

❑ 458. Be a Daredevil

Can you imagine jumping out of a plane with your family? What about bungee jumping from a bridge? Think of the adrenaline rush, the excitement, the wind whipping around you, the views, the speed—the fun. Sharing this kind of daredevil excitement, this pure thrill, is a great way to connect with your family on the most basic level.

On the other hand, jumping out of a plane or off a bridge may scare the living daylights out of you. And there's no shame in that. Remember: Sometimes a little fear can be healthy and can even bring you closer together. But only you know what's right for your children and their age levels. So brainstorm about some adventures your little group might tackle together—something outrageous and a little scary—and then go for it! Who knows? When all is said and done, you may even want to do it again!

> **TAKE A DIVE!**
>
> Want to experience the free-fall sensation of skydiving without actually jumping out of a plane? Why not give Perris Valley Indoor Skydiving in Perris, California, a try? Yes, that's right, we said indoors! How is this possible? A bank of 200-horsepower fans blows a column of air straight up a 40-foot-tall tunnel. "Flyers" with varying levels of training enter this 150-mile-per-hour environment and begin soaring.

▲ ▲ ▲ ▲ ▲

"Don't take up a man's time talking about
the smartness of your children; he wants
to talk about the smartness of his own children."

—Ed Howe

▼ ▼ ▼ ▼ ▼

❑ 459. Believe in Magic

While Santa, the Tooth Fairy, Leprechauns, and the Easter Bunny may seem silly to you, these mythic characters can add a little excitement to a child's life. Teaching your children to believe in magic sends the message that anything is possible—that anything can happen. And it will teach them to use their imaginations. Your children will thrive and grow in the land of make-believe. There they can imagine and solve all sorts of problems and work on their own natural development in the comfort and safety of an imaginary place, all while forming a bridge between imagination and the real world. After all, the land of make-believe is not the only place these creatures inhabit. In fact, they're all known for crossing over into our world, whether it's to slip money under the pillow of a sleeping child for a tooth or to hide Easter eggs around the house. Children who learn to believe in magic when they're young are better able to see the real magic in the world as they grow older. And who knows? Maybe the next time you see a rainbow, you *will* find a pot of gold!

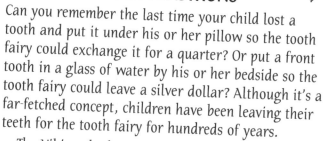

TOOTH TRADITIONS

Can you remember the last time your child lost a tooth and put it under his or her pillow so the tooth fairy could exchange it for a quarter? Or put a front tooth in a glass of water by his or her bedside so the tooth fairy could leave a silver dollar? Although it's a far-fetched concept, children have been leaving their teeth for the tooth fairy for hundreds of years.

The Vikings had a more direct method—parents would just pay their children for their recently lost teeth so they could add them to their necklaces or other jewelry. Adults believed that children's teeth gave them extraordinary power and would make them invincible in battle. Another commonly held belief is that recently lost teeth should be buried so that witches and evil spirits would not be able to use the power of the teeth to place curses on the child. Others thought that burying teeth in the garden would help children grow strong new adult teeth. But as people began to move from farms into cities, gardens became scarce; the tradition of "burying" teeth underneath pillows began as a result.

❏ 460. Watch a Solar Eclipse

The sun disappears in the middle of the day, and the sky turns dark in a matter of minutes. Is it aliens? The end of the world? Nope, it's a solar eclipse! Historically, many cultures were frightened by this astronomical occurrence, but there's no reason to be scared. Indeed, a solar eclipse is a great chance for you and your family to learn about the unique relationship between the sun, the earth, and the moon. Plus, a solar eclipse is just plain cool!

In order to view this phenomenon safely, you'll need to make a pin-hole camera so you can view the eclipse indirectly. All you need is a long box (at least 6 feet long), a piece of aluminum foil, a pin, and a sheet of white paper. Cut a hole in the center of one end of the box. Tape a piece of foil over the hole, then poke a small hole in the foil with the pin. Cut a viewing hole in the side of the box (on the end opposite that in which you made your hole). Put a piece of white paper inside the end of the box near the viewing hole. Point the end of the box with the pinhole toward the sun so that you can see the image of the sun on the white piece of paper.

ECLIPSE-OLOGY

Did you know that there are four different types of solar eclipses?

Total Eclipse: When the sun is completely obscured by the moon.

Annular Eclipse: When the sun and moon are exactly in line but the sun is visible as a ring of light behind the moon.

Hybrid Eclipse: Transitions between a total and annular eclipse depending on where on Earth you are viewing it.

Partial Eclipse: When the sun and moon are not exactly in line, and the moon only partially obscures the sun.

❑ 461. Go for a Moonlight Swim

From pool parties to swim meets to diving through the waves of the ocean, swimming is largely a daytime activity. It's fun and relaxing, and it has its place at the center of summer. But this established activity can have a twist. Take your family out for a moonlight swim in a lake or in the ocean, and turn this fixture of summer into a quiet act of mystery and daring. Things we find so commonplace under the sun are new and exciting under the moon. Everything is different. What was that noise? What was that in the water? Just the simple bellowing of a bullfrog, the gentle lap of the current, or the flutter of a bird's wings are enough to turn the world on its end and give new weight to life. There's nothing to express or discuss with your family here. It's just a simple act, the ultimate form of refreshment because it literally makes the world seem fresh again.

▲ ▲ ▲ ▲ ▲

*"It's this way with children.
It's cumulative. The more you love them,
the more you sacrifice; and the more you sacrifice,
the more you love."*
—William Graham Summer

▼ ▼ ▼ ▼ ▼

❑ 462. Ride in a Limousine

You don't need to be a celebrity to feel like one every once in awhile. Celebrate your family's importance by renting a limousine, and live richly for an evening. Get dressed in your best and see the sites in your city together through tinted windows and an open moonroof. Take turns picking places to visit, then have the limo pull up in front of your favorite restaurant. There may not be red carpets or flashbulbs popping along with every step you take, but that doesn't mean you can't have a special evening together—just because.

❑ 463. Watch the Elephants Parade into a Circus

When you think of the circus, you think of clowns, of trapeze artists, of lion tamers, maybe bearded ladies, but above all you think of elephants. They are the responsible businessmen, the men in the grey flannel suits (or in this case, the grey wrinkly, leathery skin), as the saying goes, and they provide the constant in the show, the reliable, steady, massively heavy back upon which others perform. They're something to marvel at, but you don't have to wait until

FAST FACT

When an elephant stomps its feet, the vibrations created can travel 20 miles through the ground. Elephants receive messages through their feet, too. Research on African and Indian elephants has identified a message for warning, another for greeting, and another for announcing, "Let's go." These sounds register from 80 to 90 decibels—louder than most humans can yell.

they get in the ring. You can catch the elephants before they lumber trunk to tail in their private parade into the circus. It's the big top's red carpet show, and you can witness it firsthand when you line up to watch the elephants march. Elephants are strange mammals. Their size suggests a lack of grace, but they can pack a lot of personality and humor into those tiny brains of theirs. A few minutes watching them as they ready themselves to perform will show you just how much fun they can be.

❑ 464. See *The Nutcracker* Ballet

It's the holiday season, and all you can find on TV are silly holiday movies with even sillier plots. There's something you can do about that. Raise the standards a little bit, and take your family to see a holiday classic: *The Nutcracker*. With its wonderful songs and dances, *The Nutcracker* provides memorable entertainment while elevating the minds of young children. This production is put on by local and metropolitan theater groups alike, but if you can't find it in your area, there are classic movie versions available for rent or purchase.

▲ ▲ ▲ ▲ ▲

"Pretty much all the honest truth telling there is in the world today is done by children."

—Oliver Wendell Holmes

▼ ▼ ▼ ▼ ▼

❑ 465. Visit a Wind Farm

Wind energy is widely touted as an important part of our present and our future—a way to power our homes and our lives with a renewable resource. Wind turbines also make a remarkable visual addition to a landscape. There is something simple and mesmerizing about seeing turbines lined up on a ridge or out in the ocean, their blades slowly rotating with the air. Visit a wind farm, and see for yourself what is being done to balance our needs with those of the planet. Your family may be inspired to learn more about conserving energy and recycling products. Did you know that the United States is the top wind power producer in the world in terms of sheer output? This is because the winds are stronger in the United States than in second- and third-place countries Germany and Spain. Some of the largest wind farms in the United States can be found in Texas and California, but wind farms are located throughout the country. To learn more about wind power, visit www.awea.org, the Web site for the American Wind Energy Association.

❏ 466. Visit a Bird Sanctuary

At a bird sanctuary, threatened birds are brought back to health, and their populations are expanded so they can be returned to the wild once more. Take your family to a nearby bird sanctuary to learn about the birds in your area that need help. Learn what's currently being done and what you can do to pitch in. You and your family will discover the interconnectedness of the world's creatures and places, and your kids may even be inspired to find out more about their feathered friends.

❏ 467. Visit the *Field of Dreams* Baseball Site and Play Catch

Even if you haven't seen the movie, you've heard the famous line from *Field of Dreams*: "If you build it, he will come." The film, about a baseball fan who builds a ball field among the corn on his farm, beautifully captures and expresses the poetry of baseball, the timelessness of the sport, and its importance in the lives of so many. It's main message will strike a nerve with everyone in your family—no matter how old or young: If you pursue your dreams, things will fall into place and you will achieve them, not only for yourself, but also for others. There's an indelible magic in baseball and all it stands for,

IT'S FREE!

With a runaway hit movie driving interest in their ball field, owners of the *Field of Dreams* movie site probably could have charged admission. Much to their credit, they did not. Instead, they chose to maintain the field in a non-commercial fashion, a precept that mirrors the movie's theme. All visitors are invited to bring bats, balls, and a glove and "go the distance."

and you and your family can participate in it by visiting the *Field of Dreams* ball field in Dyersville, Iowa, and playing catch together. The simplicity of the surroundings and the rhythm of the activity will remind you all of the important things in life. Be sure to watch the movie before you go!

❑ 468. Drive Go-Karts

Driving is a bore—all that traffic, crawling along like a snail with nothing but a place to leave and a place to get to. In the eyes of your children, how-ever, driving is possibly one of the most exciting things you do. You may not understand this now, but you will once you indulge

> **KNOW BEFORE YOU GO**
> There's an element of danger to go-karting, as these cars can go pretty fast. Before you go, check age and height restric-tions for the location you'll be visiting.

their fantasy and give them a chance to get behind the wheel on a go-kart track. Strap in, don your helmets, and get ready for some fierce family competition. You'll have a blast negotiating hairpin turns and giving into your lead foot on the straightaways as you pass each other and jockey for position, all in a quest for fun and victory. You'll rekindle the excitement you felt for driving when you first learned, and your kids will get to rejoice in the illusion that driving will always be like this. Best of all, you'll have fun bonding through the shared experience of beating each other on the track.

❑ 469. Visit a Volcano

How do you get to the center of the earth? Easy. Climb a volcano and jump inside. Okay, it's not quite that simple, and you'd need some pretty high-tech clothing to say the least, but that was the general idea behind Jules Verne's famous novel *Journey to the*

FAST FACT

Mauna Loa is the largest volcano on Earth, approximately 56,000 feet from the base at the bottom of the ocean to its peak. It's also one of the most active volcanoes, so it's still growing.

Center of the Earth. Counterintuitively, in order to descend to the center, one must first *ascend* into the clouds, but that's part of what makes volcanoes so fascinating. As the gateways to the interior of our planet, volcanoes are amazing. They billow smoke and spew lava at times, and then wait years and years—sometimes even centuries—to do it again. Fortunately, volcanoes tend to give some warning to scientists when they're going to have their flamboyant temper tantrums, so the rest of the time they make for fascinating destination points for family vacations. Hike or drive to the crater, enjoy the unique views from the mountaintop, then peer inside and contemplate the mysteries of the planet.

MAJOR VOLCANOES IN NORTH AMERICA
1. Mount St. Helens, Washington
2. Kilauea, Hawaii
3. Novarupta, Alaska
4. Mount Rainier, Washington
5. Sunset Crater, Arizona

❑ 470. Visit a Sand Dune

You have probably encountered small sand dunes every time you visited the beach. Where the sand piles up, blown by the wind, dunes form, protecting the land off the beach. But sand dunes can be so much more and so much grander. In fact, they are an often forgotten ecosystem found in various parts of North America. Sand dunes provide homes to many endangered species and are frequently in the protection of conservation groups. Despite their protected status, you and your family can visit and enjoy various outdoor activities together such as hang gliding, nature walks, and even sledding! Learn about the dunes by taking an educational hike, then have some fun too. Get your imaginations ready, and pay a visit to some of the major sand dunes in North America. Once you've experienced this ecosystem, it will no longer be forgotten!

MAJOR SAND DUNES IN NORTH AMERICA

1. Jockey's Ridge State Park, Outer Banks, North Carolina
2. White Sands National Monument, New Mexico
3. Athabasca Sand Dunes Provincial Park, Saskatchewan, Canada
4. Oregon Dunes National Recreation Area, Oregon
5. Great Sand Dunes National Park, Colorado

❑ 471. See a Drive-In Movie

Drive-in movies are coming back into style. That's good news because this is affordable, simple entertainment. What could be better than rolling up in the family car and watching a double feature? It's like going to see fireworks, but the entertainment lasts longer and has a plot. Drive-in movies of the past were usually associated with silly horror flicks with blobs and aliens and poorly costumed monsters from the deep, but today's drive-ins tend to show lots of family films and big hits, so consider taking your family to one near you. There are about 380 currently operating in the United States; check online for locations. Don't forget to bring the popcorn and snacks!

❑ 472. Pedal a Paddle Boat

Picture it: the sun streaming down on a warm afternoon, a gentle breeze blowing ripples across the water, and the birds whistling in the trees. What could you do on such a lovely day? Rent a paddle boat! These boats, like bicycles on the water, hold anywhere from one to four people, so they are perfect for a family outing. Get in two to a boat and race with each other, or get a larger boat and pile in together. You'll learn all about teamwork because everyone chips in on the pedals to make the boat go fast. Paddle boats are available on lakes, on rivers, and even in harbors, so there's a wide variety of things to see when you rent one. It's a simple way to put the cares of the world aside for a time and enjoy the day as a family.

▲　▲　▲　▲　▲

"The Grand essentials of happiness are: something to do, something to love, and something to hope for."
—Allan K. Chalmers

▼　▼　▼　▼　▼

❑ 473. Play Table Tennis

Eventually, in many parents' lives, there comes a time to decide whether or not to add a game table to your home. The choices are many—air hockey, pool, table tennis. Table tennis has the advantage of folding up for easy storage when not in use. As many as four can play at the same time, and the game is different each time it's played so interest remains high for a long time. The game helps in the development of hand-eye coordination, it's physical, the rules are easy, and even just volleying the ball back and forth provides hours of fun. Table tennis provides an opportunity for family

entertainment because it serves all levels of proficiency. Dad and Mom can have just as much fun in a tournament as the kids. The time you spend playing games with your children is time well spent on many levels. They learn by example, so when you exhibit good sportsmanship, safe playing habits, controlled tempers, and love of the game, your kids will mirror your behavior.

▲　▲　▲　▲　▲

"Here all mankind is equal: rich and poor alike. They love their children."

—Euripides

▼　▼　▼　▼　▼

❑ 474. Invite an Exchange Student

If you've got an extra bed in your home and an interest in introducing a student from another country to your family and lifestyle, the foreign exchange student experience might be for you. Being a host family to a student from any number of countries in Europe and Asia brings a different cultural experience into your children's lives and offers the exchange student the opportunity to know and understand an American family. Programs that promote exchange students often have a great purpose in mind—to educate through experience and foster peace among nations through personal relationships. Being a host family opens the door to a future exchange arrangement for your children as well. If you're interested in such a program, check the Internet at www.foreignexchangestudent.com for all the information you need.

▲ ▲ ▲ ▲ ▲

"There is always one moment in childhood when the door opens and lets the future in."
—Graham Greene

▼ ▼ ▼ ▼ ▼

❑ 475. Add Color to Special Days

There's no need to limit food coloring to dyeing Easter eggs. Coloring food for special occasions adds an element of surprise and creativity to meals served on such days as St. Patrick's Day, Valentine's Day, the Summer Solstice, birthdays, or any day your family treats as an occasion to celebrate. Fill Valentine's Day with red and pink foods (red velvet cake, tomato pasta, pink lemonade) and St. Patrick's Day with green (green bagels and green cream cheese, anyone?). How about using a favorite color for each family member's birthday celebrations? Pick a color, any color, then let that color set the tone for your special celebrations.

❑ 476. Turn the Tables on the Bedtime Story

Turn on the tape recorder because you won't want to miss this! For a change, ask your little one to tell *you* a bedtime story. Give your child prompts to get the story going: "It was early in the morning and the sun had just come up. I looked out my window and saw..." Or, "I went for a walk and saw a big tree filled with apples. So, I..." Once you get the story started, let your child tell the rest of it. It doesn't have to make sense, and if the story turns out to be never-ending, teach the concept of chapters: "It's time to go to sleep now, but I can't wait to hear the next chapter tomorrow night!"

Telling stories allows your child to be creative, release fears, share joys, and engage you in a warm and wonderful nighttime ritual.

❑ 477. Let Your Child Teach *You*

What kids know that adults don't could fill a book! And when it comes to new technology, the kids seem to know about it even before it reaches the marketplace. Switching roles and letting your kids be the teacher is good for everyone. You get brought into the 21st century, and they feel empowered, confident, smart, and helpful. What do they know that you don't? Just ask! The list could be long and might include:

- How an MP3 player works
- How to play the new games and use the new gear
- How to use your digital camera
- How to use an ipod
- How to use Twitter
- How to create a blog
- How to sign up for Facebook or MySpace
- How and why to go to YouTube.com
- How to use all the features on your cell phone
- How to program just about anything

❑ 478. Get Swimming!

Do you know how to swim? Do your kids? If not, it's time to learn. Sure, swimming is fun. But not knowing how to swim can also be a safety hazard. Experts recommend that parents wait until children are at least four years old before starting formal swimming lessons. Before that age, children aren't developmentally ready to learn the skills necessary for swimming. Of course, that doesn't mean you can't enroll in a parent-and-me swim class to get your toddler familiar with the water. It just means that children will do best in a swimming program independent from you once they reach the age of four. Formalized swimming lessons are good, too, because they teach children water safety along with the mechanics of swimming strokes.

Remember: Even if your child learns to swim at a young age, it doesn't mean they no longer need supervision in the water. Things can get tricky in the water pretty quickly, so always keep your eyes and ears on young kids when they're swimming.

▲ ▲ ▲ ▲ ▲

"The reason grandparents and grandchildren get along so well is that they have a common enemy."
—Sam Levenson

▼ ▼ ▼ ▼ ▼

❑ 479. Map It!

Where has your family been? If you take a lot of trips, you may start to lose track after a while. And if you haven't had a chance to travel much, wouldn't it be fun to plan ahead for places you'd like to visit? Get a poster-size map of the United States and tack it to a wall where everyone in the family can see it. Choose one color tack for places you've visited and another color tack for places you want to visit. Your children will get a kick out of this visual record of where you've been and where you're headed, and it's a great way to reinforce those school geography lessons.

❑ 480. Celebrate Mother's Day

What does Mom like best? Does the family know? Mom often shoulders the large burdens and small burdens so well that no one even realizes she's doing it. On Mother's Day, it's time for the rest of the family to do something for her in acknowledgement of her ongoing love and contributions to the family. Gather the rest of the family together to make Mom dinner and tell stories about the great things she has done as a mother and as a person. Fathers, don't forget to buy Mom some flowers or do something special early in the morning before the kids get up. Just because she's your wife, not your mom, doesn't mean she is any less deserving of your appreciation.

THE CREATION OF MOTHER'S DAY

After her mother died, Anna Jarvis started a letter-writing campaign in support of the celebration of mothers everywhere. A minister in Grafton, West Virginia, obliged and dedicated the second Sunday in May specifically to the late Mrs. Jarvis. Ironically, the woman who is credited with creating what we now know as Mother's Day never became a mother herself. Her entire life was dedicated to caring for others: first her elderly mother and then her blind sister. Jarvis never married; she died a pauper in 1948.

❑ 481. Celebrate New Year's Eve

"How ya gonna keep 'em down on the farm after they've seen Paree?" That's a line from an old World War I song, and it was written about the soldiers who had seen the world and then had to go back to their homes. How would their wives and families keep them at home once they'd seen the world? Your own home on New Year's Eve can be the mythic "Paree" for your kids if you start your traditions when they are young. It may not seem important at an early age, but when they are teens and older, you'll appreciate their desire to be at home instead of on the roads. A tradition-filled New Year's Eve can be as simple as a special set of hors d'oeuvres that become favorites, followed by a very special once-a-year dinner such as lobster, crab cakes, roast beef, meatball subs, or whatever fits into your family's budget. After dinner, make your New Year's resolutions: Write them down and save them in a box to look at again next year. Play games, watch the ball fall at midnight on TV, and stand on the front porch and bang pots and pans to ring in the New Year for the whole neighborhood. As the kids get older, invite their friends over to share your family's traditions. Later the girl-friends and boyfriends will join your family's fun. No one will want to go out after they've seen your house as "Paree!"

❏ 482. Learn CPR and First Aid Together

At some point, your children will be old enough to watch other people's kids (hard to believe, isn't it?). Whether they're interested in babysitting or working as a lifeguard or a camp counselor, they're going to need to be trained in first aid and CPR. But why wait until then? Once your child is old enough, register for a course in first aid and CPR. You'll enjoy learning together and will even have a built-in practice partner. And CPR and first aid are skills that come in handy when you least expect to need them. It never hurts to be prepared, and children enrolled in scouts can even earn a badge with the new knowledge.

▲ ▲ ▲ ▲ ▲

"Our greatest responsibility is to be good ancestors."
—Dr. Jonas Salk

▼ ▼ ▼ ▼ ▼

❏ 483. Be Grateful

Do you know how lucky you are? Do your children? Don't wait until Thanksgiving to count your blessings. Take some time out every day to be grateful for all that you have. This is a good lesson to teach children early. It will help them keep their wants in perspective by reinforcing just how much they actually have. Start a "Grateful" journal and take some time out each day or each week so that each family member can share what he or she is grateful for. Whether it's something big (like having such a great family), something little (like feeling grateful for a friendly classmate or someone who let you in front of them in traffic), or even something silly (like feeling grateful for candy!), you'll grow as a family when you take the time to appreciate how sweet life is.

❏ 484. Be a Secret Santa

Communities often have charitable organizations that sponsor Secret Santa programs. Check with churches and schools in your area to find out where you can adopt your own child in need of a Secret Santa. Even if you don't celebrate Christmas, this is a great opportunity to teach your child how wonderful it can feel to help someone in need. Oftentimes, Secret Santa programs will give you the age and gender of the child you'll be helping, along with a few items from his or her wish list. Take your children with you when you shop for the gift, and encourage them to select something they think the child will enjoy. Everyone wins when you give from the heart!

❏ 485. Visit a Wildlife Habitat

Preserving noninvasive species in protected areas has become so important that wildlife habitats now have their own council: the Wildlife Habitat Council, a nonprofit, non-lobbying group of corporations, businesses, and individuals dedicated to preserving wildlife. It's not only the migratory bird experts, botanists, and endangered species groups that are working to maintain and protect Earth's ecosystem. Families, schools, towns, communities, and individuals are learning all about the importance of preservation. When you and your kids visit a wildlife habitat near you, you'll have the opportunity to walk the trails, read the labels, see birds and wildlife in their natural habitat, and learn about the ecosystem. As your family leaves behind the sounds, sights, and hassles of life outside the sanctuary, you'll begin to appreciate the soft coos of mourning doves, the sudden flash of color on a bird's wing, and the huge variety of plantings that keep our air clean, our soil enriched, and our wildlife alive. Every visit is different as you learn to look more carefully, listen more intently, and explore new trails. Find a wildlife habitat near you by checking online or looking in your phone book.

BACKYARD WILDLIFE SANCTUARY

Our suburban homes cover a lot of land. You can give some of it back to the animals by turning your backyard into a mini-sanctuary and providing the basics: food, water, and shelter.

If you can, plant native plants that bear the fruit, nuts, seeds, nectar, and pollen that wild animals like to eat. Hazelnut trees, elderberries, service berries, huckleberries, and wildflowers are terrific.

You can also buy or build bird feeders. Fill the feeders with seeds songbirds prefer, such as sunflower seeds, white millet, and thistle.

Water is often scarce. One way to supply water is to set out birdbaths and keep them clean. Put the bowl of a birdbath on the ground for small mammals and ground-feeding birds. Give butterflies a drink, too. Fill a basin with sand and keep it wet. Place the basin near flowers, where butterflies visit.

Birds and small mammals need places to hide, build nests, and stay warm and dry in bad weather. If you can, plant a long hedgerow of native shrubs. Build piles of rocks, brush, or logs for small animals.

When you're finished, visit www.nwf.org to register your backyard refuge with the National Wildlife Federation!

❏ 486. Celebrate Kid's Day

Every day is Kid's Day, right? That's certainly the way it seems sometimes. You take them to school and to practice. You make their meals and help with their homework. Then you tuck them into bed with a few bedtime stories and a kiss on the forehead. Well, just like Mother's Day and Father's Day, Kid's Day is a holiday too, and it falls on the first Sunday in August. Make Kid's Day a special day for your kids where you do something a little different. Plan activities or stay at home watching movies. It doesn't matter what you do as long as you take some time out of your regular daily lives to let your children know how much joy and meaning they bring to you as parents. After all, they won't be kids forever.

▲ ▲ ▲ ▲ ▲

> *"Human beings are the only creatures on earth that allow their children to come back home."*
> —Bill Cosby

▼ ▼ ▼ ▼ ▼

❏ 487. Visit a Farm

You and your children probably know the song "Old MacDonald Had a Farm," but you probably don't know any Old MacDonald. Food is so easy for us to get—a stroll down the supermarket aisle or a drive-through run for burgers and fries—that we can sometimes forget where it comes from. Remind yourselves with a visit to a local farm. Farms are spread all over North America and come in all types, from large agribusiness farms that specialize in mass quantities of certain crops and food to small local growers of fresh fruits and vegetables and community-supported farms where everyone pitches in. A visit to a farm—or to several—will give you insight into what goes into your body and the different approaches toward feeding you and preserving the land. Learn how corn is harvested, how cows are milked, and how eggs are collected. Learn how to grow lettuce or beans or fruits. It's hard work, but it can be a rewarding—and growing—experience for your family. And even if farm life isn't for you, you're sure to come home with some fresh, tasty food to cook together.

▲ ▲ ▲ ▲ ▲

"Always be nice to your children because they are the ones who will choose your rest home."
—Phyllis Diller

▼ ▼ ▼ ▼ ▼

❏ 488. Attend a Movie Premiere

The red carpet is rolled out, the searchlights lace the sky, and paparazzi are scouring the area in full force. Treat yourselves like celebrities and get a glimpse of how the world works for them by attending a movie premiere. Some of the most popular theaters in Hollywood for a premiere include The Village Theatre, Bruin and Mann's National Theatre, Grauman's Chinese Theatre, and El Capitan. But if you're not near Hollywood, never fear: You and your family can be a part of a regional premiere where you can see the first showing of a new movie in the area. Local filmmakers are an important part of your community and deserve your family's support just as much as the big shots. In fact, by showing your children both kinds of premiere, you expose them to the different natures of creativity—the more business-minded creativity of Hollywood and the more art-oriented creativity of independent filmmakers. Encourage your children to think about why we make art, what motivates creativity, and how they feel about these questions. To some extent, these issues touch on the larger question of what motivates each of us in anything we do—the question we all come back to throughout our lives.

❏ 489. Watch a Meteor Shower

You can see random shooting stars at any time of the year, but a meteor shower is an entirely different spectacle. It's a gallery of shooting stars, and several occur each year. The most popular is Perseid, which can be seen flying across the night sky from late July to mid-August. Your local meteorologist will usually let you know when to watch. You'll get the best show if you head somewhere with little or no artificial light. Be sure to bring a blanket to lay on the ground and some insect repellent.

MEMORABLE METEORITES

Every day hundreds of meteors, commonly known as shooting stars, can be seen flying across the night sky. Upon entering Earth's atmosphere, friction heats up cosmic debris, causing streaks of light that are visible to the human eye. Most burn up before they ever reach the ground. But if one actually survives the long fall and strikes Earth, it is called a meteorite. Here are some of the more memorable meteor falls in history:

The **Ensisheim Meteorite,** the oldest recorded meteorite, struck Earth on November 7, 1492, in the small town of Ensisheim, France. A loud explosion shook the area before a 330-pound stone dropped from the sky into a wheat field, witnessed only by a young boy. As news of the event spread, townspeople gathered around and began breaking off pieces of the stone for souvenirs. German King Maximilian even stopped by Ensisheim to see the stone on his way to battle the French army. Maximilian decided it was a gift from heaven and considered it a sign that he would emerge victorious in his upcoming battle—and he did. Today bits of the stone are located in museums around the world, but the largest portion stands on display in Ensisheim's Regency Palace.

MEMORABLE METEORITES (*continued*)

The **Tunguska Meteorite,** which exploded near Russia's Tunguska River in 1908, is still the subject of debate nearly 100 years later. It didn't leave an impact crater, which has led to speculation about its true nature. But most scientists believe that around 7:00 A.M. on June 30 a giant meteor blazed through the sky and exploded in a huge ball of fire that flattened forests, blew up houses, and scorched people and animals within 13 miles. Scientists continue to explore the region, but neither a meteorite nor a crater have ever been found. Conspiracy theorists contend that what actually hit Earth that day was an alien spaceship or perhaps even a black hole.

Michelle Knapp was idling away at her **Peekskill, New York,** home on October 9, 1992, when a loud crash gave her a start. When she ran outside to investigate, she found that the trunk of her red Chevy Malibu had been crushed by a football-size rock that passed through the car and dug a crater into her driveway. When Michelle alerted police, they impounded the stone and eventually handed it over to the American Museum of Natural History in Manhattan. Turns out the meteor was first spotted over Kentucky, and its descent was caught on more than a dozen amateur videotapes. As for Michelle's Malibu, it was purchased by R. A. Langheinrich Meteorites, a private collectors group, which has taken the car on a world tour of museums and scientific institutions.

❏ 490. Practice Fire Safety

No one wants to think about something bad happening to their home, but that doesn't mean you can't be prepared as a family and grow closer doing it. Gather together and discuss what you would do in the event of a fire. Plan how you would escape the house, when you would call 911, and where you would meet outside if you got separated. Get flashlights, fire extinguishers, and rope ladders ready. Practice your plans, and take turns leading the exercises. This will teach your kids not only about emergency preparedness, but also about the value of foresight in all situations. Reinforce the fact that you all look out for each other and that you are all responsible for each other's well-being. This is a lesson that will last forever.

STAYING SAFE

Have you checked your smoke alarms lately? If not, you should. Statistics show that of the deaths that occur from home fires each year, approximately two-thirds happen in homes with no smoke alarms or with smoke alarms that aren't working properly. That's scary stuff! Take steps to ensure your family's safety by taking action now:

1. Check to be sure there is a smoke alarm on each level of your home.

2. Check the batteries in your smoke detectors monthly to be sure they're working. You're more likely to remember if you test the alarms on the same day of each month.

3. Replace the batteries in your smoke alarms annually. Consider doing this on the same day you move the clock forward (or back) so you won't forget.

4. Remember that smoke alarms don't last forever. Replace yours every ten years to ensure effectiveness.

❑ 491. Make a Date

What's better than time spent together as a family? Time spent alone with Mom or Dad! Your kids will jump at the opportunity for a special solo date. Take this opportunity to explore your child's talents and interests. For instance, if your daughter really enjoys her dance class, consider a trip to the ballet. If your son really likes baseball, take a trip to the batting cages. Make sure to give each of your children a chance to have a special date with Mom and then with Dad. You'll all have so much fun that you'll want to make this a monthly occurrence.

▲　▲　▲　▲　▲

"You know your children are growing up
when they stop asking you where
they came from and refuse
to tell you where they're going."
—P. J. O'Rourke

▼　▼　▼　▼　▼

❑ 492. Break the Rules

Want to turn an ordinary day into an extraordinary one? Serve pie, ice cream, cookies, soda, or pizza for breakfast. Break your routine just this once. Do it to celebrate a birthday or simply for no reason at all. Breakfast is the most important meal of the day. Why not celebrate it?

❑ 493. Play with Water Balloons

Is the heat getting to you? Time to fill up a bucket of water balloons and head to the backyard for a fight to remember! Give everyone a chance to arm themselves with balloons. Once everyone's ready, it's time to let loose. Who has the best aim? Who will end up the wettest? How quickly will you go through all of the balloons? This is a great way to vent frustrations, blow off a little steam, and cool off at the same time. What could be better? Once all the balloons have been tossed, make a game out of picking up the debris. You'll be the coolest family on your block!

❏ 494. Watch the Clouds Roll By

Life is so busy. School, work, chores, soccer games, grocery shopping. Sometimes you need to call a time-out. Choose a calm day when the sky is clear and sprinkled with clouds. Then grab a blanket and head outdoors. Have everyone lie on their backs staring up at the sky. Ask your kids if they see pictures in the clouds. Doesn't that one look a little like a dog? What about that one? Doesn't it look kind of like a tree? Once your kids get the hang of this game, you'll be amazed by where their imaginations take them. The sky's the limit in this dreamy game! Take this opportunity to talk about perspective and how enriching it can be to see things from someone else's point of view.

❏ 495. Say "I Love You"

We love our kids. If we didn't, we certainly wouldn't be interested in a book about 500 things to do with them! But how often do we tell them? Make a point of beginning and ending each day by telling your kids just how much you love them. Slip little love notes into their lunches. Write "I love you" in the steam on the bathroom mirror after you take a shower. They'll get the message loud and clear!

❏ 496. Celebrate an "Unbirthday"

Throw an "unbirthday" surprise party for your children on any date other than their actual birth dates. Think about how surprised they'll be! Tell guests to bring cards for any occasion but a birthday. Use any holiday decorations except birthday ones. Serve a cake with lollipops on it rather than candles. Have everyone make a wish for the guest of honor before they cut the cake.

❑ 497. Switch Roles

There's a children's book titled *Freaky Friday* in which a mother and daughter somehow end up in each other's bodies. The chaos that ensues is pretty funny, and both mother and daughter learn to appreciate each other a bit more after spending a day in different shoes.

Why not try that with your own children? Designate a morning or afternoon—or even a whole day if you're feeling brave!—and let your kids call the shots about what to do, where to go, and what to eat. But they don't get to have all the fun! They'll also be responsible for any chores you would normally take care of: the breakfast dishes, laundry, cleaning. When it's time to switch back to your typical roles, you'll do so with newfound understanding. For extra fun, rent *Freaky Friday* and see how their experience compares to yours!

▲ ▲ ▲ ▲ ▲

*"The great man is the one who
does not lose his child's heart."*

—Mencius

▼ ▼ ▼ ▼ ▼

❑ 498. Ride in a Convertible

Whether you own one or are just renting, there's nothing quite like the feel of sun on your face and the wind in your hair as you drive along a scenic road with the top down. Get out of town. Head for the ocean, the mountains, or the woods. Just don't forget your sunglasses and sunscreen!

❑ 499. Color Together

When's the last time you broke out the crayons and coloring books and colored with your child? Give yourself (and your children) permission to go outside the lines and to let creativity reign. A blue tree? Why not? Red grass? Sure! No matter how old your kids are, coloring can be a relaxing activity and a nice time-out from life's hectic moments. While you're coloring, talk to your children about their life's ambitions. Tell them what yours were when you were their age. Don't forget to put everyone's creations on the refrigerator door when you're done!

▲ ▲ ▲ ▲ ▲

> "Adults are always asking kids what they
> want to be when they grow up because
> they are looking for ideas."
> —Paula Poundstone

▼ ▼ ▼ ▼ ▼

❑ 500. Brainstorm

So you're up to the very last Thing to Do with Your Children Before They Grow Up. But it's not the end, it's just the beginning! The beginning of what? Quality time spent doing, seeing, talking about, and learning about quality things. Now it's your turn to add to the list and keep it going and growing for your children. Is it possible there's anything that's been left off this list of 500? Why not brainstorm as a family and see what else you can come up with? Brainstorming gives your brain cells a workout and, in this case, it will give your family a new list of things to do and traditions to start. Give each family member paper and a pencil/pen and decide on a topic to brainstorm. For example, you could all be thinking of new traditions to start for Thanksgiving. Or perhaps the list would be of new foods to try, new places to visit, new family things to do on Saturday night, or new ways to help your community. Set a timer and begin. When the timer goes off, read your lists aloud and then decide which things to do first. It's a family decision made by a family who knows the value of each other.